THE PSYCHOTHERAPY MAZE

A Consumer's Guide to Getting In and Out of Therapy

Revised and Updated

by **Otto Ehrenberg, Ph.D.**
and **Miriam Ehrenberg, Ph.D.**

JASON ARONSON INC.
Northvale, New Jersey
London

THE MASTER WORK SERIES

New printing 1994

Library of Congress Cataloging-in-Publication Data

ISBN: 1-56821-245-3
Library of Congress Catalog Card Number: 94-70252

Manufactured in the United States of America. Jason Aronson Inc. offers book
cassettes. For information and catalog write to Jason Aronson Inc., 230 Livingston S
Northvale, New Jersey 07647.

To Vivienne W. Nearing
our counsellor at law and other things as well

ACKNOWLEDGMENTS

WE WOULD like to express our appreciation to Deborah Bergman, whose suggestions and thoughtful editing made this a better book. Three people helped us in this revision by supplying updated information: Howard M. Cohen, Ph.D., on new developments in psychotherapy insurance, and Reuven Closter, C.S.W. and Ronnie Lesser, Ph.D. on gay and lesbian therapy. We are grateful to them for their time and comments. To Sarita Mendoza, for her generous assistance in preparing the manuscript, we offer many, many thanks.

CONTENTS

7

1 | Getting Oriented to the Psychotherapy Maze

THE PRACTICE and scope of psychotherapy has grown enormously since its beginnings almost a century ago. Originally associated in the public mind with the alleviation of emotional disturbances, psychotherapy is now also seen as the road to emotional fulfillment. Psychotherapeutic theories, techniques, and practitioners have proliferated, holding out the promise of self-actualization and joy along with the hope of freedom from disabling symptoms. New books on self-assertion, living and loving, or great sex are constantly finding their way to the best-seller lists, and the classified sections of newspapers and magazines offer a variety of therapies ranging from the traditional to the occult. There is now a therapy for every taste, whether it is psychoanalytic therapy, gay therapy, feminist therapy, primal therapy, or even past lives therapy, to name but a few. From 1976 to 1980 alone the number of psychotherapy "brands" grew from 164 to 250. Psychotherapy has not only become big business, it has become one of the steadiest growth industries in the country, described by the *Wall Street Journal* as a "booming, $17 billion-a-year market." The National Institute of Mental Health estimates that the utilization rate for mental health services went from 1 percent of the population in

1955 to 10 percent in 1980. The number of outpatient mental health visits similarly grew from one-half million in 1960 to four and one-half million in 1980.

With an ever-increasing number of therapies and practitioners to choose from, the public has been subjected to a growing state of confusion and uncertainty in which abuses flourish. In such a climate, the psychotherapy consumer needs guidelines and protection. The inherently high risks of psychotherapy make it just as necessary to spell out consumer rights in this field as in law, medicine, or automotive repair, and there has been a growing consumer movement to meet this need. Organizations of mental patients, such as NAPA, the Network Against Psychiatric Assault, have been formed to fight hospital abuses, the Public Citizens' Health Research Group has developed written contracts spelling out client rights and therapist obligations, and individual therapy consumers have been bringing more malpractice suits to the courts. Psychotherapists themselves, aware of the need to protect consumer interests, have begun to write consumer guides to psychotherapy. When *The Psychotherapy Maze* first appeared, it found a wide audience of perplexed therapy clients who needed help in making their way through the psychotherapy maze. We received a lot of appreciative mail from them, along with reports from therapists that their clients were reading the book and were, as a result, becoming more assertive within the therapy relationship.

People have, and should have, questions about what psychotherapy can and cannot do for them. Rather than responding to these legitimate questions, there is still a tendency among many practitioners to ignore such concerns and to put clients on the defensive for voicing them. It is often assumed that clients, as lay persons, have no basis for evaluating either the credentials of psychotherapists or the effectiveness of their own therapy. Many psychotherapy systems have built into them a "client trap": the psychotherapist, as the expert, knows the client better than the client knows him- or herself and, therefore, the client must accept as correct what the therapist says. If the client agrees with the therapist, that proves the therapist is right. If the client disagrees with the therapist, that also proves the therapist is right because the client's resistance reveals the therapist has hit target. The therapist, being the expert on interpersonal relationships, is defined as healthy, always acting in a proper way, and above being questioned by one who is "neurotic," "sick," or "paranoid."

Clients have traditionally been relegated to the underdog position in the psychotherapy relationship, thereby perpetuating a fundamentally countertherapeutic attitude. This attitude has fostered intimidation rather than emancipation and growth. If you are in psychotherapy or about to take the plunge, you can protect yourself from authoritarian therapists, quacks, needless therapy, excessive costs, and other abuses. We think that it is not only your right but also your responsibility as a psychotherapy client to look after your self-interest. To get the most out of psychotherapy you must know what is reasonable to expect and unreasonable to accept. Awareness of what psychotherapy entails—its scope as well as its limitations—will provide you with the basis for a meaningful psychotherapy experience.

WHAT IS PSYCHOTHERAPY?

Psychotherapy is a process that helps people resolve their emotional problems, usually through the self-awareness that is gained in the therapeutic relationship. How the process works will emerge throughout this book as the various aspects of therapy are discussed.

People bring a variety of problems to psychotherapy. Some suffer from disabling anxiety attacks or headaches, some from compulsive habits such as excessive drinking, overeating, or refusing food altogether, some from feelings of worthlessness or depression, some from inability to have intimate relationships. Others do not feel particularly troubled but feel that life is empty and unsatisfying. Psychotherapy's immediate concern is helping people overcome these problems and the unhappiness they cause, but psychotherapy is also aware that these problems have a common base. In each condition the person does not feel free to be him- or herself and to live productively because of constriction from within. While this lack of freedom manifests itself differently in different people, it is always a fundamental issue for psychotherapy.

Psychotherapy recognizes that one has the innate capacity to grow, to know oneself, and to make choices consonant with the development of one's potential. Growth—the unfolding of one's core—is a natural condition of being alive and is synonymous with psychological well-being. Conversely, when growth is blocked and one is not free to be oneself, one experiences a sense of disharmony. Psychotherapy explores the ways people limit their lives and undermine their autonomy. By revealing obstacles to growth, psychotherapy can help free people from self-restricting attitudes and patterns of behavior and bring nascent qualities to the fore.

The process of psychotherapy must be compatible with its goal of expanding your autonomy. It is not a process in which the psychotherapist "cures" you or does something to you. Rather, it is a collaborative educational process based on your active participation. The therapist's role is not that of a doctor but of a teacher who acts as catalyst and guide in your efforts to understand the ways in which you hinder your own development and avoid possibilities for growth. The therapist must help you expose the ways you flee from your own affirmation and also help you gain control over your existence. The psychotherapist must not validate your fears of helplessness and powerlessness by doing things for you that you can do for yourself. Any process in which you relinquish responsibility for growth to the therapist is not authentic psychotherapy.

WHO SHOULD GO INTO PSYCHOTHERAPY

People go to psychotherapy for a variety of reasons. Most go because they are seriously distressed and need help coping with day-to-day life. Some are not particularly distressed but go to psychotherapy because they want to get more out of life. Others go because they are curious about psychotherapy or because they want to do the "in" thing. Still others go not really wanting psychotherapy: they want to get reassurance that they are not "crazy," to fix blame on somebody else, or to meet the demands of an authority such as a parent, spouse, school, or probation officer. Sometimes, too, people go to psychotherapy on the pretext that they are doing it for someone else, to camouflage their own interest in doing so. If you are considering psychotherapy, think about your reasons for wanting to go. The more genuinely you want psychotherapy, the more helpful it will be. People who go only at the insistence of others are not really open to the possibilities of exploring themselves or of changing themselves.

Being aware of your discomfort and anxiety is a positive sign. People who are in touch with their feelings rather than blocking them out are already one step ahead in psychotherapy. The more you are aware of your distress and of not being able to be what you want, the stronger will be your desire for change.

There is a popular saying among psychotherapists that the ideal client for psychotherapy is the person who needs it the least. This ideal type is known as the "yavis": young, attractive, verbal, intelligent, successful. Probably one reason that therapists feel a "yavis" makes a better client is that it is easier for them to establish a good relationship with this type. They prefer to work with such persons and equate their preference with necessary client characteristics. However, these characteristics are not essential in order to benefit from psychotherapy. The belief in the importance of verbal and intellectual ability is particularly widespread. The ability to put feelings into words can be of value, but verbal facility can just as easily be used to hide one's feelings behind a wall of intellectualization. Furthermore, words are only one way to express oneself. The assumption that psychotherapy is particularly beneficial to the intellectual elite for a long time hindered psychotherapy from tapping nonverbal modes of experience or making itself available to lower socioeconomic groups. With new approaches, such as body therapies, behavior modification, and family systems therapy now available that are less dependent on verbalizations, there is a modality to suit every need and with it a growing market for psychotherapy services in all sectors of society.

What really matters in being a client is your interest in psychotherapy. Psychotherapy is most helpful to those who really want help. It can benefit all people who are willing to expend the effort to make meaningful changes.

WHEN TO GO TO PSYCHOTHERAPY AND WHEN TO TRY ALTERNATIVES

How do you know when your problems belong in a psychotherapist's office? One indicator is your ability to handle your feelings. It is not unusual to experience anxiety, confusion, or depression from time to time, but these feelings become significant when they are recurrent or extreme. If you cannot shake off these or similar feelings of psychological stress by yourself, it is time for psychotherapy. Another indicator is the cause of the problem. Everyone experiences emotional problems occasionally and some people, such as those undergoing prolonged unemployment or suffering chronic illness, are faced with more stress than others. That does not necessarily mean, however, that they should go into psychotherapy. Psychotherapy does not eliminate the difficulties of living, nor is it by itself a solution when the external conditions of life are so oppressive that you are not free to exercise any options in dealing with your problems. When you are laid off and have no money to live on you need help getting a job, not treatment for your insecurity. But when you are afraid to go on a job interview because you feel inadequate or are sure beforehand that someone else will be hired, you should consider psychotherapy.

When feelings of stress result from externally created problems rather than inner conflicts, the psychological discomfort can be alleviated by psychotherapy but such problems are better handled through the alternative helping methods described below. These methods can offer more effective support systems and direct help in dealing with the situational difficulties, which might include rape, single parenthood, physical illness, overbearing employers, or other problems. A wide range of alternatives exists, although availability depends somewhat on the community in which you live. Some of the typical ones are:

- Crisis intervention services (for example, rape crisis centers, AIDS hotlines, or battered women shelters);
- Peer self-help groups, usually organized around specific problem areas (for example, Parents Without Partners, men's or women's consciousness-raising groups, or Overeaters Anonymous);
- Training in personal effectiveness (for example, assertiveness training classes, relaxation training, or Parent Effectiveness Training);
- Counseling and planning services (vocational guidance, Planned Parenthood, or financial advisory services);
- Self-help (acquiring information necessary for improving a situation, initiating changes in work or personal relationships, or obtaining medical care or services from a social agency).

Sometimes severe situational problems put undue strain on our psychological weak spots. When that happens, people who tend to be tense, for example, may become exceedingly anxious, or people who are easily discouraged may lapse into a major depression. Under these circumstances psychotherapy is called for in addition to, rather than in place of, an alternative helping method. The alternate helping methods can also be useful for people already in therapy when they come up against difficult external problems. These alternatives free therapy time to work on the psychological rather than the practical aspects of one's problems, and the two approaches tend to support each other: insights gained from psychotherapy often make the experience with alternative methods more meaningful, and what is learned through the latter stimulates further exploration in psychotherapy.

A question is often raised about the merits of discussing emotional problems with a friend instead of going to a psychotherapist. If there is someone you respect and trust, that is certainly an avenue to try, provided you keep certain caveats in mind. A friend can help you clarify a problem and, perhaps, encourage you to face it. Even if your friend cannot help you resolve the problem, research has shown that just confiding in someone can be useful by reducing stress. However, if your problem is a very serious one or if it persists, relying solely on friends for help has its limitations and could even be harmful. A social relationship does not lend itself to extended working through of problems because, unlike the professional relationship, it is based on mutuality of obligation, as is explained later on in Chapter 9. When discussing problems with a friend you still need to think of the other person's feelings. After a time friends may resent the demands being made on them or expect "equal time," which you might not be prepared to offer. Friends, unlike therapists, are not trained to keep a certain degree of emotional distance when listening to you. While friends can be very supportive when they agree with you they can also be very critical when they do not. Potentially the greatest difficulty in using friends as therapists is that friends are not trained to pick up possible serious underlying personality problems, and thereby could delay you in finding necessary professional help.

DOES PSYCHOTHERAPY WORK?

Much research has been conducted to evaluate the effectiveness of psychotherapy. The results of these studies show that psychotherapy works, that psychotherapy does not work, and that psychotherapy can have harmful effects. These contradictory findings stem from different views of what constitutes success in psychotherapy, different views on how this success is determined, and bias in doing the research. Many studies have been motivated by the desire either to debunk or to defend psychotherapy, to acclaim one new approach or to discredit another.

The first source of confusion in research is the differing determinants of what constitutes success in psychotherapy. Is it removal of a disturbing symptom, achievement of a specific goal, disappearance of problems, greater awareness of oneself, an increase in happiness, or the freedom to make fuller use of life? The varied approaches labeled psychotherapy emphasize different goals. Effectiveness can therefore be measured only against psychotherapy's success in reaching its stated goals.

The next problem is how to determine whether success has been achieved. Does one use the evaluation of therapists, of clients, of family or friends, or of psychological tests? All of these sources have been used, and each presents limitations. The therapist's or client's reports are mistrusted by some because they are considered to be biased, with both therapist and client needing to justify their efforts. Other, presumably more objective, people are not suitable judges since they may not be aware of changes that are significant to the client, and psychological tests often miss the point altogether. Another problem is when the results of psychotherapy should be measured. Should it be evaluated after two months, a year, after termination, or later? Some therapy systems aim at fairly rapid observable changes, others at laying groundwork for changes that may not become apparent until much later. The effects of therapy do not end when therapy stops: benefits may continue to accrue as insights and changes have a chance to solidify.

In light of all these variables, the inconsistency of results is not surprising. With the vast array of psychotherapy approaches, psychotherapists, and clients, it is more useful to ask, not if psychotherapy works, but which approaches work under what conditions and with whom. Research is now addressing itself to those questions. Even when more definite answers are available, it will still be hard to quantify the benefits of psychotherapy. Sometimes just a little bit of help at the right time can be of immeasurable importance.

Not all systems are beneficial to all people all the time, but there is enough evidence to conclude that some systems are beneficial to some people some of the time. Just how useful psychotherapy will be depends on many factors that are discussed in this book. The most important issues are your reasons for going into psychotherapy, the suitability of the therapy you choose, the competence of your therapist, and the way in which you apply yourself in psychotherapy.

THE CHALLENGES AND REWARDS OF PSYCHOTHERAPY

Psychotherapy is a life-expanding undertaking and, like all such ventures, is both challenging and exciting. The broader your goals and the more you want to accomplish, the more demanding it becomes. For starters, you have to sift through the maze of options and make a choice compatible with your needs and life situation. Once in therapy, you have to be ready to deal with things you would rather forget, to keep working even when you do not seem to be making much progress, and to tolerate the anxiety of putting your new understanding into action.

It can be difficult to accept the demanding aspects of psychotherapy, especially if you start while very distressed. When you are feeling very anxious or depressed, you want to feel better fast. You want somebody to take care of you and get you over the hump. The therapist will be sorely tempted to settle for giving you what you want at the moment: to patch you up with moral support, advice, or a tranquilizer and send you home happy for a while. This kind of care may make you feel better, and it may be a needed step to put you in a frame of mind to be ready to face your problems, but it is not really psychotherapy. Letting the therapist take over for you may be temporarily reassuring but it also undermines your confidence in your own capacities. Excessive interventions of that nature by the therapist are a potential hazard in that the comfort they provide can seduce you into compromising your basic need for autonomy. The ability to resolve the conflict between wanting to be cared for and learning how to care for yourself is a crucial factor in avoiding disappointments in psychotherapy later on.

Meeting the challenges of psychotherapy does provide important rewards. If you are with the right therapist, you may begin to feel better after only a few sessions. When starting therapy, you tend to feel less anxious because of the supportive relationship with the therapist. Then, as your problems are clarified and you learn new ways of dealing with them, your sense of security and self-confidence begins to build up. Corresponding to the growing feelings of well-being that psychotherapy can provide, one recent research study found that slightly more than half of the therapy clients interviewed felt better after only eight sessions, almost two-thirds felt better after thirteen sessions, and three-fourths felt better after twenty-six weekly sessions. While therapy can not eliminate life's problems, it does help you face them, and while it can not make hostile, competitive, or overly demanding people in your life disappear, it can give you the means to deal with these and other problems of life in a more productive way. Actually, as you change, people around you are likely to change too. When you become more secure and confident in your dealings with others, they will probably begin to accommodate themselves to you.

A generally unrecognized side benefit of psychotherapy that is now being corroborated by large-scale research is the improvement of clients' physical health. This comes about in two ways: reducing psychological stress and increasing positive feelings about oneself reduces vulnerability to disease, and resolving psychological problems prevents them from being expressed in somatic symptoms. Although business organizations at one point considered dropping psychotherapy coverage from employee insurance policies because of its cost, some are now adding this benefit, as it has been established that medical costs drop by anywhere from 37 to 75 percent when employees have access to psychotherapy. In the long run, the savings in medical costs are expected to more than make up for the cost of psychotherapy.

OBSTACLES TO PSYCHOTHERAPY

Despite these important potential benefits, only a small proportion of people for whom psychotherapy could be useful ever go to a psychotherapist. To start psychotherapy, one not only has to have an appreciation of what it has to offer but also has to overcome fears about the process and cultural prejudices against it.

Going into psychotherapy means, first of all, facing personal shortcomings. Many people consider it demeaning to have problems in living, problems they seem unable to cope with, and are reluctant to admit that they do, even to themselves. As most people who start psychotherapy have poor self-esteem, it is particularly threatening for them to have to acknowledge their difficulties by seeking the help of a psychotherapist. Recognizing one's limitations is made even more difficult by the custom of labeling people with emotional problems as "sick." While people no longer think "you have to be crazy to see a shrink," there still is some stigma attached to being in psychotherapy.

A related stumbling block to psychotherapy is the reluctance to reveal things about oneself that carry a sense of shame. In a mistrustful society, it is worrisome to think of exposing oneself to others. Although we live in a society in which it is increasingly acceptable to share one's feelings, value is still placed on "keeping a stiff upper lip" and dealing with problems on one's own. This attitude makes it especially difficult for men to start psychotherapy, because they fear that it will mark them as "unmasculine."

Another fear, also more common among men, is that psychotherapy means surrendering independence. Many people are afraid that they may become too needy of the psychotherapist. Some psychotherapists do foster dependency by encouraging clients to rely on them rather than on inner resources, but authentic psychotherapy always aims at developing your independence and ability to take responsibility for your own life. On the other hand, some people are scared away by this very striving for self-responsibility. They do not want this responsibility, preferring that others continue to take care of them. Even though it is uncomfortable to have problems, they can still count on indulgence from others: "Don't bother me—I can't cope."

Still others are afraid to start psychotherapy because they are not sure they are up to the task. They doubt their ability to participate meaningfully in the therapy process or their potential for change. They fear a further exposure of their inadequacy. Their feelings of worthlessness may also make them afraid of rejection by the therapist.

Occasionally people fear that psychotherapy can cause a loss of creativity. This concern is based on a popular misconception that creative persons are "neurotic" and that eliminating the neurosis will make them "normal" and dull. Since the essential qualities of the genuine creative act—openness and spontaneity—are also basic goals of psychotherapy, psychotherapy is more apt to liberate than to block creative forces.

Some people, especially those with radical political views, shy away from psychotherapy because they think the goal of therapy is to make them adjust to the status quo. It may or may not be the intention of the psychotherapist to influence you to conform to certain societal values that you might not share, and this is an issue that could be important to explore with a therapist before deciding to work together. However, labeling all psychotherapists as upholders of the establishment may be a smoke screen that keeps a person from having to take a closer look at his or her own problems.

Still other doubts about psychotherapy revolve around its time and cost. The emergence of such methods as encounter, marathon, and sensitivity groups, and more recently assertiveness training and *est,* attests to the desire for quicker and less costly routes to self-development. For some people, such approaches are helpful, but for others these attempts to bypass the more encompassing process of psychotherapy are woefully unsuccessful and, at times, even harmful. Being well informed about psychotherapy and using it intelligently is the best way to get the most for your psychotherapy dollar.

Apart from these personal hurdles, various social influences discourage a serious psychotherapeutic effort. Paradoxically, a frequent barrier results from the needs of close friends and relatives. Although these same people may initially urge a person to enter psychotherapy, they often become its enemy instead of its advocate. If they find it hard to accept the growing independence of the person in therapy, they might try to sabotage the therapy. The woman who realizes that her "pussycat" role is degrading cannot discard the décolletage and dish towel without resistance on the part of her mate. The son who rejects his mother's sacrifices to be rid of the accompanying guilt may find that she refuses to forsake her martyrdom. It may even happen that friends and relatives become jealous of the therapist's influence on the person in therapy.

The cultural climate also functions as a barrier to psychotherapy. A pervasive theme of the culture is the veneration of quick and easy routes to feeling good. We are urged to take aspirin for "fast, fast, fast relief," antihistamines "at the first sign of a cold," and tablets for "safe and restful sleep, sleep, sleep." We want a quick cure for our discomfort, being seduced by the easy way out and blinded to its dangers. A climate that embraces all convenience items despite their dangerous side effects—aerosol cans, birth control pills, instant foods, plastic wraps—hardly promotes a willingness to engage in a process, like psychotherapy, that may prove arduous and long.

In still more fundamental ways, society discourages us from aspiring to more autonomous ways of life. People who are not willing to confine their possibilities for growth are apt to find new pathways that can disrupt established patterns. One common concept of psychological normalcy is, in fact, culturally defined, with "normal" being behavior that is conventional and "abnormal" being behavior that departs from the usual acceptable social standards. This makes it easier for most people to "adjust" to things the way they are than to risk change and have to buck society.

The push to adjust to society is reinforced even by those professions that are ostensibly devoted to promoting the integrity of the individual, including psychotherapy. As R. D. Laing and many others have pointed out, psychotherapy does have political implications and can be a repressive political act. At times psychotherapists may unwittingly use therapy as a tool of conformity when they are unaware of repressive cultural influences from which clients need to free themselves. More often, the "helping professions" knowingly act as agents of the culture by labeling as immoral, illegal, or abnormal that which is threatening to the status quo. For example, it is not accidental that abortion and homosexuality were immoral and illegal acts when society needed a growing population but became individual "rights" when society needed zero population growth. The professions set the stage for conformity by fostering authoritarian relationships in which the individual is treated like a child, to be protected by a knowledgeable adult: the priest or "father" ministers to his "son" while the "doctor" calls the patient by his first name. One is encouraged to let the professional assume responsibility for essential decisions in one's life. At the extreme is the professional who arrogates the right of clients to make basic decisions about their own lives; physicians, lawyers, and ministers have conspired to keep people unaware that they were suffering from a terminal illness and have kept others living, in agony, against their wishes.

The concept of mental illness, dubbed by Thomas Szasz "the myth of mental illness," is yet another barrier to psychotherapy. Labeling emotional and behavioral problems as mental illness not only serves to stigmatize people, but leads clients to expect that in treatment "the doctor" will cure them of their problems rather than help them learn to overcome their problems by their own efforts. The concept furthers a constitutional-organic explanation that suggests the person is a victim of genetic inheritance rather than a social-environmental explanation that sees a person as limited by poor support systems and faulty early learning. At the very least, the mental illness concept fosters dependency on therapists, shifting responsibility for change to the therapy, but, at the extreme, it provides the rationale for forcing people into mental institutions against their will. Because some people have found themselves involuntarily subjected to hospitalization, medication, and electric shock, others have avoided seeking psychotherapeutic help out of fear that they, too, may be forced to accept more than they are looking for.

These personal fears and cultural barriers keep many people from seeking therapy and make it difficult for others who do enter therapy to start in a constructive frame of mind. The combined effect of these attitudes on potential clients is to foster unrealistic expectations that therapy will provide quick relief from painful problems and that the expert will do the work for them.

GET READY, GET SET, GO

Even without the cultural barriers, it's not easy to get started in psychotherapy. To begin with, there is the uncertainty about how to go about doing it: how do you pick a therapist, what do you say when you go to one, and what do you have to do once you're in therapy? If you are thinking of therapy for yourself, you probably feel anxious about starting off on a new experience in which a lot is at stake and the outcome is uncertain. You are not sure what is going to happen to you and how you are going to take to it. You might be worried about what other people are going to think of you. On top of all this, you have to overcome a certain amount of lethargy. Getting started means putting in time and effort, it means planning and committing yourself to a new routine, and it usually means having to make financial sacrifices.

With these attitudes to overcome, no wonder there is a tendency to put off starting therapy until stress and discomfort force you to act. But waiting till then puts you at a disadvantage: you will have lost the freedom to look around for a suitable therapist, needing instead to accept the first one you come across. When you are very upset your emotional resources become dissipated, leaving you less capacity to work at the therapy. And, the longer you wait, the more your problems and reactions to them become crystallized, making it that much harder to bring about changes.

Getting started is easier the clearer you are on what kind of therapy you want and how to go about getting it. This will narrow down the possibilities to manageable proportions and eliminate obviously inappropriate approaches. With a framework in mind for judging the suitability of therapists, you will be better prepared for the choices you'll have to make.

2 The Psychotherapy Catalogue

CHOOSING A therapist is complicated not only by the array of different kinds of professionals offering this service and by the different personalities of the therapists, but also by the many theories and methods of psychotherapy employed. This chapter summarizes the major approaches to psychotherapy, both old and new, currently being used. We have excluded psychotherapy systems that are not generally available or have too few adherents for them to constitute a practical choice for you.

Most of the theories and methods described here were evolved for individual therapy but can also be applied to group, family, or child therapy. The usefulness of these other forms of therapy is discussed later in the chapter. Medical treatment, which is sometimes used as an adjunct to psychotherapy and sometimes used as the sole means of treating emotional problems, is also discussed separately.

Besides the various labels applied to each school of therapy (such as gestalt therapy, primal therapy, transactional analysis) there are broader terms that characterize several systems of psychotherapy (for example, psychoanalytic approaches, behavioral approaches, cognitive approaches). Perhaps no two terms generate as much confusion as psychoanalysis and psychotherapy. Psychoanalysis is one school of psychotherapy, and historically the term refers only to the theory and methods developed by Sigmund Freud. Some people think of psychoanalysis as distinct from psychotherapy and define it as a long-term depth approach to personality change, in contrast to psychotherapy, which they define as a shorter-term and more superficial approach. For this reason, some persons look for a psychoanalyst rather than a psychotherapist, thinking they are thereby getting something more valuable and prestigious. As you will see in the summaries provided, there are many other schools of psychotherapy, in addition to psychoanalysis, that aim to restructure the personality and work on an intensive level.

The theoretical orientation of the therapist and his or her view of your problems and their cause will affect how that person works with you in many important ways. These include:

- The emphasis placed on such factors as inner life versus interpersonal relationships, understanding versus feeling, past versus present and future, growth versus elimination of symptoms, insight versus behavior change;
- The nature of your interaction with the therapist;
- The kinds of methods used in therapy—discussion, dream analysis, role playing, body exercises, or other techniques.

The multitude of schools of psychotherapy is taken by some to indicate that psychotherapy is not a valid scientific tool but rather a conglomeration of unproven theories, some brilliant, some far-out, some just plain ridiculous. If psychotherapists really know what they are about, why is there so much disagreement, and if psychotherapy is a bona fide process, is that process psychoanalysis, primal screaming, or a nondirective "uh-huh"? A lot of the confusion comes from the fact that each theoretician develops a system based essentially on the distillation of his or her own personal needs and experiences and those of the persons he or she deals with as revealed in their relationships. None of the theories is completely right or wrong; each reflects a certain approach to the world and, as that world has changed, psychotherapy has changed to meet the new needs and interests that have emerged.

A major trend in psychotherapy has been a shift from personal to interpersonal and now toward transpersonal problems. The newer approaches, in keeping with the tempo of the times, emphasize immediate awareness in lieu of worked-through insight. Accordingly, the pitfalls of psychotherapy have shifted from "interminable" psychoanalysis, as Freud called it, to the substitution of apparent for real gains. With the advent of mass media there has also been a dramatic change in the way new psychotherapy systems come into being. Formerly, new systems were built up painstakingly and offered bit by bit to the professional community. Now, new systems are promoted on a mass basis and burgeon overnight. Innovators do not look for the approval of their colleagues but take their wares directly to the public marketplace. Books on psychotherapy are often on the best-seller lists and television popularizes the faces of all the latter-day psychotherapy innovators. As a result, fads in psychotherapy take hold much like new products, with new therapy systems giving way to still newer "brands" every few years. The charisma of a therapist on television often becomes more important than the soundness of his or her system, and visibility becomes confused with validity.

When you shop for a psychotherapy system, try not to be misled by status symbols or by promotional campaigns. By familiarizing yourself with the different emphases provided by each system as well as the different methods you can expect the psychotherapist to use, you will become able to choose an approach that makes sense to you and is compatible with your needs. The brief review of theoretical systems that follows is intended as an introduction. For those wanting more information, further reading is suggested at the end of this book.

THE MAJOR SCHOOLS

Freud and Psychoanalysis Psychotherapy started with Sigmund Freud, who both enunciated a theory of personality development and formulated a therapeutic technique he called psychoanalysis. Even though it is the oldest system, it is still very much in evidence and, indeed, some people are drawn to it just because it has the prestige of being the original.

According to Freud, people are motivated by their instincts, the sexual instinct (libido) being the most basic. The personality is organized into three parts: the id, which represents the instinctual needs and constantly seeks their gratification; the ego, which tries to satisfy the id according to the realities of the life situation; and the superego, which internalizes the parents' moral prohibitions as one's own. Life is a constant struggle of id versus ego and super-ego, and the integration of the needs of these three factions deter-mines one's state of mental health. To the extent that one represses the instinctual needs, they create anxiety as they threaten always to break through. The individual must create "defenses" against this eventuality, but they are never more than partially successful and the repressed urges surface in the form of neurotic symptoms or, more innocently, in dreams, slips of the tongue, or jokes.

As the individual grows from infancy to adulthood, the libido seeks gratification in different ways corresponding to the level of development. These "psychosexual stages" are known as the oral, anal, phallic or Oedipal, latent, and genital, the name indicating the medium through which the libido is expressed. In normal de-velopment the baby will pass from the oral stage, in which it is fo-cused on sustenance and gratification through the mouth, to the anal stage, in which it is focused on toilet training and control. In the Oedipal stage (ages two to six), phallic strivings emerge but are repressed and remain latent until the genital stage (puberty), when the individual is focused on gratification directly through the sexual organs. If the course of development at any stage does not run smoothly, the individual may become "fixated" at the level, showing symptoms of an "oral" personality, for example, or may later regress to that level under stress. While all these stages are significant for one's emotional development, the Oedipal stage is regarded as the most critical, as it is at this stage that the superego is developed. During the Oedipal phase boys and girls become fo-cused on their sexual organs—boys on the penis and girls on the clitoris, according to Freud. The boy develops sexual fantasies in-volving his mother and sees the father as a powerful rival who is capable of castrating him for such incestuous wishes. As a result, sexual feelings toward the mother are repressed. The boy develops pure love for his mother and forms an identification with his fa-ther, adopting their moral prohibitions as his own. Thus the super-ego comes into being, an internal policeman to guard against un-acceptable impulses and resolve the Oedipal crisis. The case with girls is a bit more complicated and has engendered a great deal of controversy, sparked especially by the feminist movement.

Freud maintained that the awareness of anatomical differences that occurs in the phallic stage creates "penis envy" in the girl: she feels deprived of the male organ and blames the mother for the in-sufficiency. To compensate for her lack, she turns to her father in a wish for his penis. Unlike the boy, the girl's Oedipal wishes are never fully resolved nor is her superego ever fully developed. Even in adulthood the woman continues to be motivated by her feelings of deprivation of the missing organ. She may marry to obtain the organ vicariously, but never feels content unless she gives birth to a boy and possesses a penis through him. Freud's theory of the primacy of the vaginal over the clitoral orgasm related to his belief that the desire for clitoral stimulation was unresolved penis envy while the ability to be satisfied through vaginal orgasm represented coming to terms with female sexuality.

The goal of Freudian therapy is to resolve the conflict between the id, ego, and superego. This is achieved when the client recognizes the existence of the instinctual urges and learns to gratify them in more socially accepted ways, such as sublimating in creative endeavors. Women are encouraged to relinquish their penis envy and accept their biologically determined passive and nurturing role in life.

The process of therapy relies heavily on free association and dream interpretation. In free association, the client is encouraged to say everything as it comes into his or her head, no matter how irrelevant or silly it seems. The client lies on a couch with the therapist out of sight. The therapist says very little so as not to interfere with the associative flow. When certain patterns become clear, the therapist will interject an interpretation. Dreams are encouraged and interpreted as distorted statements of repressed wishes. Part of the therapy is devoted to the analysis of the "transference" by which the client is seen as relating to the therapist as he or she did to early authority figures. Freudian therapists usually insist on a minimum of three sessions a week, more often four or five. Some therapists also lay down certain rules governing outside behavior, including prohibitions against talking to anyone about the therapy and making any changes in life-style during therapy.

Among the criticisms of Freudian therapy is that the prescribed authoritarian relationship with the therapist is not conducive to the development of autonomy. The Freudian therapist is more likely than others to follow set procedures rather than bend to the client's needs. These procedures govern such major issues as setting goals for the client consonant with Freudian theory and interpreting disagreement as resistance rather than as rationally based, as well as such relatively minor issues as expecting the client to adjust vacation schedules to the therapist's. Women, especially, find Freudian therapy hard to take unless they accept that true happiness lies in passive nurturing and renunciation of their "masculine" strivings.

Those who are drawn to Freudian therapy often feel reassured by the intensity of their feelings toward the therapist, either positive or negative, and the focus on the "transference." They accept the authoritarianism as a necessary component of the elitist aura of Freudian therapy, which many of its practitioners have tried to maintain. Despite Freud's strong objections to medical analysis, most of the early psychoanalysts in the United States tried to restrict training opportunities to physicians, with the result that psychoanalytic societies became exclusive enclaves. Such noted nonmedical analysts as Theodor Reik and Erich Fromm were instrumental in setting up new training institutes open to other qualified professionals, but sibling rivalry continues.

Ego Psychology and Object Relations Theory Many therapists who are strict adherents of Freudian theory have sought to enlarge upon his original doctrine. Although they have established new approaches of their own, these are elaborations on Freudian psychoanalysis rather than departures from it.

The ego psychologists, one of whose proponents was Anna Freud, daughter of Sigmund and a "lay (nonmedical) analyst," while accepting the important role of the id, focus their attention on ego functions. In addition to the ego's role in resolution of conflict with the id, they are also concerned about its autonomous functions such as cognition, imagination, and perception, which are viewed as developing according to an innate biological timetable. The object relations theorists, an offshoot of the ego psychologists, focus on one particular ego function, namely object relations, an oddly impersonal term that means relationships with other people. Many object relations theorists, including Melanie Klein, John Bowlby, and Margaret Mahler, concentrate on early childhood relationships with primary caretakers. Those dealing with adult relationships, particularly Heinz Kohut and Otto Kernberg, are best known for their work with narcissistic character disorders and borderline personalities, two conditions defined by distorted object relations and sense of self.

In practice, the experience of therapy with an ego psychology or object relations therapist is not unlike that described for a classical

Freudian. Therapy frequency is usually set at a minimum of three times weekly. The client is still expected to use the couch and free-associate, while the therapist remains impersonal to foster the "transference neurosis." Silences on the part of the client are usually regarded as resistance to therapy and most often greeted with corresponding silence by the therapist or interpretations of the silence. Some clients experience object relations therapists as cold and nonfacilitating and continue to struggle with these feelings throughout therapy; some accept their discomfort as a necessary part of the psychotherapy process while others want a climate in which they are free from direct interaction with the therapist.

Adler and Individual Psychology Alfred Adler was the first of Freud's colleagues to split off and develop a new system. Adler was interested in the capacity of the body to compensate for organic damage. From this he developed his basic thesis that all human striving is directed toward compensating for feelings of inferiority. According to Adler, the striving for superiority and power, rather than the sexual instinct, determines human behavior. Human problems are therefore social rather than sexual in nature, with neurosis resulting when the drive to power is blocked.

As children grow they become aware of their inferiority to and dependency on adults. This "inferiority complex" can become exaggerated in many ways: by parents who are rejecting, by sibling position, or by actual "organ inferiority." A person can compensate for feelings of inferiority either by competitive achievement and gaining power over others, or by retreating from direct competition and social interaction. The individual's manner of striving for power or superiority is his or her "life-style," which is always unique. The goal of therapy is to understand this life-style and develop ways of achieving a sense of power without losing one's "community feeling."

Although Karen Horney usually gets the credit, Adler was the first disciple of Freud to develop a theory of female psychology based on woman's social role rather than on her anatomy. Women are jealous of men, according to Adler, not because of the latter's sexual organ but because men have social advantages and power.

The focus in Adlerian therapy is on understanding present lifestyle and future goals, rather than on the past. The therapy relationship is regarded as a model for other relationships and is aimed at developing positive feelings for other people. The therapist, in face-to-face encounters, helps the client to substitute realistic for unrealistic goals and encourages social consciousness and activism. Power strivings are unblocked and steered into socially useful channels. Adlerian therapists are directive and active, and usually see clients two times a week for several years.

Jung and Analytic Psychology Carl G. Jung, the favorite and the only prominent non-Jewish student of Freud, could not accept what he considered to be Freud's excessive emphasis on sex. The system he developed was both desexualized and more esoteric and elaborate than that of his mentor.

The basic motivating force in Jungian theory is the "life-force," which is similar to Freud's libido but not exclusively sexual in nature. The psyche has three levels: consciousness, the personal unconscious, and the collective unconscious. The outer crust of the personality is the "persona" or façade, which is the part exposed to others. This conscious self has different ways of apprehending the world (either by introversion or by extroversion) and different functions in so doing—thinking, intuition, feeling, or sensuousness. The personal unconscious is a mirror-image of the consciousness and compensates for what is weak in the consciousness. For example, an introvert has an extroverted side of which he or she is not aware. The personal unconscious thereby contains the potential for richer functioning. The collective unconscious consists of memories inherited from earlier generations, which provide a reserve of wisdom on which consciousness can draw. Emotional problems arise from an imbalance between the various aspects of the self. The goal of therapy is to integrate those aspects of the personal unconscious that are repressed and underutilized and to bring the client into contact with the collective unconscious.

Jungian therapy focuses on present and future strivings rather than on the past. Much attention is given to dreams, which are considered to be a source of revelation leading to integration of the personality. The therapist takes a directive role and introjects his or her own associations to help the client progress to the point the therapist has reached. Jung felt that his therapy was most appropriate for people past the age of forty. He thought that two times a week was adequate and that clients needed at least twenty-four hours to assimilate the material covered in a session. While some people are drawn to Jungian therapy because of its concept of the collective unconscious and the striving for self-transcendence, others reject it for being too mystical.

Reich and Vegetotherapy Although Wilhelm Reich was originally one of Freud's favored students, the two men came into conflict over Reich's radicalism. Reich was concerned with the relation of political repression to character formation, an idea that was mocked by the psychoanalytic establishment. He was also held in disfavor by political radicals for his attempts to introduce sexual reforms. After coming to the United States, Reich continued to find himself at odds with practically everyone. Events culminated in his arrest and imprisonment by federal authorities in connection with FDA curbs imposed on his marketing of therapeutic devices.

Reich felt that character is formed in order to meet the needs of the existing social order, and that individual needs have to be repressed to meet the demands of authority. Sexual needs, as the first to come into conflict with society, are the first to be suppressed. This suppression lays the groundwork for a permeating restrictive pattern running through the entire personality. Restricting the sexual impulse cripples the whole personality and it is only through sexual freedom that the individual can find personal freedom. Sexuality, as expressed in the orgasm, is the key to healthy personality functioning. The goal of therapy is to restore the motility and flow of biological energy or "orgone."

Character traits such as ambition or passivity, which form the "character armor," are developed to protect the individual from his or her instincts and constitute the roots of psychological disturbance. The character armor has a corresponding muscular armor, which is evidenced in idiosyncratic postures and movements of the body.

Therapy proceeds on both a verbal and a body-contact level, although most Reichians focus on body work. The therapist must penetrate the character armor by pointing out to the client characteristic attitudes that are used as defenses. The therapist focuses on how a person walks, sits, looks, breathes, and talks, and reads the emotions through their physical expression. The therapist also works through the layers of muscular armor, using yelling, pounding, and kicking to have the client experience the physical aspects of emotions. The client lies disrobed on a couch to make visible the areas of body tension and to make them available for manipulation that, combined with deep breathing exercises, leads to relaxation. The therapy must also work toward mature sexual functioning by helping the client achieve full orgasm.

Reichian therapy has a reputation of being "far-out." Reich's reputation as a "kook" is related to the nude body work, a concept that was far ahead of its time, and to his orgone theory and orgone-accumulating boxes. Reactions to Reichian therapy seem to be strongly positive or negative. On the positive side, people have found it helpful in putting them in touch with feelings and bodily sensations that would not emerge otherwise. Clients who have reacted negatively tend to find the therapy either too intrusive or too sexually oriented. People tend to go to Reichian therapy after becoming disillusioned with conventional psychoanalytic approaches.

Horney and the Cultural Approach Originally an orthodox Freudian analyst in Germany, Karen Horney later became a leader of the "cultural school" of psychoanalysis in the United States. According to Horney, the search for security is the basic human drive. When the individual's security is threatened, he or she develops anxiety. To cope with these feelings of helplessness and isolation, the individual develops various strategies, which tend to differ according to the particular culture. Horney described ten coping patterns, which can be reduced to three basic strategies: moving toward people (in which the individual may accept his or her basic helplessness and look toward others for affection and support), moving against people (in which the individual acknowledges the hostility of others and fights back), or moving away from people (in which the individual just tries to keep apart). Although one strategy predominates in any individual, all are present to some degree. Some persons can create balance among the strategies, but others are unable to resolve the clash, which results in neurotic conflict. This is intensified by the inflexibility of the neurotic, who sticks to a particular strategy even though it is inappropriate. The neurotic creates an idealized self-image that denies or condemns shortcomings in the actual self and prevents the "real" self from emerging. The goal of therapy is to help the real self in each individual come to the surface. This is accomplished by facing the idealized and actual selves and creating a balance among the three different ways of approaching the world (to, against, and away).

Horney became prominent in the 1940s and 1950s as a result of several books on therapy for the general public. Her popularity among women was especially strong: not only was she a woman but she developed a theory of female sexuality based on women's cultural role. She proposed that Freud's conception of female sexuality was based on his male vantage point and Victorian upbringing. In her view, as in Adler's, women's feelings of inferiority and jealousy toward the male stemmed from envy not of his penis but of his social advantages. She went on to suggest that the notion of penis envy might have evolved from male envy of the female capacity to create and nurture life. Her ideological break with the psychoanalytic establishment and her initiation of a rival psychoanalytic society also won her many adherents.

The therapy process is similar to Freud's, consisting of free association, interpretation, and working through. However, the therapist is more directive, focusing on fighting the prideful ideal self and on realistically facing the actual self. Therapy frequency is about three times a week, generally for a period of several years.

Sullivan and Interpersonal Relations Harry Stack Sullivan was the first American psychiatrist to develop a prominent psychoanalytic theory. Together with Horney, he broke from the ranks of the Freudians to help establish what became known as the cultural school of psychoanalysis.

People's primary strivings are, to Sullivan, the pursuit of satisfactions and the pursuit of security. Satisfactions include all physical needs; security needs are culturally determined. The environment regards the child as "good" or "bad" depending on its behavior; security comes from the approval one receives from being good, while being bad leads to disapproval and a sense of insecurity. These basic attitudes about oneself are always experienced in relation to interpersonal situations, and the self-concept is based on the perceived reactions of others. These perceptions can be accurate or they can be distorted. Once the self is developed, it maintains its form and is directed toward avoiding anxiety. People therefore tend to block out everything that threatens the way in which they have organized the self-system and that provokes anxiety. Even "hateful" self-systems are maintained by misinterpreting or ignoring friendly overtures from others.

One of the major goals of therapy is to help the client see the way in which his or her relationships are based on distorted perceptions of others. The therapy must be an interpersonal process with the therapist in the role of "participant observer." Therapy focuses on childhood experiences that have created distortions, and there is a back and forth between analysis of distortions in past situations and distortions that occur between therapist and client. The relationship between therapist and client is intensified in order to release the distortions and ease resistance to change.

Because of this intensification of the therapist-client relationship, there is a potential for overly intimate involvement. In recent years, a group of Sullivanian therapists has achieved considerable notoriety with its attempt to reshape interpersonal relations by active intervention in clients' lives, including the promotion of relations within the Sullivanian community and the exclusion of others. The appeal of Sullivanian theory is thus weakened by the excesses of some of its practitioners.

Rogers and Client-Centered Therapy The first major psychotherapy system developed by an American psychologist was Carl Rogers's nondirective approach. The basic drive of every human being, according to Rogers, is the drive toward self-actualization. Actualization, however, can occur only in accordance with an individual's perception of him- or herself. It is the perception of self that determines one's behavior and relationships with other people. Preserving and enhancing the self-concept and obtaining positive regard from others are basic motivations. Experiences not consistent with one's self-concept can be disowned, and an individual may also take over values from others that are not directly experienced or are contradictory to direct experience but more congruent with the self-concept. The need to enhance the self-concept in this and other ways may come in conflict with the drive for self-actualization.

The goal in therapy is to help the client resolve this conflict by reorganizing perceptions of self and actualizing potential for growth. The therapy process rests on providing a permissive atmosphere conducive to acquiring understanding, one in which the client's potential for constructive change is respected. The therapist tries to understand reality as experienced by the client. The client is left free to work out the course and direction of the therapeutic situation according to his or her needs. The therapist does not offer interpretations to the client but may provide summaries of material presented by the client to make sure the client is being clearly understood and to reflect back what has been said.

The major appeal of Rogerian therapy is its nonauthoritarian approach. It is better suited to clients who have the psychological resources to explore their own feelings, needing very little direction from the therapist. On the other hand, those who need more from the therapist than encouraging warmth and understanding are apt to be disappointed with this approach.

Existential Analysis (Daseinsanalysis) Existential analysis is derived from existential philosophy and phenomenology. It was developed primarily by Ludwig Binswanger, a Swiss psychiatrist, and introduced to the United States by Ulrich Sonnemann. Existential theory is best known to therapists through the works of Medard Boss and to the public through the books of Rollo May. Although this system has great simplicity, paradoxically many people find it hard to understand, probably because it does not deal in the usual categories and terminology, attempting to describe experience rather than explain or classify it.

The existential therapist holds that the essence of human existence is the awareness of "being-in-the-world" (the German word for which is *Dasein*). Awareness of being carries with it the awareness of one's ultimate nonbeing, the basis of existential anxiety. Human life is also characterized by awareness of oneself as someone who exists in time, with a past, present, and future. Many disturbances are related to disturbances in the experience of time. When there is no future horizon or it is blocked, as in depressive states, life seems to come to a standstill. Other disturbances may lie in an inability to relate comfortably to the past: the past may be discarded as too painful, or one may be unable to give it up and live in the present.

According to existential analysis, each person has a unique way of being-in-the-world, which is characterized by that person's openness to the world. The more a person denies the fundamental traits of being and does not confront existential anxiety, the more unauthentic and the less a person one becomes. Authentic existence requires facing one's condition and accepting responsibility for all of life's possibilities. To the extent that people can at any given moment fulfill only one of the many new possibilities that are always opening up, they experience the existential guilt of "being in-debt" to themselves. The goal of existential analysis is to help the client understand his or her possibilities *as* possibilities and thereby permit them to unfold. The therapist does not ask why the client behaves in a certain way but rather "why not" in more daring and less restrictive ways.

Unlike other therapists who try to draw the client out, the existential therapist tries to enter the world of the client. The therapist has to shed all attempts to explain the client's behavior, reach behind it, or translate it into such categories as ego or id, which may not be part of the client's world. Instead the therapist, by being affectively present, helps the client come face to face with his or her immediate experience. Through such genuine encounter the client can participate with the therapist in a discovery of self in which awareness expands along with choices. Existential analysis is not an intellectual recognition or explanation of a problem but an opportunity to experience new ways of living and relating.

Despite the general interest in existential concepts, existential analysis has caught hold with relatively few therapists, probably because it is contrary to the American predilection for systematization and dispenses with the usual classifications and labels. Though the framework is different, however, the procedures used in existential analysis are similar to those of other analytic systems: discussion, association, and dream analysis. Clients who want an explanation for their behavior may be disappointed by existential analysis, but those who want to broaden their awareness and, therefore, possibilities, will be attracted to it.

Gestalt Therapy Gestalt therapy was developed by several persons, but has become most associated with Frederick S. ("Fritz") Perls. *Gestalt* is the German word for "meaningful whole."

According to gestalt therapy, human life has a basic wholeness in which thinking, feeling, and acting are integrated. In the course of development, this unity of the self may become split. The individual also exists in the context of his or her environment and it is the interplay of both that provides a key to understanding. A disturbance or a lack of unified experience in the self leads to a disturbance in the individual's relation to his or her world. An integrated person can engage freely with the world, while persons whose experiences are split tend to relate in unproductive ways. The goals of therapy are to help the individual achieve wholeness and a flexible interaction with the environment. By becoming aware of needs and acknowledging them, a person also becomes free to choose and to take responsibility for changing.

The therapy process is oriented toward developing awareness of, and responsiveness to, immediate experience. Emphasis is placed on the "here and now," the current experience, rather than the past or "why" of behavior. Many exercises, called "experiments in awareness," are utilized toward this end. A client may be asked to complete the statement, "At this moment I am aware . . ." by filling in a description of what is in his or her immediate awareness. Another experiment instructs the client to select a recent memory and with closed eyes visualize and reconstruct the scene, noting all that is there. A body awareness exercise instructs the client to lie down and feel the body, noting aches, tension spots, and uncomfortable positions, and to adjust the body smoothly. Role playing and the "empty chair" exercise are described in Chapter 8, "Making Therapy Work." The therapist engages the client actively, directing exercises, challenging statements, rejecting certain behaviors such as asking "why" questions, but also reacting sympathetically.

The awareness experiments and confrontational approach of gestalt therapy enable many people to experience feelings that were formerly blocked, and it can be effective with persons who tend to overintellectualize. However, in the process, gestalt therapy lends itself to intrusive and arrogant behavior on the part of therapists. They may also blame the client for lack of progress, as responsibility for change is placed on the latter. Gestalt therapists usually encourage their clients to enter a group in addition to individual sessions.

Lowen and Bioenergetic Therapy Bioenergetic therapy was developed by Alexander Lowen, an American psychiatrist who was a student of Reich. Like Reich, Lowen believes that emotional problems express themselves in the body in the form of muscular tensions, with "bioenergy," the fundamental body energy, manifesting itself on both an emotional and a muscular level. In the normal person, bodily impulses can flow to the surface, keeping the body emotionally alive and ready to respond. In others, the body is ignored and becomes a repository of repressed feelings. Therapy aims at "reclaiming" the body and enabling energy to flow freely through the organism. As physical tensions are an expression of emotional tension, dissipating the former will help to resolve the latter.

The therapy consists of acting out emotional processes in the language of the body. Several specific exercises are employed, and clients generally wear leotards to facilitate this work. Sessions usually start with taking "stress positions" that place the muscles in a position of steady stretching. These stretch positions highlight the areas of tension and arouse bodily feelings that can be utilized during the session. Further exercises are directed toward working out inhibited reactions: a client may be asked to pound on a table while shouting "Mommy," or to grab the end of a towel held by the therapist and tug while shouting "I want it." These activities are used to develop the capacity for emotional expression, thereby increasing self-assertiveness, releasing negation, and developing affirmative feelings.

Bioenergetics appeals to people who feel they are not really at one with their physical selves and want to achieve a unity of experience. For this group, it has generally proved to be a satisfying approach. Others have found its focus too narrow to help them deal with complex problems of living.

Janov and Primal Therapy Primal therapy was developed by Arthur Janov, an American psychologist. To Janov, the origin of emotional problems is in the daily attitudes of family life. Parents and others demand certain responses from children to fulfill their own needs, giving the child little or no opportunity for self-initiated activities and a real life. The child's primal needs for food, warmth, physical contact, and so forth are denied, resulting in primal pain. This pain accumulates and is warded off by developing various neurotic defenses: clouded memories, reflex habits, avoiding feelings. Neurosis is a defense against primal pain.

The goal of therapy is to unearth and release the primal pain. The method used is "direct talk" to the sources of primal pain—to the authoritarian father or the overprotective mother. This direct talk goes beyond the verbal to the "primal screams" and a reexperiencing of key scenes. "Primals" are intense experiences that differ from person to person and may include screaming, writhing, sweating, and trembling. Primal therapy requires three weeks of continuous individual work, usually up to three and a half hours daily, during which memories, breathing techniques, and direct verbal confrontations are utilized to bring back early experiences. Therapy is preceded by the client's spending twenty-four hours in isolation indoors to deprive him or her of usual tension outlets and to weaken defenses. The therapist works with only one client for the three-week period. The client stays in therapy for up to nine months in a group setting, continuing to have cathartic experiences. Some therapists and clinics offer primal therapy on a regularly scheduled basis without the concentrated three-week period, and without total therapist availability.

Going through "primals" is emotionally demanding and not to many people's taste. There is some possibility that clients may become overwhelmed by the intensity of the experience and there is considerable question whether the release of primal pain itself is enough to be lastingly therapeutic without reintegrating uncovered feelings into the personality. Janov supports his therapy with claims of success based on physiological changes and the unabashed statement that primal therapy is *the* cure for neurosis. The dogmatism of the system and the condemnation of other approaches raises questions about the primal therapist's ability to respect clients who may be at variance with aspects of the therapy.

Transactional Analysis Transactional analysis was developed by Eric Berne in *Games People Play* and popularized further by Thomas Harris in *I'm OK—You're OK*. It is based on the conception that people are motivated by important social hungers as well as by biological drives. These hungers are satisfied by "stroking," which is any act that recognizes the presence of another person. The first is stimulation hunger, which is satisfied by physical stroking. Recognition hunger can be satisfied by positive strokes such as applause, smiles, or kisses, or by negative strokes such as frowns or disapproval. Negative strokes, while not as satisfying as positive strokes, still afford some recognition. "Crooked" strokes are mixed messages combining both positive and negative elements. Structure hunger is the need to organize one's time, and people arrange their activities to obtain the most strokes. There are six basic ways of structuring time, going from the safest to the most exciting: withdrawal, in which the individual avoids others and satisfies him- or herself with "stored" strokes, which may be relived from previous situations; rituals or stylized ways of interaction; activities or work; pastimes; games, which are social transactions leading to a "payoff"; and, finally, intimacy, which is an open give-and-take between people. These ways of structuring time are incorporated into a larger structure called the life plan or "script," which is developed in childhood.

Each individual has three aspects of personality: the Child (impulse aspect), the Parent (critical aspect), and the Adult (mature aspect). A stable person can change from one state to another depending on its appropriateness to the situation, but others may be stuck in a particular state or have one state contaminated by another. In social transactions, people can communicate satisfactorily only when these states are complementary to one another. When the states are crossed, for instance one person's Child talking to another person's Adult, this leads to conflict. Most transactions are complex and ulterior, with more than two states activated at the same time, one covering up the other. Ulterior transactions are the basis for games, which always involve a con.

The goal of therapy is to help the client move from games to intimacy and to avoid self-destructive scripts. The methods of transactional analysis consist of "structural analysis" in which the interaction of the three states of the client are analyzed, and in analyzing scripts. Therapy can be individual, but is usually conducted on a group basis because the latter provides greater opportunity for analyzing transactions. The therapist is active and direct in pointing out the three different states in which clients are interacting, in diagnosing their games and scripts, and in convincing clients that they need not be victims of these problems.

Transactional analysis has appeal because it is relatively easy to understand, not very demanding of the client, and supportive in unraveling difficulties in interpersonal relationships. However, in its focus on interpersonal behavior and its labeling, transactional analysis often bypasses the inner person and deeper levels of feeling.

Ellis and Rational-Emotive Therapy   Rational-emotive therapy was developed by Albert Ellis, an American psychologist, and is the best known of the cognitive approaches. The therapy is based on the view that emotions are a form of evaluative thought. Positive emotions result from experiences labeled "good" and negative emotions are caused by the label "bad." Controlling one's emotions is accomplished by controlling one's thoughts. Emotions can be changed from negative to positive by reevaluating or relabeling situations. Emotional disturbances result from repeating to oneself negative and illogical thoughts. The individual develops these thoughts in relation to the environment. Parents and the larger culture provide many damaging evaluations and irrational beliefs, which are then internalized.

The goal of therapy is to show the client the nature of these irrational beliefs and induce him or her to adopt more rational ideas. To achieve these goals, the therapist takes an active and persuasive role.

Ellis feels his system is most appropriate for intelligent younger people who are not very disturbed and who are willing to work and discipline themselves. Some clients welcome the directness and firm opinionated stand of the therapist, but others find it not very conducive to reflection or to getting in touch with one's own feelings.

Behavior Therapy/Behavior Modification Although behavior therapy is often considered a form of psychotherapy, it is a system apart because it is exclusively concerned with changing behavior and not with increasing awareness. What the psychotherapist sees as emotional problems to be clarified, the behavior modifier sees as maladaptive habits to be changed. Behavior therapy asserts that all behavior is a learned response to the environment. The goal of behavior modification is to extinguish old maladaptive responses and to elicit new responses. Its methods are based on the principles of learning theory, which hold that people persist in behavior that is rewarded and desist from behavior that is punished. By punishing negative responses and reinforcing positive responses, the therapist conditions the individual to respond in new ways. This is done in two steps. First, the behavior therapist conducts a behavioral analysis, which is a study of events leading up to and following a particular unwanted behavior. Next, the therapist designs and carries out a program of treatment to modify that behavior.

Several techniques have been developed to modify behavior. "Systematic desensitization" is used to reduce the anxiety associated with a certain situation and thereby eliminate avoidance of the feared situation. Fear of snakes, or of riding in elevators, are examples of maladaptive behaviors that are treated by systematic desensitization. Treatment involves exposure by progressive steps to the feared situations. The client's fears are ordered from the least to the greatest, and he or she is exposed to them one by one.

This is done either by imagining the feared situations or by actual exposure. Fear of snakes might be treated by first talking about snakes, then looking at snake pictures, then looking at live snakes, then touching a live snake held by someone else, and finally handling a live snake oneself. Each new step is undertaken only after fear at the previous step is dissipated.

"Operant conditioning" is used in conditions that require complex behavior change, such as school failure or stuttering. Operant conditioning is based on the premise that behavior is affected by its consequences. It changes conditions in the environment that reward unwanted behavior and introduces positive reinforcement for desired behavior. "Token economies," a form of operant conditioning, are used to reward positive behavior. When the client makes a desired response, he or she receives a token that can be exchanged later for some direct reward. For example, a child who wets the bed may be given a gold star each night he or she stays dry; after getting seven stars in a row, the child may trade them in for a toy. Or, a couple may give each other tokens for exhibiting desired behavior (washing dishes, not smoking), which, in sufficient quantity, may be exchanged for dinner out or sex in.

"Aversion therapy" involves punishing the undesired behavior in order to extinguish it and is usually reserved for severe difficulties. For example, a transvestite is asked to dress in women's clothes while in the therapist's office. While doing so he is given electric shocks until the clothes are entirely removed. This procedure is repeated during office visits until the client finally refuses to wear women's clothes outside as well as inside the therapist's office.

Behavior therapy has been successful in treating specific behavioral problems such as phobias, sexual deviancy, and enuresis, but it has had little effect on complex emotional problems. Because such problems are beyond the scope of behavior modification, behavior modifiers are turning back to a consideration of the processes that go on within a person. To the extent that they do, they can be more successful in helping people come to terms with their problems, but to the same extent they are no longer doing behavior therapy. Many psychotherapists incorporate behavior modification techniques into the psychotherapy process. When used as an adjunct to psychotherapy, these techniques can facilitate therapy by relieving anxieties and other symptoms and leaving clients freer to focus on underlying problems. They can be and often are used informally to encourage a client to exercise new capabilities. The critical difference between the supplementary use of behavior modification techniques in psychotherapy and their exclusive use is the difference between changing one's life and changing one's habits.

Sex Therapy Sex therapy is a form of behavior modification that concentrates on sexual problems such as premature ejaculation, impotence, and orgasmic dysfunction. The usual procedure is for clients to work in pairs. Clients who are engaged in a sexual relationship, marital or otherwise, come with the partner. Other clients, depending on the clinic, may be provided with a "surrogate" partner by the clinic.

The couple works with two therapists, one male and one female. Although there is variation in procedure, a common pattern is for the couple to engage in an intensive two-week treatment period during which they are seen daily. The therapy is a reconditioning process aimed at reducing performance fears. Through a series of graduated homework assignments, the couple goes on to different levels of sexual activity, moving on to a new level only once comfort and satisfaction have been achieved at the previous level.

Sex therapy has achieved its best results when the sexual problem is grounded in a lack of information, in misinformation, in lack of technical know-how, or in reluctance to deal with associated anxiety, as in the case of men who ejaculate prematurely and women who have never had orgasms. It demystifies sex and instills confidence in the partners by teaching them how to gratify each other and reassuring them about their own entitlement to pleasure. When the sexual problems are expressive of deep-seated emotional attitudes, as in the case of erection and "desire" problems, and the sex therapy isolates sexual behavior from the feelings involved toward the sexual partner and toward oneself, it is not very successful. Impotency, for example, can reflect various attitudes: it could be a statement of feelings of guilt in having sex and the expectation of punishment, or of general feelings of incompetence and powerlessness, or of feelings about the sexual partner as being undeserving, or it could be a way of getting back at one's partner. Because sex therapy does not work well if the sexual dysfunction is based on unresolved feelings and attitudes, it is best for clients who are in a committed relationship and does not work well for those in distressed relationships. To broaden its utility, some sex clinics now offer psychotherapy in addition to sex therapy. Of course, it is also possible to get help with sexual problems from a psychotherapist in the context of psychotherapy.

In considering sex therapy, utmost care must be used in checking the credentials and reputation of the therapist as the field of sex therapy has become one of grave abuse and commercial exploitation. Many so-called sex clinics are but thinly disguised procurement agencies and individual sex therapists may seek to have sexual relations with you.

Neuro Linguistic Programming Neuro Linguistic Programming (NLP) was developed by Richard Bandler and John Grinder, two American psychologists. NLP describes itself as a model of human experience and communication. The developers of this system maintain that by applying its principles one can describe any behavior in a way that makes it possible to effect lasting changes quickly. Examples of such changes are curing phobias in an hour, eliminating unwanted habits (smoking, overeating) or curing many physical problems in a few sessions, changing interactions of couples, families, and organizations to become more satisfying. In addition to remedial change, NLP promises generative change by determining the structure of any talent or exceptional ability so that it can be taught to others.

This system is not concerned with the theory of therapy but with how therapy is done. The developers of NLP studied successful therapists to extract their method. They found that all successful therapists follow the same sequences and patterns, regardless of their theoretical orientation. The central technique is to "match" the client by using his or her representational system—visual, kinesthetic, or aural—which the therapist can do by noticing the total behavior of the client, including in which direction the client looks when talking about an experience: up, down, sideways, right, or left. These different directions provide accessing cues. People who look to the right and upward when answering a question, for example, are experiencing a visual image, while those looking down and to the right are experiencing kinesthetic feelings. When the therapist can access the meaning of what is being said and knows what images, sounds, and feelings are involved in any given problem situation, it is possible to help the client change the system and thereby resolve the problem. If it is determined by this method, for example, that a client with a height phobia has a visual image of falling down, the therapist then rivets the client's attention to a representational system other than the bothersome visual one. The client might be asked to go to a high window and look down while singing the national anthem. Because the visual response is blocked, the phobic response is also blocked and the problem resolved.

Another way of matching the client is by "pacing" his or her behavior. This can be done by "direct mirroring," such as breathing at the same rate as the client, or by "crossover mirroring," matching the tempo of the client's breathing through hand movements or through speech. Once the therapist paces the client it is possible to lead him or her to new behavior and anchor these new responses to old situations by using a variety of conditioning techniques.

As is the case with other behavioral approaches, NLP seems to work well in helping people overcome troublesome symptoms. However, remedial change (stopping unwanted behavior) is, as NLP states, a very limited goal. Generative change (actualizing one's potential) is a much broader goal, and it is not clear that the mechanistic approach of NLP is able to achieve it.

Hypnotherapy Hypnotherapy is the application of hypnosis to alleviate psychological distress and problems. According to one of its major proponents, hypnosis by itself has no permanent psychotherapeutic effects but it can be of specific benefit in conjunction with psychotherapy. Hypnosis has been used to remove temporarily such incapacitating hysterical symptoms as paralysis, tics, and amnesia. While relieved of such symptoms, a client may be able to work psychotherapeutically to get at the causes of the symptoms. Hypnosis is also used to reduce resistance and to help bring repressed memories to the surface. Some hypnotherapists use it as a form of persuasion, trying to have the client accept attitudes and values in a trance state that are being resisted in a waking state. Hypnosis has also been used as a way to break undesirable habits such as smoking and overeating.

Hypnotherapy is limited in application to persons who are suggestible and can be hypnotized to the necessary depth. Hypnotic suggestions have a limited life-span and unless the problems a symptom is expressing are worked through in a waking state, the symptom is apt to reappear. Similarly, repressed material that emerges in a trance is helpful only to the extent that it can be integrated into one's waking state and consciousness.

Some hypnotists teach clients self-hypnosis to enable them to continue the benefits on their own. For example, a very tense client who has been hypnotized to achieve a state of deep rest that counteracts the tension may be taught to put him- or herself into a trance whenever he or she needs relaxation and control over tension.

Although some mental health professionals have been trained in hypnosis and use it as an adjunct to psychotherapy, many hypnotists have no training or expertise in psychotherapy. While they may help you learn new ways to respond to certain stimuli and control unwanted habits, they may be unable to help you with any broader issues or to integrate your new behavior into a different life pattern.

Eclectic Psychotherapy Many psychotherapists describe their approach as "eclectic," meaning they do not ascribe to any one theory or method but avail themselves of what works best in the various approaches. While eclecticism in some therapists may indicate flightiness and a need to swing with each new fad, in most it indicates openness to new techniques and a capacity to work with clients in a flexible manner. Usually, an eclectic therapist will favor a particular view, say the interpersonal approach, but will not be closed off to using other methods, such as behavior modification, when they seem appropriate.

Research has shown that despite different theoretical emphases, in practice, experienced psychotherapists turn out to be more similar than dissimilar in their approach. As therapists gain in experience they tend to become less doctrinaire and more eclectic, putting their personal stamp on the type of therapy they practice. Good therapists, even if they do not consider themselves eclectic, sense the limitations of the particular theories they subscribe to and reach out to clients in ways that cut across theoretical lines. Because of their training and experience they are able to modify their approach depending on the client's problems, responsiveness, or stage in therapy. Less secure therapists tend to be more rigid in sticking to a theory and less able to respond in spontaneous ways. Choosing a therapy system that makes sense to you is, therefore, only the first step: it is also important for you to evaluate any potential therapist on a personal basis, as we will describe in the next chapter.

THE DIFFERENT MODALITIES

Psychotherapy is practiced in different forms to meet different needs: individual therapy, group therapy, family therapy, couples therapy, and child therapy. These different therapy modalities, as they are called, may be used alone, or sometimes in combination with one another. In addition to a choice of theoretical approach, you also have a choice of modality, and the purpose of this section is to help clarify which is most appropriate for you.

Individual Therapy Psychotherapy started as a one-to-one endeavor and this form has remained the most prevalent. In part, people gravitate to this mode because it is the prototype of therapy, but individual therapy has a number of advantages compared to the other modalities. Many people, because of the intensity of their emotional disturbance, need the individual attention and support of an exclusive relationship, especially when they start therapy. Also, because therapy is usually seen as a personal matter, most people prefer individual therapy for the privacy that it provides. Another advantage of individual therapy over the other modalities is that it offers a greater opportunity for getting in touch with intrapsychic difficulties as the client is the sole focus of the therapy. Such problems as depression, chronic anxiety, confused thinking, inability to function at work, or feelings of lack of fulfillment are more readily explored in individual therapy. In addition, the individual therapy setting lends itself better to introspective therapeutic methods, including free association and reflecting on dream imagery, that require isolation from the unexpected intrusion of others. Yet another advantage of individual therapy stems from the relationship between client and therapist that emerges. The one-to-one relationship is the most basic and primary relationship people have and individual therapy, by recapitulating it, enables client and therapist to study it in vivo. This is particularly important for the psychoanalytically oriented approach, which regards the "transference" relationship between client and therapist as critical to the therapy process.

Individual therapy is sometimes supplemented by group therapy. The latter can be used as an adjunct to individual therapy when the client cannot afford more frequent individual sessions but wants to have a more extensive therapy experience. Or group therapy may be used as an adjunct for people who have difficulty in their interpersonal relationships, as described in the section on group therapy. Sometimes people who have been in individual therapy will leave to join a group as new goals, more appropriate to the group setting, are formulated.

Group Therapy All major psychotherapy systems have adapted their methods of individual therapy to group use, since a group setting has several advantages that individual therapy cannot provide. Although some practitioners structure group therapy essentially as individually centered therapy within a group situation, most try to capitalize on the unique therapeutic possibilities inherent in group interactions.

Group therapy offers a ready-made circle of people who are willing to try to understand, accept, and share feelings with one another. It is especially sensitive to interpersonal difficulties, as these are readily revealed in the group interaction. Uninhibited interactions are encouraged and, when achieved, inevitably lead to emotionally arousing confrontations. As a "living laboratory," groups focus on helping participants to perceive their habitual ways of dealing with interpersonal stress and to try out new ways.

While providing a greater range of stimulation, group therapy also offers greater opportunities for response. The participants have to cope with the reactions of others and can give as well as receive help. Group participation facilitates transfer of newly learned behavior into daily life.

Though there must be mutuality of purpose for group cohesion to develop, groups can be heterogeneous or homogeneous in such member characteristics as age, sex, or psychological problem area. Heterogeneous groups offer a wider range of stimulation and are intended to function as a microcosm of the larger world, while homogeneous groups (couples, divorcées, adolescents) facilitate sharing of common experiences. Therapy groups usually consist of from six to ten people and meet weekly for an hour and a half. Some groups have a predetermined time when they will end. Others continue for as long as group interest persists. Such groups are likely to undergo changes in membership, with some leaving as their goals are met and new people joining at different times. Most groups meet with one therapist, some with two, and some occasionally without the therapist. When two therapists are present, they are usually one of each sex to provide both "mother" and "father" figures.

Therapists vary greatly in the role they take in the group, depending on their theoretical approach and personality predispositions. Some remain neutral arbiters, some actively promote group interaction, and some become group participants. The therapist's main responsibility is to ensure that a therapeutic atmosphere is maintained and that painful experiences are utilized constructively. The influence of the group is very strong and can have important positive or negative effects. It can support a member through a critical moment in the therapy and it can foster conformity by pressuring people to participate when they want to be aloof or to accept feedback when they want to reject it.

Compared to individual therapy, group therapy provides a greater diversity of stimulation, greater opportunity to try out new ways of relating, and more time in therapy for less cost. On the other hand, group therapy offers less time for individual problems, particularly those that do not relate to interactions with others, and it provides little opportunity for examining personal experiences or for reflecting on new experiences. For that reason group therapy is frequently combined with individual therapy, although it can be and often is used by itself.

Family Therapy In family therapy, the focus is on bringing about changes in family relationships rather than in individuals. To accomplish this, families are seen as a unit, with all members attending what is known as conjoint therapy. Children are included in the therapy, although the age at which they are included varies from therapist to therapist. Some want children as young as four to attend, others do not want them below nine or ten years of age. In addition to children, other relatives living in the home, such as grandparents or aunts, are included in therapy sessions as are resident nonrelatives who play an integral part in family life. Variations on the practice of conjoint therapy, such as concomitant or collaborative therapy, in which two or more family members may see the same therapist individually or different therapists who consult each other, tend to focus more on changing the individual as he or she relates to the family than on changing the family system.

Although conjoint family therapy involves a group of family

members, it differs from group therapy, in which more attention is given to the individual's problems, even though in a group environment. Further, unlike the group, which exists only in therapy, the family group has a life of its own, which continues with or without a therapist. This means both that the family group can put constructive new ways of relating into immediate practice after a session and that unresolved frictions are left hanging and can become aggravated between sessions.

Family therapy encompasses all the theories and methods of individual and group therapy, as well as a few new ones of its own. The approaches vary in the emphasis each gives to defining the causes of the problem, improving communications, finding better ways of coping with disagreement and other forms of stress, involvement of children in the process, and attention given to the needs of individual family members. Available forms of family therapy range from the older psychoanalytic approach aimed at analyzing unconscious conflicts that disturb the family relationships and the behavioral approach aimed at changing behavior in the family by realigning reward and punishment systems to new approaches that challenge the structure of the family.

The most prominent of the more recent innovations, systems therapy, structural therapy, and paradoxical therapy, owe their development to several persons. Nathan Ackerman is considered to be the grandfather of the family therapy movement, and it was he who first urged the therapist to participate emotionally in sessions to shake up the family and jar it out of its unproductive patterns of interaction. Other important innovators in family therapy include Virginia Satir, John Bell, Jay Haley, and Salvador Minuchin. Many family therapists have found it difficult to define what, exactly, they do as their response is generally quite personal and spontaneous. Among specific strategies that are employed are teaching family members how to communicate with each other (how to ask a direct informational question, how to ask for and receive feedback, how to express covert questions overtly, how to answer questions), taking a family member's place in the system (acting like the indignant parent, the negative child), allying oneself with the family underdog, confirming family members (kneeling when talking to a child, forcing oneself to notice positive qualities in an unpleasant family member), and having family members reverse roles (asking the mother to act scared to encourage the child to protect her).

Because these new family therapies are based on very active emotional participation of the therapist, some therapists feel they are in danger of losing their therapeutic maneuverability by being drawn too closely into the family system. To avoid this possibility, they utilize a cotherapist or even a cotherapist and an additional team of therapists who act as observers behind a one-way window. Needless to say, these variations can become quite costly for the family, as more than one therapist's time is involved.

Other variations on the family therapy theme concern involvement of more persons on the client side. Sessions may be expanded to include other people important to the family, such as neighbors, friends, or employers (this is called network family therapy), or several families may meet as a group in what is called multiple family therapy.

Most therapists see families on a weekly basis, usually for an hour-and-a-half session. The duration of therapy ranges from a few weeks to several years; on average, it lasts about one year.

Many families who enter therapy do so with one family member, usually a child, pinpointed as the cause of difficulties. Family therapists, however, are committed to the proposition that the family interaction is where the problem lies and will proceed accordingly. In considering family therapy, be prepared to have everyone's behavior explored, challenged, and changed.

Couples and Marriage Therapy In couples or marriage therapy, the focus of the therapy is the relationship between the partners rather than the individual people involved. In that respect, it is very similar to family therapy, except that the latter includes all members of the family unit. Couples therapy is intended for marital, premarital, extramarital, and homosexual couples, as the problems in these relationships tend to be similar and best resolved by working on them as a dyad. Historically, troubled marriages used to be handled in the offices of marriage counselors, but more partners are now turning to couples therapy, which offers a more dynamic approach to problematic relationships.

Therapists with different theoretical orientations approach couples therapy in different ways. In addition to the theoretical systems already outlined in the section on psychotherapy schools, couples therapy also utilizes the new methods of family therapy, including systems therapy and paradoxical therapy (described in the section on family therapy). Generally speaking, these new orientations make for more active interventions and manipulations on the part of the therapist, geared toward encouraging the partners to adopt new ways of relating to each other. The therapist will bring up sensitive issues that the couple tends to avoid and encourage them to confront their difficulties rather than to make their feelings known indirectly through angry behavior or withdrawal. Sometimes the therapist will stage interactions or give assignments that heighten the couple's experience of the impasse in their relationship in a manner that induces change. If the resistance to change is very strong, the therapist might encourage one partner to behave in a way that typically distresses the other, which paradoxically often helps the partner to relinquish the behavior. The new therapies place less emphasis on insight and more on creating an environment in which the couple is forced to abandon old ways that cause conflict and learn new ways of relating that lead to harmony.

Couples therapy is usually conducted on a once-a-week basis, and sessions tend to run for an hour rather than the forty-five- or fifty-minute sessions common in individual therapy. The total length of time couples spend in therapy varies depending on the nature of their difficulties, but usually major problems can be resolved in one year or less. If couples therapy continues beyond that point it generally indicates that the couple is not invested in maintaining the relationship or that the approach is not working for them.

Couples therapy is appropriate when there is a commitment to each other and a commitment to change in relation to each other. As the goal of couples therapy is to improve the relationship, if an individual is not committed to that goal and secretly "wants out" but agrees to therapy because of guilt, such therapy may not serve his or her best interests. More often than not, individuals are confused and unsure of their motives. Under these circumstances, therapy that aims at discovering or actualizing individual goals may be more appropriate.

Child Therapy   Psychotherapy, in the usual sense, cannot be used with young children, as exploration of one's feelings and attitudes requires a degree of conceptual development beyond the scope of the younger child. Furthermore, children are often too intimidated by adults to talk about their feelings. This fear is intensified when children are brought to therapy by parents because of some "complaint" about them. The child then sees the therapist as an agent of the parents rather than as an ally and source of support.

Play therapy was developed as a way to overcome these obstacles. It offers children a natural medium through which they can express themselves and work out troubling feelings. Through the use of games, dolls, and drawing, or by just being with the therapist, the child can give vent to painful emotions. Feelings of rejection by the family, jealousy of siblings, and anger toward the parents may all come to the fore. Acting out conflicts and reliving frightening situations through play helps the child to assimilate these experiences into his or her personality. It also helps the child attain some understanding of these difficult feelings and offers an opportunity to experiment with more appropriate ways of expressing them. Older children can engage in the more usual type of psychotherapy when they are able to talk about their problems.

Therapy with children, when limited to the child, is a partial solution. Just as with adults, the problems experienced by children arise from the situation in which they live and their interactions with others. Unlike adults, however, children have very little control over others and cannot shape their own worlds. If a child has difficulty expressing anger to his or her parents, chances are it is because the parents do not want to hear it. Enabling a child to unburden him- or herself of angry feelings will have only a limited benefit if he or she has to continue living with parents who will not tolerate any expression of anger. A child with emotional problems does not have the wherewithal to resolve these problems without the active participation of the parents. Therefore it is important that the child's parents work with the therapist as well.

Child therapy is practiced by therapists using many different psychotherapy systems. More important than theoretical orientation is the therapist's ability to work with a child at the child's own level of self-expression and to incorporate the parents into the therapy. The therapist who does not work with the parents will most likely not be able to offer help of lasting benefit to the child. Child therapists vary in their attitudes about working with parents. Some encourage it, others discourage it. Those who discourage it see parent contact as inimical to establishing a trusting relationship with the child. This attitude implicitly defines the parents as the common enemy and further alienates child and parent. It is also easier for the therapist because he or she does not have to deal with the parents. Yet the child's fears that confidentiality may be destroyed by therapist-parent contact can be allayed by having such contacts in the presence of the child. Occasional family sessions are, in any event, a preferred mode of therapy for children since the focus of the emotional problems usually lies in the family interaction.

THE PLACE OF MEDICAL TREATMENT

Medical treatment is often prescribed in addition to, or instead of, psychotherapy in order to reduce the symptoms that accompany psychological disturbances. There are two major types of treatment currently in use: psychoactive drugs and electric shock (electroconvulsive therapy). Psychosurgery, which was a mode of treatment until the early seventies, has been virtually discontinued because of public outcry. Although there is some evidence that the more serious psychological disturbances, such as schizophrenia, may have biological components, this is not yet clearly understood and cannot be directly addressed through treatment. As a result, medical treatment for the major disorders as well as for the less severe problems of living is limited to symptom relief. The one exception is orthomolecular treatment, discussed in a special section below. For people who are experiencing severe symptoms—frightening hallucinations, extreme rage, major depression, loss of judgment—medical treatment is used to alleviate their psychological pain or to protect them and those around them from irrational, harmful behavior. For people who are experiencing less severe symptoms such as insomnia, low-level anxiety, or minor depression, medical treatment is sometimes used to help them maintain their level of performance at important activities such as work or child care, but more often it is used as a convenient antidote to discomfort.

A good deal of controversy surrounds the use of medical treatment for psychological disturbances, and the major positions can be summarized as follows:

- Medical treatment is the treatment of choice because it is the most likely to provide quick, possibly permanent, relief from symptoms and because a psychological approach is expected to be useless or to take too long.
- Medical treatment is an appropriate adjunct to psychotherapy because by surpressing symptoms it makes clients more accessible to the therapy process.

- Medical treatment, except for extreme disturbances, is detrimental because suppressing symptoms reduces a client's motivation to deal with underlying problems and thereby perpetuates the difficulties.
- Medical treatment is too dangerous and too little understood to be used for any but the most severe psychological disturbances, and then only as a last resort.
- Medical treatment is appropriate if it addresses itself to the biochemical basis of the disorder but not if it only addresses itself to symptom relief.

To make an informed decision as to what is best for you, should you ever be in a situation in which medical treatment is recommended, it is important to be aware not only of the potential benefits, but also of the limits and the substantial risks inherent in this approach.

The application of medical treatment to psychological problems is a logical outgrowth of the medical view that such problems are a form of illness akin to bodily illness. In line with this orientation, the American Psychiatric Association has codified a very broad range of psychological problems under the medical umbrella, giving each one a special diagnostic number and label. Historically, medical treatment was limited to persons hospitalized with the more severe disorders and consisted of the more radical techniques, mostly various types of shock treatment and psychosurgery. With the "psychopharmacological revolution" drugs started to replace these older techniques and to be used for a wider variety of symptoms. At the same time, medical treatment became popular outside the hospital as well as within it. As psychopharmacology grew and began to be used for relatively minor symptoms, there was a corresponding growth in the number of psychological problems that became categorized as mental illnesses. In the most recent psychiatric classification system, known as the DSM-III (*Diagnostic and Statistical Manual of Mental Disorders,* 3rd edition) the number of official mental illnesses has grown to 230, from 145 mental illnesses which were listed in the DSM-II. Such diverse problems as difficulty in giving up smoking, lack of interest in sex, nervousness resulting from situational factors, and hallucinatory behavior combined with deteriorated functioning are all similarly viewed as mental illnesses amenable to psychiatric treatment. The psychiatric terms for these problems of living are "Tobacco Dependence, Continuous, 305.11," "Inhibited Sexual Desire, 302.71," "Adjustment Disorder with Anxious Mood, 309.24," and "Schizophrenia, Undifferentiated Type, 295.92."

If you receive psychiatric treatment, you will be given a diagnosis corresponding to one (or more) of the mental disturbances listed in the DSM-III. Usually the diagnosis is made on the basis of relatively little information obtained through a list of routine questions that are oriented more to determining *what* is wrong with you than *if* something is wrong with you. Nevertheless, a great deal of importance is attached to the diagnostic process, which, because of its impersonal and pejorative nature, was called a "degradation ceremonial" by R. D. Laing. The diagnosis you receive, in addition to determining your treatment, also colors how people regard you. Once you are labeled, the tendency among both mental health professionals and others is to think of you as a representative of a diagnostic category rather than as a human being with unique problems. To keep you from pigeonholing yourself in the same manner, it will be helpful to maintain a perspective on what diagnosis is really about.

Any diagnosis you receive constitutes at best a working hypothesis about you and your problems that is subject to change as more is learned about you or as you change. Unfortunately, once made, a diagnosis tends to take on a life of its own: psychiatrists tend to notice signs that confirm their diagnosis and not to notice or to dismiss as insignificant evidence that questions the diagnosis.

Because the diagnostic labels and numbers have a scientific ring to them, people tend to ignore the fact that there are serious doubts concerning the validity of the various diagnostic entities. There is a considerable lack of interrater agreement on some of the diagnostic categories and different psychiatrists can and do diagnose the same person in different ways. We see this happening in the courtroom when the "experts" offer opposing testimony. The subjective nature of mental illness diagnoses, and the way they can be influenced by the biases of the evaluator, has been demonstrated in a number of experimental studies. In one international study, when therapists from different countries were shown a videotaped interview of a "disturbed person," they provided different diagnoses. In a study conducted in this country, therapists' diagnoses varied depending on what they were told about the person's social class: people were diagnosed differently if they were seen as poor rather than affluent. Because many of the diagnostic symptoms are elusive and based on inner states rather than observable behavior, it is relatively easy to "fake" a mental disorder and, therefore, to impute one incorrectly. In a notorious experimental study, eight "normal" volunteers (including three psychologists, a pediatrician, a psychiatrist, a painter, a housewife, and a student) arranged to have psychiatric evaluations to gain admission at various mental hospitals. During the intake interviews, they compained of hearing unclear voices saying words such as "empty" and "hollow," but in all other respects the information provided was accurate and consistent with their lives. On the basis of these interviews, all but one of the volunteers were diagnosed as schizophrenic and admitted to inpatient care. Immediately upon arriving on the psychiatric wards the pseudopatients reported that they were feeling fine and no longer heard any voices, and behaved in a friendly and cooperative manner. Nevertheless, they were given medication and could not obtain their release for between seven and fifty-two days, the average time being nineteen days. When they finally were released, the original diagnosis was changed, not as one would expect to "normal," "sane," or even "malingerer," but instead to "schizophrenia, in remission." Once made, the diagnosis carried more weight than the pseudopatients' reports and the direct behavioral evidence.

In addition to the problems in applying the diagnostic criteria, there is the problem of defining the various entities or illnesses. The development of the diagnostic categories has been influenced by political and economic concerns as well as by psychological and scientific concerns. For instance, "homosexuality," which used to be listed as a mental disorder in the old DSM-II, was eliminated from DSM-III, not because of any new scientific evidence but because of political controversy and public pressure. Similarly, "chronic minor affective disorders" was excluded from DSM-III, as the chairperson of the task force explained, because it was felt "that insurance companies would not reimburse for treatment of a condition that appeared to be both incurable and trivial."* At the time this book was going to press, discussions were being held by the American Psychiatric Association task force with invited professionals on revisions for a new DSM-III. Of three new mental disorders proposed for inclusion one, "masochistic personality dis-

* R. L. Spitzer, "Nonmedical myths and the DSM-III," *APA Monitor* (October 1981), p. 3.

order," was already discarded because of the strong objections of women professionals who maintained this diagnosis would offer a legal defense to wife beaters. This diagnosis was replaced with "self-defeating personality." Two other proposed new diagnoses, rapist and "premenstrual dysphoric disorder," were facing similar objections, the first because it, too, would offer a legal defense to male offenders and the second because it would stigmatize women with premenstrual problems. In commenting on the discussions regarding the inclusion of "masochistic personality disorder," psychologist Renée Garfinkel said, "The low level of intellectual effort was shocking. Diagnoses were developed by majority vote on the level we would use to choose a restaurant. You feel like Italian, I feel like Chinese, so let's go to a cafeteria. Then it's typed into the computer. It may reflect on our naïveté, but it was our belief that there would be an attempt to look at things scientifically."*

Just as the diagnostic categories are expedient labels with doubtful validity, the medical treatments prescribed for "mental illnesses" are expedient measures that have doubtful efficacy. The medications and other treatments may have palliative benefits but they are nonspecific measures that do not achieve a permanent remedy. It is often unknown how these various treatments work and most entail undesirable side effects, some of which are serious and irreversible. Despite these dangers, medical treatment continues to be used rather indiscriminately for psychological distress. Many clients find medical treatment attractive because it provides them quick relief from psychological discomfort, and many professionals find it attractive because it is convenient and profitable to administer. Some clients also opt for this form of treatment for financial reasons: their insurance policies may not reimburse for psychotherapy but only for medical treatment. Heavy promotion of medication for psychological disturbances helps keep this form of treatment in the minds of doctor and patient alike. The appeal of medication is so great that in 1980, for example, about 10 percent of the population received a prescription for Valium or other minor tranquilizers; this comes to over two billion tablets of Valium alone. Unfortunately, drug dependence can result after only a few weeks of therapeutic doses of tranquilizers, and doctors are reluctant to recognize addiction when it occurs. Research has

* As quoted in *Time,* December 2, 1985, p. 76.

shown that when a patient manifests withdrawal symptoms as the dosage is decreased or discontinued, physicians tend to interpret this as a return of the original anxiety and advise the patient to return to the usual daily dosage, thereby perpetuating a drug habit they have created. The equivocal benefit-risk ratio of the minor tranquilizers also applies to other medical treatments, and the convenience of such treatments may exact a high price: not only do addiction and overdose result more commonly from the use of prescribed drugs than from the use of illegal drugs, but the more effective treatments are those with the more dangerous side effects and discontinuance of treatment usually results in a reappearance of symptoms.

There are several important things to keep in mind if you are considering medical treatment.

- Do not consent to such treatment just because a psychiatrist or physician tells you it is necessary. The decision to accept medical treatment is yours, and you should agree only if it makes sense to you. It is a good idea to obtain a second opinion before consenting to treatment consisting of anything more than temporary administration of mild tranquilizers or megavitamins. Many psychiatrists want you to take medication because they are uncomfortable with your anxiety, but you should take medication only when *you* cannot deal with it.
- Do not accept medical treatment if it is not prescribed in conjunction with a medical checkup and history or if no provisions are made for monitoring you while undergoing such treatment. The prescribing physician should be aware of any medical problems, allergies, or drug reactions you have, as well as any other medications you are taking. When in psychotherapy, whether with a psychiatrist or a nonmedical therapist, it may be preferable to obtain medication, if necessary, from your regular physician. That person will be able to prescribe more safely, having a better knowledge of your bodily functioning and the facilities to monitor your reactions.
- Do not accept any treatment before finding out possible side effects. People are increasingly and properly concerned about the harmful effects of taking medication or undergoing other treatment. Physicians tend to take the attitude

that side effects are statistically improbable, and that the potential benefits are worth the risk. Since the decision concerns you and your body, you are the one to determine how much risk you want to take.

- Do not undertake medical treatment with the expectation of a permanent cure. Most benefits are temporary and the treatment may have to be continued or repeated.

The four basic categories of medical treatment are as follows:

Psychoactive Drugs Psychoactive or mood-altering drugs fall into several broad categories. The minor tranquilizers or sedatives (the best-known brands being Valium and Librium) can be helpful in reducing anxiety. Their side effects include drowsiness, lethargy, and withdrawal reactions after large doses. They should not be used in conjunction with alcohol, or with a variety of other drugs. These drugs can lead to habituation and dependency.

The major tranquilizers or antipsychotic drugs are used to calm overexcitement and hyperactivity and to reduce such symptoms as anxiety, thought disturbance, and withdrawal. The most popular brand names are Stelazine, Thorazine, and Mellaril. Dangerous side effects, including faintness, palpitation, Parkinson's disease–type symptoms, and tardive dyskinesia (involuntary muscle movements in the jaw or limbs), may occur even from small doses of these drugs and the latter effects may be irreversible. Extreme caution must be used in prescribing them and they should be considered only for severe disturbances and if milder medications have been unsuccessful. They are often prescribed in conjunction with other drugs that can counteract some of the side effects, but the counteractive drugs can produce side effects of their own.

The antidepressants form another category of drugs and, in turn, break down into three subgroups. The tricyclics (Elavil and Tofranil, among others) and the MAO inhibitors (Marplan, Parnate, Nardil) are effective in relieving simple depression but they should not be used in combination with each other or when there are signs of cardiovascular disease or high blood pressure. They can take weeks or months to have effect. The MAO inhibitors are also dangerous to use in conjunction with various foods including cheese, chocolate, and certain fish. Adverse side effects from both groups include constipation, urinary retention, and dryness of mouth. In addition, tricyclics can cause palpitations, tremors, excess sweating, and blurred vision, while the MAO inhibitors can cause dizziness, loss of appetite, inhibition of ejaculation, and jaundice. The third group is the amphetamines or "speed" (including Benzedrine and Dexedrine), which are prescribed for narcolepsy, for children diagnosed as having minimal brain dysfunction, and for adult weight reduction. The amphetamines can be habit forming and should not be used for long periods of time. They should also not be used if there is any indication of heart disease or high blood pressure. Other side effects include insomnia, restlessness, palpitations, and dependence. When abused these drugs can produce bizarre symptoms including extreme aggressiveness and thought disorders.

Another drug family, derived from lithium carbonate, is frequently characterized as antidepressant but is intended only for blocking the manic phase of manic-depressive disorders. Because of its sudden popularity it is now being promoted for other forms of depression as well. Lithium's side effects include fatigue, slurred speech, muscle weakness, unsteady gait, tremors, nausea, vomiting, and diarrhea, and it should not be used by persons on a salt-free diet. Popular brand names are Lithane and Lithonate.

A frequently prescribed drug not falling into any of the above categories is Ritalin, which is used primarily for treatment of minimal brain dysfunction in children. It should not be used in cases of marked anxiety or agitation, in the presence of seizures, or for children under six. Side reactions include insomnia, nervousness, loss of appetite, nausea, palpitations, and headache. Ritalin may cause drug dependency.

Electroconvulsive Therapy While originally administered only in hospital settings, electroconvulsive therapy (ECT) has spread to private psychiatric practice. It declined in popularity for a while but is now on the upswing again, being used by 16 percent of the nation's psychiatrists. One possible reason for increased usage is the growing awareness of the limitations of psychopharmacology. ECT consists of the induction of an electric current through the brain, causing convulsion and coma. It is usually administered in series of six to ten treatments, which may then be repeated. ECT is mainly useful in the treatment of depression but it is also used for some schizophrenic reactions. Although ECT can wipe out some symptoms temporarily it is a dangerous technique that can result in lasting memory loss and, perhaps, irreversible damage to the brain. Nobody understands how ECT works or why it relieves symptoms but that it does so is considered sufficient rationale for its use. ECT is a handy form of therapy for unscrupulous psychiatrists. Using this technique, they can handle a large number of patients who are charged a high fee for each treatment, which lasts only minutes. Psychiatric offices specializing in this technique are known as "shock mills."

The use of ECT has been a subject of controversy ever since its introduction, and that controversy continues unabated. There has been a consistent effort on the part of the medical profession as a whole to downplay the dangers of ECT and many nonmedical writers in the field of mental health have gone along with this trend. One consumer guide to mental health, for instance, takes the position that people who complain about memory loss from ECT do not really have a memory loss but only *feel* they have a memory loss. The disadvantage of ECT, according to the guidebook, is the negative feeling about the treatment rather than the treatment itself.

Some of the people who have undergone ECT have provided a harrowing picture of the experience and its effects that differs radically from that provided by its practitioners. In fact there is a group of formerly hospitalized mental patients who have organized NAPA (Network Against Psychiatric Assault) to fight the abuses of ECT and other medical treatments. They publish *Madness Network News* for consumer protection, which maintains a "Roster of Shock Doctors" and the hospitals at which these people work. Several psychiatrists and neurologists have also joined the movement to stop the administration of ECT, with Peter Breggin and John Friedberg being among the most vocal. As they point out, even when consent is obtained, it is not truly informed consent, as few people are aware of the fatality rate of ECT, for example, or of the fact that it is not just a shock to the brain but one to the entire body, affecting the cardiovascular and hormonal systems as well as other bodily functions. While many psychiatrists consider ECT to be an "efficient" way to treat symptoms, its dangers are too great for you to submit to such treatment wtihout fully understanding what you are in for. Suggested reading on ECT is provided at the back of this book.

Psychosurgery In psychosurgery parts of the brain are destroyed to alter a person's behavior; it is used mostly to control aggressive behavior. Psychosurgery is the most hazardous form of medical treatment because the effects are irreversible. Afterward, a person can never be the same again. Psychosurgery generally leads to apathy, mental impairment, a blunting of the personality, and sometimes to convulsive seizures. Though psychosurgery gained a modicum of public support as a treatment of last resort for chronic psychiatric patients, the technique has been used experimentally with a much wider range of patients. It has even been used on children to reduce hyperactivity.

The dangers of psychosurgery received some public attention through legal suits brought by people who had been subjected to psychosurgery when hospitalized. Some of these people spearheaded attempts to control the use of psychosurgery, which eventually prompted the National Institute of Mental Health along with the National Institute of Neurological Diseases and Stroke to issue guidelines declaring psychosurgery to be an experimental therapy that should not be made available to the public. This was followed by the creation of a congressionally mandated body, the National Commission for the Protection of Human Subjects of Biomedical and Behavioral Research, which was to establish further guidelines for psychosurgery. Unfortunately, the commission watered down the earlier guidelines, stating that psychosurgery was less hazardous than previously thought, and potentially of significant therapeutic value. Although the use of psychosurgery has been curbed dramatically by virtue of adverse public opinion, it is still a procedure that may be legally performed.

Orthomolecular Psychiatry Recognizing the possibility of a biochemical basis to some emotional disturbances, orthomolecular therapy is oriented to restoring the proper biochemical balance with various nutrients. The therapy consists of diet control, usually through the elimination of sugars and starches and the use of megadoses of various vitamins (primarily B's, C, and E) and trace elements (primarily zinc). The typical American diet is conspicuously lacking in B vitamins and very high in sugars, which destroy the limited B's in today's processed foods. Dietary deficiencies, as, for example, in scurvy conditions, are known to create psychological disturbances that disappear when the deficiencies are corrected.

While orthomolecular psychiatrists are greeted with derision by the medical profession, some have reported dramatic results with patients, including those with schizophrenic symptoms. Orthomolecular therapy has been particularly effective with children diagnosed as hyperactive or as having minimal brain dysfunction. Orthodox psychiatric treatment puts such children on a program of amphetamines or Ritalin to reduce the symptoms. Dr. Benjamin Feingold, whose work in this area is most widely known, has found that many of these symptoms can be made to disappear by eliminating from a child's diet all foods containing chemical additives, such as colorants and flavorings, and by introducing essential foods that might be lacking. Many so-called problem children have become "normal" once given a sound diet.

Until recently very few health practitioners in this country cared about nutrition, and there are fewer still who are adequately informed about it or able to work with you or your child in this way. Nevertheless it would seem to be a safe alternative to try with anybody whose diet suggests biochemical imbalance and whose psychological problem has proven amenable to such treatment in others, for example, hyperactivity, general irritability, and learning disability.

POPULAR ELECTIVES

A good number of growth systems have come into being that are identified with psychotherapy, though their aims are different, being predetermined and less individualized. These approaches do not claim to be a substitute for therapy or suitable for dealing with emotional disturbances. Rather, they address themselves to people who feel they are not getting enough out of life or using their potential fully. Nevertheless, some people in need of therapy are drawn to these systems in the mistaken belief that psychotherapy is what is being provided. Perhaps some of the attraction of these approaches to potential clients lies in the way they are marketed. Unlike most therapy systems, growth techniques are "packaged" and heavily promoted. While these techniques may be effective in what they do, the promotion and packaging may serve to confuse consumers as to the applicability of these techniques to their personal needs.

Encounter Groups The purpose of encounter groups is to provide intense emotional experience through encounters with others. Encounter groups aim at openness of communication and stripping of façades so that people come to know one another as they really are. This permits trusting relationships that foster individual growth. Encounter groups are intended to offer intimacy as an antidote to isolation, a therapeutic "experience" rather than psychotherapy. In many ways the encounter movement represents a rebellion against conventional psychotherapy: psychotherapy systems, methods, and training are considered irrelevant to people's basic need for deeply experienced relationships with others.

With the founding of Esalen Institute, a "growth resort" at Big Sur, California, encounter groups became part of the pop culture and started mushrooming all over the country during the 1960s. This explosion was triggered in large part by the appeal of the psychological "turn on" encounter groups offered and their ability to satisfy people's hunger for closeness and relationships. But, more important, this was the first therapeutic-growth system that was widely promoted. Esalen was a major step into an organizational big-business approach to therapy.

Encounter groups consist of ten to fifteen people who meet for several sessions within a short period of time, ranging from several days to several weeks. Marathons are a form of encounter group, staying in session continuously for anywhere from the better part of a day to a weekend. A variety of verbal and nonverbal techniques (confrontation, massage, hugging) and structured exercises (telling the person next to you what you think of him or her, clapping at different rhythms, "trust" falling—falling backward into another's arms) are used to encourage uninhibited interaction among group members. Encounter groups stress the expression of feeling and bodily awareness and enjoyment; they play down intellectual understanding.

Encounter groups started waning with the appearance of new group movements such as Arica and *est*. Evaluative studies have shown little evidence of lasting therapeutic benefit and considerable evidence that they can be harmful. While most group leaders agree that seriously disturbed people should not be in encounter groups, little or no attempt is made to screen participants beforehand, nor is there any follow-up after the group sessions. The encounter group's lack of permanence works against experiencing genuine trust and intimacy, avowed to be a primary goal. Group leaders disclaim any responsibility for what happens to the participants, who are considered to be totally responsible for themselves both in and out of sessions. Encounter groups have been satisfying for people without serious problems who welcome interesting experiences that stimulate emotional growth, but they have been a disappointment for people who sought them out as a substitute for psychotherapy.

est *est* was the most popular of the packaged approaches to self-realization in the seventies, when it was first introduced. Founded by an American salesman who renamed himself Werner Erhard, Erhard Seminars Training centers on communicating the message that each person is responsible for his or her own life. The *est* program takes two consecutive weekends during which a group of approximately 250 people are led together, in a large room, through a variety of experiences by a trainer. These experiences consist of many techniques borrowed from Esalen, gestalt, Dale Carnegie, zen, and other movements, but put together in a structured format. Unlike the more indulgent atmosphere at Esalen, *est* is austere and Spartan, with physical discomfort as an integral part of the program. Participants sit for long hours on hard chairs with minimal breaks for food or bathroom. During the course of the session the message is constantly repeated, sometimes in rather derogatory fashion, that each participant is the cause of his or her own experience and responsible for everything that has happened.

Run like a large business organization, *est* reportedly grosses millions annually. It has attracted many dedicated volunteers who claim that *est* has changed their lives and who help the paid staff spread the message. Others, however, have found the seminars to be a naïve assortment of borrowed techniques with nothing new to offer. The popularity and appeal of *est* is undoubtedly related to its well-organized marketing approach and the coverage it has received in the media. Its promise of a sixty-hour transformation seems to be the panacea people have been searching for. A good number of *est* enthusiasts feel it has changed their whole approach to life, and others, although less enthusiastic, credit *est* with helping them to experience themselves more fully. But while many people have found help in coming to grips with their problems by accepting the message, most people's problems are not amenable to such a simplistic approach. Readiness to accept responsibility must be followed up by the hard and slow process of doing so. A more disturbing aspect of *est* is the worshipful attitude trainers and converts hold toward Erhard. Any system that thrives on such adoration of the leader does not seem consonant with the development of positive attitudes about one's self.

Arica Arica was developed by Oscar Ichazo and named for the town in Chile where he was born. It describes itself as an educational experience that can put you in touch with your inner resources. According to Arica, each person has an inner self that radiates energy, love, and wisdom. This inner radiation may be blocked by negative experiences of the past so that instead of projecting this inner glow the person projects negativism into everything he or she sees, hears, and touches. Reality is only a reflection of the self and the individual has to accept responsibility for the way he or she is and for changing.

Arica training is based on four hundred exercises designed to make the "student" aware of the positive inner self and remove the negative blocks to its expression. These exercises aim to develop every aspect of being, including the body, mind, emotions, and spirit. Training may be done in or out of residency. Exercises include meditation, relaxation, breathing, and encounters. A high-protein diet, including a special drink called Dragon's Milk, is utilized to maintain high energy levels during training, which, at its most intensive, is accomplished during a forty-day residency.

As with all growth techniques, Arica has its adherents and detractors. Some find it has enhanced their efficiency, vitality, and relationships. Others find that it does not deal with sources of negativism and that these continue to interfere with adjustment after the training is completed. In addition, the cost of related materials sold at Arica stores, such as Dragon's Milk and meditation robes, has evoked considerable criticism.

Silva Mind Control This system was developed by José Silva and has attracted hundreds of thousands of students. It aims to help people make the most of their mental powers by teaching them to think on an alpha level. The brain has many different patterns of electrical activity, and its alpha waves are associated with creativity. Alpha levels can be achieved by many different systems, such as meditation or biofeedback. Silva Mind Control uses suggestion and conditioning to attain it. The standard program consists of four twelve-hour sessions. Students lie on the floor in a comfortable position while the trainer describes the mental powers to be achieved. As the trainer counts backward, the students are to descend into deeper levels of consciousness until they reach the alpha state. During this time the trainer repeats such messages as "Every day in every way, I am getting better and better." While in the alpha state, students are given different assignments to carry out. One is to picture a scene in which you are content and at ease, and then to think about a problem or difficult situation and visualize it fully, experiencing the tension and anxiety. This picture is then framed and canceled out with an X. The next step is to imagine this problem situation with a happy solution, frame it, and look at it. As you replace negative images with positive images your mental energies are expected to zero in on achieving success. Another exercise is to visualize a series of objects such as a penny or a wall and then visualize yourself entering and exploring these objects until you become them. You then move on to animate objects and to people so that you can experience their moods and feelings. You can then influence others by projecting positive thoughts toward them.

Silva Mind Control has been used to eliminate compulsive habits, to solve problems, to master academic material, and for other similar tasks. Some people have found it very helpful on a short-term basis but with impermanent results. Silva Mind Control, however, offers its students repeat courses at no charge and many say they find the second go-round more productive than the first.

Transcendental Meditation Of all the growth techniques, Transcendental Meditation (TM) is by far the most popular and it is widely used not only in this country but worldwide. Training at TM centers consists of a brief exposition on the benefits, both physiological and psychological, of meditation, and classes in the technique of meditation. TM is not unlike other forms of meditation, yogic or zen, but has its own unique characteristics, developed by Maharishi Mahesh Yogi. Training is usually done in four sessions. During the first, individual session, the instructor gives you a personal mantra, one of several used by TM, which is never to be revealed to anyone else. Upon receiving the mantra, the trainee is expected to kneel before a picture of Guru Dev, the Maharishi's teacher, and place an offering of fruit or flowers on the altar while the instructor chants. The mantra is a Sanskrit word on which you focus during meditation until it completely fills your awareness so that all else is blocked out. At this point your mind is quieted and you can transcend it, reaching your source of thought and energy. The following three group sessions are used for practicing meditation. Thereafter you are on your own and are instructed to meditate two times a day for approximately twenty minutes each.

TM, like other forms of meditation, has proven very effective in combating stress by lowering blood pressure and anxiety. Criticism of TM recognizes its efficiency but centers on its "hype." Its ritual regarding the mantra, its initiation ceremony, and its commercialization seem to be the only things differentiating it from the meditational techniques of other yogis and gurus. Dr. Herbert Benson has even developed a very Spartan and utilitarian version of meditation known as the "relaxation response" that provides many practitioners with the same benefits.

3

How to Pick
a Therapist

THE COMPETENCE of the therapist and his or her compatibility with the client are the most important factors determining the outcome of psychotherapy. Yet most people entering psychotherapy never really choose a therapist, but take the first name they get. They are afraid to "shop around" because they feel intimidated and unsure of what to look for. But it is possible to choose a therapist and to pick a person who is suitable for you. If there is a lack of choice in your locale, you might want to travel farther to get the right therapist rather than settle for whoever is close at hand. In looking for a therapist, remind yourself that you are buying a service, that you are a client to be satisfied, that you have a right to ask questions about the service you are buying. The more particular you are in your choice, the better your chances for good psychotherapy.

WHAT TO LOOK FOR

Your therapist should be a person with the particular knowledge, skills, and personal characteristics necessary to conduct psychotherapy. Specifically, the therapist should be educated in personality theory, be experienced in conducting psychotherapy, have had personal psychotherapy, and be a wholesome, sensitive person who respects others.

While these requirements might seem obvious, they cannot be taken for granted just because a person hangs out a shingle. Unfortunately, the diplomas on the wall or the string of degrees after the name do not necessarily tell you whether a potential therapist meets these basic requirements. These are matters you are going to have to investigate for yourself, in ways that will be discussed in this chapter.

PROFESSIONAL BACKGROUND

As there is no primary profession of psychotherapy, psychotherapists enter the field from one of several related disciplines. Medicine, psychology, and social work are the most prominent but other professional routes to psychotherapy have been taken, including nursing and the clergy. The absence of a separate profession of psychotherapy has resulted in rivalry among the different professions that enter the field. The medical profession is the most combative, taking great pains to try to restrict the entry of other professionals into the practice of psychotherapy. This position stems from the view that emotional problems are a subset of medical illnesses and are treatable only by physicians. The major efforts of the psychiatrists have been directed against the psychologists, whom they see as the most threatening. Psychologists usually have the title of "doctor" and are licensed for independent practice whereas social workers, until recently, worked mostly in institutional settings under psychiatric supervision. The competition between psychiatrists and psychologists has taken place on many fronts, including the psychiatric lobby's continuing attempts to prevent insurance companies from reimbursing for psychotherapy services when administered by a psychologist. This issue is being resolved, not on a professional level, but through antitrust action in the courts, where it has been found that such limitations were in restraint of trade. As the psychotherapy market has grown and the number of suppliers has also grown, the competition among the professions has been intensifying. Social workers are becoming more active in trying to establish their rights to practice and to be eligible for third-party payments, psychologists continue to work to protect their professional independence, and psychiatrists continue to lobby to restrict the activities of nonmedical practitioners.

Another consequence of the absence of an independent profession of psychotherapy has been the lack of professional standards of practice. There is a tendency among professionals from the allied professions to view their professional training as sufficient for entry into the distinct profession of psychotherapy, but this is not the case. Besides the professional training required to become a psychiatrist, psychologist, or social worker, a psychotherapist needs to have specific training in psychotherapy, including personal psychotherapy. The lack of licensing or regulation of psychotherapy as a profession means that many persons practice psychotherapy without adequate training in that field, a fact that is obscured by the extensive training they may have received in their primary profession.

Each profession approaches people and their psychological problems with different degrees of relevant expertise, as well as with different perspectives: medicine through the body, psychology through the personality, and social work through the society.

Medicine and its subspecialty psychiatry see emotional problems as a form of illness to be treated like other diseases. Psychiatry thereby falls prey to using technologically oriented medical treatment for psychological conditions. Medication and electroconvulsive therapy are the natural consequences of this orientation. While some emotional disturbances can be alleviated by medical treatment, that is not psychotherapy. Unfortunately, many psychiatrists are not clear on the difference and consider a ten-minute session in which medication schedules are checked as "psychotherapy."

As Freud first suggested, medicine and psychotherapy are basically incompatible. In the medical approach, the individual becomes a "patient" to be treated, not a person to be engaged in an active psychotherapy process that stimulates growth. It stands to reason that psychiatrists call persons to whom they render psychotherapy "patients" while therapists from other professions, although generally adopting this custom, sometimes call them "clients." Another difficulty inherent in the medical approach is that physicians are trained to focus on the disease rather than on the individual in order to retain "objectivity" and stay personally uninvolved. But psychotherapy as an interpersonal process requires the therapist's active engagement with the client, and the psychiatrist must therefore learn to drop his or her shield to relate in a personal way.

Of course, some psychiatrists overcome these medical attitudes as they practice psychotherapy. Indeed, many prominent advocates of genuine psychotherapy have been psychiatrists, and members of that profession have been in the forefront in developing new theories and approaches in psychotherapy.

Psychology's route to understanding emotional problems is through a study of the personality. Among all the professions, it is the most directly related to psychotherapy since its subject matter is psychological processes.

Clinical psychology has taken two major roads. It can be credited with the development of the humanist—existential—client-centered approaches that are oriented toward enabling people to reach their potential and recover responsibility for their own existence. These approaches have helped to dispel the archaic and dangerous notions implicit in the mental illness concept, while also restoring dignity to the person with emotional problems.

Psychology is also largely responsible for the development of behavior modification. This technique grew out of the belief that all disorders are the result of maladaptive habits that have to be eliminated and replaced with adaptive behaviors. It has been effective in eliminating many unwanted symptoms and freeing the person of the emotional burden they entail. However, in focusing on habits rather than the person who has them, this approach adopts an overly simplistic view of people that tends to ignore individual responsibility for behavior and places it instead in the hands of a technician.

Social work tries to understand human problems through their relationship to society. The field has, as its primary focus, making social services available to those in need. The bias from which social workers must free themselves in order to practice psychotherapy is that of helping the client by direct intervention rather than through working toward changes that emerge from the client. Social work has also been more concerned with the individual as he or she relates to others and the emphasis in psychotherapy is therefore apt to be on interpersonal processes rather than on intrapsychic difficulties. The major contribution of social work to psychotherapy has been in the application of family therapy and other therapy forms that work with interpersonal networks rather than individuals.

Related to these differences in orientation are differences among the practitioners in the major professions in terms of motives for entering the field, affiliations, and attitudes toward one another.* Psychiatrists tend to enter the field because of parental influence and the desire to gain identity and professional status. Psychologists are more influenced by teachers and the intellectual stimulation provided by psychotherapy and enter the field because of a desire to understand people. Social workers are influenced by co-professionals and enter the field out of a desire to help people. Most psychotherapists have other work in addition to private practice: psychiatrists work more frequently in hospital settings, psychologists as academicians, and social workers in clinical or social agencies. Of all the professions, psychiatrists have the highest proportion of political conservatives, with the more conservative being more prone to administer drugs and shock. The rivalry among the professions, especially between psychiatrists and psychologists, colors the images and attitudes the three professions have toward each other. The psychiatrists are seen as having an authoritarian and rigid personality with a godlike complex. Psychologists are seen as intellectual and conceptual and as aggressive and competitive. Social workers are seen as dedicated people concerned with helping others.

EDUCATION AND TRAINING

The training offered by these professions varies substantially in how close it comes to meeting the basic requisites for psychotherapists. None is adequate by itself. Therefore, responsible therapists supplement their preparation with specialized training in psychotherapy. Usually such training is obtained through postgraduate psychotherapy training institutes, many of which accept only candidates with a doctoral degree (PhD or MD) although some accept candidates below this level. They offer a certificate in psychotherapy based on the completion of theoretical course work in personality and psychotherapy, a specified number of hours providing psychotherapy under supervision, and personal psychotherapy.

A description of the training given by medicine, psychology, and social work shows what is provided and what is left out, which

* For the actual researches that support the observations that follow, see the suggested reading list at the end of this book.

credentials are relevant and which are not. Examining the assumptions implicit in the training will also help you evaluate the compatibility of the different professional backgrounds with your needs in psychotherapy.

Medicine The training of psychiatrists is basically in medicine. It generally consists of four years in medical school leading to an MD degree and one year in an internship. Since psychiatry is a branch of medicine, to practice psychiatry one must have a medical license, but beyond this the title "psychiatrist" is not controlled and no approval from an accrediting body is necessary to assume that title.

After the basic medical degree, most psychiatrists go through a three-year residency training program in psychiatry. In the past, many residencies were limited to medical treatment of chronic hospitalized patients and provided little or no experience in psychotherapy, but more recently there has been greater emphasis on teaching psychotherapy skills in residency programs.

About one-third of all psychiatrists are board certified. Certification is awarded by the American Board of Psychiatry and Neurology if the psychiatrist has passed special examinations that he or she is eligible to take after three years of residency and two additional years of practice. Some psychiatrists were awarded their certificate without this examination under the "grandfather clause" because they were in practice before the initiation of the board. However, since the board examinations focus on psychiatric issues such as diagnosis and medication rather than on psychotherapy skills, board certification does not necessarily indicate competence in psychotherapy.

The psychiatrist who wants to obtain specialized training in psychotherapy generally attends a training program at a psychotherapy institute.* The need for this training diminishes as the quality and relevance of the residency programs improve.

Membership in the American Psychiatric Association indicates professional responsibility but is not a sign of competence in psychotherapy. Physicians with one year of experience in psychiatry can join as associate members; those with three years can join as full members. Membership in psychotherapy or psychoanalytic associations is usually more meaningful.

---

* Some psychotherapy institutes are known as psychoanalytic institutes, indicating a particular theoretical approach.

If you are considering a psychiatrist, the more of the following credentials you find, the greater confidence you can have:

- Residency in psychiatry;
- Full (not associate) membership in the American Psychiatric Association;
- Board certification;
- Graduation from a psychotherapy institute;
- Membership in a psychotherapy or psychoanalytic society.

Psychology The typical training of psychologists practicing psychotherapy consists of four years in graduate school with one year in an internship to get a PhD in clinical psychology. Clinical psychology programs include theoretical courses on personality and psychotherapy and supervised practicums in rendering psychotherapy. Some psychologists now obtain a PsyD (doctor of psychology) degree. This is a new practice-oriented degree offered in various mental health services, including psychotherapy. The title "psychologist" is controlled by state laws and only a person meeting certification or licensing requirements (usually a PhD in psychology, two years supervised experience, passing special examinations) can call him- or herself a psychologist. Some psychologists were certified or licensed under a "grandfather clause" if they had been in practice before the laws went into effect.

Not all psychologists are trained to do psychotherapy. Psychology has several other disciplines in addition to clinical psychology that incorporate clinical skills, such as school or counseling psychology, but many more disciplines that do not. While psychologists are legally free to work in all areas of the field, the American Psychological Association's code of ethics requires its members to function only in their area of competence.

Some clinical psychologists have diplomas awarded by the American Board of Examiners in Professional Psychology. This is the only board of all the professions that tests for competency in psychotherapy. Diplomas are awarded after the candidate has passed examinations that he or she is eligible to take after five years of postdoctoral experience. Relatively few clinical psychologists apply for the diplomate status although qualified to do so. Recognizing this reluctance and wanting to meet the need for a directory of qualified psychotherapists, the Board of Examiners in 1975 developed a *National Register of Health Service Providers in Psychology*. All psychologists who are licensed or certified in their state and have a PhD in psychology and two years of supervised experience (one postdoctoral) in mental health services, may be listed in the *Register*. These standards are relatively low, but the directory does provide that a psychologist has at least had some experience in offering mental health services, though not necessarily directly in psychotherapy.

Psychologists without clinical training can obtain such training by attending a training institute in psychotherapy. Clinical psychologists also attend such programs to further develop their psychotherapy skills.

Membership in the American Psychological Association, although of some protective value for clients because of its ethical restraints on members, is not a sign of psychotherapy competence. Membership in a psychotherapy or psychoanalytic association is more relevant to psychotherapy skills.

If you are considering a psychologist, check for the following credentials:

- A PhD in clinical psychology;
- State certification or license;
- Full membership in the American Psychological Association;
- Graduation from a psychotherapy training institute;
- Diplomate status in clinical psychology;
- Membership in a psychotherapy or psychoanalytic association.

Social Work The typical training for social workers is a master's degree (MSW) in social work, generally completed in a two-year program that includes field placement. It is possible to obtain a doctor's degree in social work (DSW) but very few social workers do. Social workers are certified (CSW) in their profession by many states on the basis of an MSW and passing an examination, and by the Academy of Certified Social Workers (ACSW) on the basis of the usual state requirements plus two years of supervised postdegree experience and an examination. Both certifications were awarded under a "grandfather clause" to already established social workers. The social work curriculum focuses on casework. Some schools offer a concentration in what used to be called psychiatric social work, with courses in personality, family interaction, and child development. This concentration also requires field placement in a mental health facility. The National Association of

Social Workers publishes a *Register of Clinical Social Workers,* which lists ACSW members whose two years of post-master's experience was in clinical social work practice.

Social workers can go beyond the training offered in their field to get specialized training in psychotherapy. There are a number of training programs in psychotherapy, mostly in the large metropolitan areas, which accept people below the doctoral level.

Membership in the National Association of Social Workers is useful only as an indicator of professional responsibility with no bearing on psychotherapy skills, whereas membership in a psychotherapy or psychoanalytic association is relevant.

If you are considering a social worker check for the following credentials:

- Master's degree in social work with a clinical concentration;
- Certification by state or Academy of Certified Social Workers;
- Graduation from a psychotherapy or psychoanalytic training program;
- Membership in a psychotherapy association.

Nonprofessional Therapists An increasing number of therapists have been practicing without training or accreditation. Because the practice of psychotherapy is not controlled by law, anyone who wants to can offer psychotherapy services and use the title psychotherapist.

Therapists who practice without credentials usually come from one of two groups: those who believe their nonconformity represents a better way, and those who do it out of opportunism. The first are often principled persons with radical social philosophies. They shun the professions and training institutes because they consider such groups to be self-serving and socially regressive. They see clients' problems as stemming from the oppressiveness of society. Therapy to them is a process of education and political action. Although they do not deny the importance of skills, they believe that therapeutic skill consists of human qualities rather than technical expertise; a good therapist is simply a warm, open, and accepting person. Because they do not consider education in psychotherapy relevant, many have little or no training, although some have trained within "establishment" institutions and some have trained privately. Radical therapists work primarily at "alternate counseling centers," which aim to provide a new life pattern for counselors and clients. These centers, catering primarily to the needs of youth and minority groups, function as communities; members help one another and share experiences as well as fees. Many radical therapists also go into private practice.

For the other group, the opportunists, setting oneself up as a psychotherapist without having earned credentials is a shortcut to the status accorded the profession and to the possibility of a lucrative practice. This group reflects a range of different people and motives. Some may have started but not completed their training, some may have intentions of completing their training and becoming accredited, and some may be outright frauds with neither talent nor intentions to train.

Regardless of what group the therapist falls into, you should be aware of the risks involved in being in therapy with a person who does not have recognized credentials. It is true that credentials by themselves are not enough to make a competent therapist, nor are they the ultimate criterion. But with the abundance of incompetent therapists, whether officially qualified or not, and the increasing occurrence of unethical practices, it is more important than ever that you have the added protection of working with a recognized practitioner. The accredited therapist practices under several regulatory bodies, including the state agency that sponsors his or her certificate or license, the ethics committee of the profession of which he or she is a member, and the judicial system through which legal action could be brought against him or her. Though in the past action has not often been taken against a professional, the possibility does function as a restraining influence. These sources of control do not exist for the nonaccredited therapist, and it is not possible to prosecute a malpractice suit against someone who is not licensed to practice. Credentials do not ensure a good therapist, but do offer you some protection and recourse from abuse.

If you are considering a nonprofessional therapist, ask:

- What skills and capabilities does that person possess that can be helpful to you?
- What experience has he or she had doing therapy?
- Do the skills this person has to offer outweigh the added risks?

WHAT DO ALL THOSE TITLES MEAN?

In addition to the titles of the major professions in psychotherapy, which have been discussed, people working in the field call themselves by many other titles as well. Below is a short rundown on various titles being used, what they mean, and what kind of assurances, if any, they provide.

Psychotherapist Psychotherapist is a title anyone can use; it is not protected by law. It gives no indication of training or competence. Qualified practitioners sometimes use it as an adjunct to their professional title of psychiatrist, psychologist, et cetera. The term psychotherapist is also widely used by people without qualifications. If a person calls him- or herself a psychotherapist without further clarification, be sure to probe on training, credentials, and approach to therapy.

Psychoanalyst This is another term that has no legal standing and can be used by anyone. Historically, a psychoanalyst was a person trained in classical Freudian theory and technique at a psychoanalytic institute. The term psychoanalysis today is used in two senses. Some use it to refer exclusively to Freudian analysis, while others use it to mean a specialized type of psychotherapy that goes more deeply into the roots of the personality structure and works more intensively, taking a longer period of time with a client. There are now many psychoanalytic institutes: some are Freudian, some are specific to other theories like Jungian or Sullivanian, while others are eclectic, not limiting themselves to any specific system. Some institutes (mostly Freudian), accept only physicians as students, while others accept students from other professions. As with the title psychotherapist, psychoanalyst gives no indication of competence, and is used by qualified and unqualified persons alike.

Psychiatric Nurse A person with a degree in nursing can become registered (RN) by passing state examinations, but there is no specialty licensing or certification of psychiatric nurses. This title is usually employed by nurses who work on psychiatric wards of hospitals, but it is also used by nurses who are in private practice. Some schools offer graduate training in psychiatric nursing and some state nursing associations grant a certificate in psychiatric nursing, based on training and experience. Use of the title, in itself, does not indicate that the person has had any training in psychotherapy.

Pastoral Counselor This title is not controlled by law, but is generally used only by members of the clergy. Some may have had training in counseling or psychotherapy in addition to, or as part of, their religious training, but this cannot be taken for granted.

Marriage Counselor or Marriage Therapist These terms have no legal standing in most states, and cover a multitude of practitioners and approaches. Although anyone can call him- or herself a marriage counselor, the American Association of Marriage Counselors does set minimum standards for membership in its organization. Persons from a variety of professional backgrounds, including psychology, social work, and medicine, are admitted to membership. Chances are, however, that a practitioner trained in one of these disciplines would identify him- or herself by that profession rather than as a marriage counselor.

Family Counselor or Family Therapist These labels also have no legal standing. Some marriage or family therapists use the two terms interchangeably and see marriage therapy as part of family therapy. Family therapy usually refers to situations in which all members of the family are involved in the therapy process, often as a group. There are some training institutes for family therapy, and graduates from such centers should be suitably qualified.

Child Psychotherapist Another unprotected term, this label tells you nothing, and the practitioner may or may not have any relevant training and experience.

School Psychologist As already noted, psychologist is a title controlled by law, and a school psychologist has had to meet state licensing or certification requirements, including education, experience, and examinations. School psychologists generally work with children who have behavioral or academic difficulties at school and make referrals and recommendations for remediation or therapy.

Counselor, Guidance Counselor, Vocational Counselor Although graduate schools offer programs in counseling, these titles are not controlled by law and can be used by anyone. Career counselor is a more recent addition to titles in this area. These counselors generally provide specific advice in making vocational or career choices, but anyone, with or without training in this area, can use these titles.

Sex Therapist This title is open to use by anyone because it is not licensed or otherwise controlled. There has been a proliferation of organizations and individuals describing themselves as sex therapists, but only a small minority of these have any training or credentials in the field. If you are considering seeing a sex therapist, it is important that you go to a practitioner who operates under some professional license, such as medicine or psychology, or to a clinic associated with an accredited hospital or university.

THE THERAPIST'S PERSONALITY, SEX, RACE, AND AGE

Training and credentials in psychotherapy are not enough to make a good therapist. A therapist must also have the personal characteristics that enable him or her to work closely with you in an atmosphere of mutual respect. The therapist must have not only the ability to understand you and your problems, but also the sensitivity to communicate this understanding in a manner that is acceptable and meaningful to you. This makes you the only judge of the suitability of the therapist's personality to your needs. If you are not comfortable with the therapist, the therapy process cannot take place.

In our status-conscious society, we tend to be overly impressed by experts and authorities. If you go into therapy with a shaky sense of your own self-worth, you are apt to accept as natural that the therapist sets the rules for your relationship and that you are expected to follow his or her cues. But this is not a genuine relationship and certainly not a therapeutic one. What you need is a therapist with whom you can feel at ease, someone with whom you do not have to screen your thoughts and feelings, someone whom you are not afraid to approach or to question. You should be able to enjoy and respect the therapist as a person—and know that the feeling is mutual.

What are some of the qualities you should look for? You need a therapist who is eager to know you as you are, not as a theory would have you. He or she should be genuinely concerned about your welfare, but in a supportive and nonrestrictive manner. Respecting people's need to live in their own way, the therapist has to grant you, in therapy as well as out, the freedom to be what you want to be. The therapist should not be afraid of your feelings and anxieties. He or she has to be ready to stand by you and help you face them rather than shield you both from experiencing them. The therapist should be nonjudgmental of you as a person, but also ready to challenge you when you are not being true to yourself. A therapist has to be able to confront you in a positive manner, without hostility, derision, or sarcasm.

Most clients find it helpful if the therapist is expressive of his or her feelings and relates in a genuine way rather than hiding behind a mask of objective detachment. A good therapist can react in a spontaneous, natural way and is not too stiff to laugh. You want a therapist who is able to recognize his or her own mistakes rather than deny them and pretend perfection. The therapist should not demand trust by virtue of his or her role, but earn it through the ability to be helpful and to respond to your needs.

Clients who have found their therapy helpful generally report that the therapist was a warm and caring person, while clients who did not find their therapy helpful report that the therapist was detached and aloof. Research studies on therapist personality characteristics that relate to positive results find that empathy (the ability to understand another person's feelings), warmth (care and concern for another), and genuineness (openness and directness) are the most important qualities. In one study conducted among clients in an outpatient clinic, "good" therapists were described as attentive, natural, and willing to engage in small talk, to give direct reassurance, to not be critical, and to not leave doubt about their real feelings; "bad" therapists were seen as making the individual feel like just another patient, as causing the patient to experience anger, as being passive and neutral, and as using abstract language.

The therapy relationship is particularly prone to exploitation of clients, so you must be on guard to protect yourself from any destructive personal needs of the therapist. These often do not become very apparent until the therapy is under way, but there are several signs to watch out for. A therapist who "comes on strong," uses jargon or quick interpretations, or otherwise awes you with his or her brilliance, may need to use the relationship to build up self-importance at your expense. The therapist who takes over the sessions may derive satisfaction from being in an authoritarian role and, in so doing, keep you from emerging. The therapist who is overly friendly may need to entice you into a relationship that will feed his or her needs for admiration or intimacy. A therapist who is overly formal and aloof may use that role as an excuse for his or her incapacity to relate, and thereby will deprive you of a meaningful relationship.

Unresolved personal needs and a lack of maturity are suggested by a therapist's attempts to impress you with a particular "style." In the desire to win a client over, therapists have a tendency to take up whatever traits are in vogue. Some wear the latest fashions to show they are successful or jogging clothes to show they are into holistic health; others are inappropriately informal, assuming the role of "good Joe" to show they are antiauthoritarian. Some indiscriminately use the latest methods to show they are professionally avant-garde, while others maintain whatever therapeutic style they were taught in school under the guise of professional rigor. Any of these stylized postures is a sign of a defensive rather than genuine approach to life and therapy. To become a real person, you need a therapist who is real.

It may be that you want a therapist who has certain personal characteristics that you consider to be important for your therapy. For example, some women want only women therapists, many blacks want black therapists, many married people want married therapists. Some people feel that only an older therapist who has lived long enough to experience life's problems can be helpful, and others want a therapist who knows what it is like to live with children. If you have strong feelings about any such personal characteristic, feel free to look for a therapist who has what you want. There are, however, practical limits to what you will be able to find since therapists form a rather homogeneous group. Most are white, middle-aged men reared in middle-class urban areas, and a high proportion come from Jewish backgrounds. They tend to be politically liberal and nonreligious. Keep in mind, however, that similarity of experience is not as important as the therapist's ability to empathize with the meaning of those experiences to you. It is more important that you share basic values than common experiences. If a woman avoids a male therapist because she's afraid a man will try to push her into a passive "feminine" role and chooses instead a female therapist who then directs her into an active professional role, the client is not necessarily better off. With either of these therapists the consequences would be the same in that both would try to propel the client where they thought she belonged rather than exploring what was most appropriate to her. Similarity of background does not guarantee respect for your right to determine your own life.

THERAPY FOR THERAPISTS

Experiencing therapy personally is an important aspect of the therapist's preparation. Textbook familiarity with the process and techniques is not enough. Going through therapy enhances the therapist's ability to empathize with the client's feelings about going through therapy and, more important, helps the therapist understand his or her own limitations, fears, and ways of restricting life. It is essential for the therapist to appreciate fully personal feelings and defenses against them if he or she is to know when and how they interfere with the therapy. Although some people can have much insight into themselves without the benefit of therapy, a therapist should not take the chance that such self-understanding is sufficient. Personal therapy also helps prepare therapists to deal with the emotional strains of their work. Therapists often engage in emotionally demanding encounters, immersing themselves in the clients' problems and becoming the butt of client feelings and accusations. The therapist not only has to accept these feelings but also must be able to turn them to therapeutic advantage. If the therapeutic interaction is not productive, therapists are apt to blame themselves and feel ineffectual. When that happens, therapists need enough inner strength to confirm a sense of self-worth. The nature of therapy demands that therapists live in close touch with their feelings. This closeness helps some live in greater harmony with themselves but for others it is a source of stress. There is evidence that not all psychotherapists have sufficiently strong foundations to withstand these emotional strains: the suicide rate among psychiatrists is disproportionately large, the highest of all the professions.

Despite the importance of personal therapy, not all therapists agree that it is necessary for themselves. There appears to be a difference among the professions in their attitudes toward this issue. Psychologists are more apt to have received therapy than psychiatrists and social workers. Of those psychiatrists who have had therapy, most report having done so for professional, or for a combination of professional and personal, reasons. In contrast, psychologists and social workers mostly sought out psychotherapy for personal reasons rather than viewing it primarily as a part of their training. Some therapists, like a lot of other people, think that they should not have personal therapy since this would be tantamount to saying that the therapist was just as "sick" as the clients. The old joke that you have to be crazy to see a psychotherapist is very much a part of that thinking. But a therapist who has not been in therapy may well be one who is unwilling to face him- or herself. And a therapist who claims to have had therapy for training purposes only (a "didactic analysis") has a need to make you think he or she is "healthy," thereby revealing an unbecoming defensive posture as well as a basic lack of understanding of what psychotherapy is about. It is highly unlikely that anyone who is unable, unwilling, or uninterested enough to get know him- or herself is going to be able to help you get to know yourself. Such a therapist is not going to be willing to explore his or her feelings as they relate to you either. Under these conditions you will not be able to experience your therapy as a genuine encounter between two persons, because one of them will be in hiding.

CLINICS AND TRAINING CENTERS

People tend to make unwarranted generalizations about clinics and training centers. A typical one is that you are safer in an organizational setting than with an independent practitioner because there is some control over the therapist: while you may not get the best, at least you won't get the worst. Another generalization is that clinics have lower fees, which in turn leads to the feeling that clinic therapists will not be very good.

Contrary to common belief, institutional status does not guarantee good or even acceptable standards for rendering service to the public. The requirements for an operating certificate are confusing and, once it is issued, the supervisory influence of the regulating state agency is usually minimal. As a matter of fact, clinics do not even have to be licensed to operate, though most are. That leaves the standards under which a clinic or psychotherapy center operates up to the institution's directorship. As a result, there are enormous variations in the quality of service provided by such institutions.

Psychotherapy clinics are the typical training grounds for therapists of all professions. The directors know that inexperienced therapists are less capable than experienced ones and, for that reason, reputable clinics provide intensive supervision for their less experienced staff members. Others, to maximize profits, seek out therapists with substandard qualifications who are willing to work for low fees and provide them with little or no supervision. The quality of supervision offered is often a major consideration in a therapist's decision to affiliate with one, rather than another, psychotherapy institution.

Although fees can be considerably lower at a clinic, some clinics charge just as much as if not more than private practitioners. Similarly, while one is likely to get a relatively inexperienced therapist in a clinic, this is not always the case. Not all therapists at clinics are beginners in training. For different reasons, some therapists prefer to stay at a clinic rather than going into independent practice, even though their apprenticeship is over and they have acquired the necessary experience and accreditation. Some psychotherapy centers, especially those affiliated with advanced training institutions, maintain high standards, selecting therapists who already have substantial prior qualifications. Such therapists, though still in a training capacity, may possess qualifications superior to those of some independent practitioners.

Clinics also vary in the kind of psychotherapy service they render. Some, particularly those connected with advanced training institutions, want to provide their trainees with experience in intensive psychotherapy and prefer to accept clients who are ready to commit themselves to long-term therapy. Clinics connected with universities are usually eclectic in orientation and those affiliated with analytic training schools (such as Freudian, Jungian, and so on) specialize in their particular approach. Most unaffiliated psychotherapy clinics encompass a variety of psychotherapy approaches. Of late, some clinics have adopted behaviorist methods and a few even specialize in them.

Clinics affiliated with hospitals are generally of one of two types. Most are "outpatient" clinics that operate close to the medical model. Though psychotherapy may be offered to various degrees, these clinics are inclined toward psychiatric methods, including drug and shock treatment. They tend to draw seriously disturbed persons who anticipate a need for medical treatment. Some teaching hospitals, on the other hand, have psychoanalytic training institutes with associated clinics that are specifically geared to rendering psychotherapy.

Social service, religious, and charitable organizations sometimes offer psychotherapy, but generally their services are limited to the more practical problems of living. Crisis centers specialize in sudden, transitory upsetting experiences in life including, but not limited to, suicidal urges. With the recent interest in family therapy, centers have emerged specializing in that modality. They focus on working with the whole family, preferring to treat it as a unit rather than through its individual members.

The anxiety of having to make choices is in no way bypassed by going to a clinic. The danger of your falling into the wrong situation is just as great as with an independent practitioner. You have to find a psychotherapy clinic that seems to be right for you and to assess its quality. While some clinics are good, many exist primarily as money-making operations. It is reasonable to generalize that chances for obtaining good psychotherapy are better at a clinic that has accreditation from an appropriate state agency and is affiliated with a well-known training institution like a university. Even after finding a suitable psychotherapy institution, you still have to select the therapist or, if you are not given choices, at least approve of him or her. The usual procedure at such institutions is for you to have an "intake" interview conducted by a social worker. At a hospital clinic you will probably have two preliminary interviews: an "intake" with a social worker and a psychiatric evaluation at which the psychiatrist will conduct a mental status examination and decide what your diagnosis is. After these preliminaries you are assigned to a particular therapist. Sometimes these assignments are made with special consideration for your needs and sometimes on purely administrative grounds. If you have any special preferences for a therapist, the intake is the time to make them known. The same basic requirements discussed earlier apply just as well to therapists in a clinic as to those in independent practice. If the therapist does not meet all of the training requirements, you can find out if he or she is in the process of completing training and working under the active supervision of a fully qualified practitioner in the meantime. If the therapist is not a person you like or feel comfortable with, you will have to ask to be assigned to someone more acceptable to you.

Most psychotherapy institutions keep records on you. If licensed, they are generally required to do so. A file is kept on each client, usually including diagnosis, summaries of the intake interview and of subsequent sessions, progress reports, and termination reports. Clinics vary in the extent to which the privacy of these records is guarded. In some, they are used with proper discretion and serve only supervisory purposes on the part of either the clinic's management or the state accreditation agency. In others, the records are used with less discretion for research, training, or demonstration purposes. You have a right to ask what information is being recorded and to know who has access to your file.

FEES AND INSURANCE

Money is one of the factors that is bound to influence your choice of a therapist. Fees charged for psychotherapy vary widely, but most psychotherapists in private practice charge between fifty and one hundred dollars per session. Higher fees are charged by well-established or prominent psychotherapists. Psychotherapists whose clientele comes from a moneyed field, such as the entertainment world, also maintain higher fees in accord with the income of the people with whom they deal. In smaller communities, less prominent therapists are apt to charge higher fees because there is less competition. West Coast therapists, on the whole, have a higher base fee than those in other regions of the country. Many therapists in private practice adjust their fee to the client's financial status, but usually within a fairly limited range, such as 10 percent or 20 percent of the regular fee. Some clinics with a sliding fee scale may offer psychotherapy for as little as five or ten dollars per session, but their fees at the upper end match those of private practitioners. Hospital clinics tend to have a wider range of fees than other clinics. A fee of fifty dollars is a fairly common clinic charge. The average fee for group therapy with a private practitioner is thirty dollars; lower group fees are generally available at clinics.

Fees vary by professional background, though these differences are narrowing. Psychiatrists as a group charge higher fees than psychologists as a group, and the latter charge more than social workers. This fee differential stems, in part, from the salary hierarchies among the professions in institutional settings. Since most mental health institutions are based on the medical model, they pay the highest salaries to physicians. Another reason is the public's willingness to pay higher fees to psychiatrists because of the medical mystique.

The size of the fee is not necessarily a measure of competence.

The lower fees of a clinic can include an unusually talented though not yet established therapist as well as an inexperienced student. The middle range of fees can include a beginner in independent practice trying to bluff his or her way into the image of an established practitioner or a very accomplished but modest practitioner. The high-fee therapist can have special talents or may possibly just be a good entrepreneur.

If you choose a therapist with a low fee, the chances are that his or her experience or training will be limited. If this is the case, be sure that such lacks are compensated for through active supervision and continued training. Your attitude toward low-priced services is also important. If you feel that a "cheap" therapist can't be good, that attitude, although unrealistic, may impede the therapy more than any limitations in the therapist's training or experience.

If you can afford it, it is probably best to choose a therapist in the middle range since he or she is apt to have solid qualifications at a reasonable cost. It will still be necessary for you to check this out. If a high-priced therapist does not have specialized capabilities important to you, be careful not to choose such a therapist for snob appeal—that is just as poor a basis for choosing a therapist as it is for going to therapy. Do not pay for reputation or image, but for quality of services. Also, remember that fees are often negotiable. If you like a therapist but the fee is too high, do not be afraid to ask if the therapist will see you for less.

Many major medical and health insurance policies cover part of psychotherapy expenses. If you want to start therapy, check your policies to see if you have coverage. If you do not have insurance that includes psychotherapy benefits, it is possible that you might qualify through the policy of a spouse or parent. The kind of coverage provided by these policies varies greatly. Some provide very limited benefits and others pay up to several thousands of dollars. Some policies insure only for psychotherapy rendered in a hospital setting, but many cover clinic and office visits. Some cover private psychotherapy only if administered by a psychiatrist or another physician, some cover for psychologists and physicians, and others cover for psychologists only if referral has been made by a physician. Many states have passed "freedom of choice" legislation that requires insurance companies to reimburse policyholders for psychotherapy rendered by psychologists. Because of legal precedents, some insurance companies, currently allowed by state laws to restrict psychotherapy benefits to policy-holders who see medical practitioners have reimbursed for psychologists' services when requested. Very few policies cover services rendered by social workers, although this is changing. New York, for example, recently upgraded the requirements for social worker certification as psychotherapy providers so they would be eligible for third-party payments.

Medicare pays only for psychotherapy services rendered by physicians. Medicaid benefits cover psychotherapy rendered by psychiatrists and psychologists.

When your therapist completes an insurance claim form, it is necessary to include a diagnosis, usually from the *Diagnostic and Statistical Manual of Mental Disorders* (see page 59). Many clients object to being given a psychiatric label and some are concerned about these labels getting into their personnel files if they are receiving insurance through a place of employment. Therapists tend to make allowances for their clients' concerns and use labels and diagnoses that have a less derogatory ring to them. The problem with this procedure, aside from its dishonesty, is that the milder the label, the more likely the insurance company will be to cut off benefits after a given period. Insurance companies are concerned with the high costs to them of reimbursement for psychotherapy and have instituted procedures to minimize their costs. One of these is the process of "peer review." The insurance company may require your therapist to provide written documentation about your mental condition and course of therapy for review by a committee of professional peers, usually paid appointees of the American Psychological or Psychiatric Association. At their discretion, they may deny coverage if they feel the condition does not warrant therapy or does not warrant continued therapy, or if they feel that the therapy procedures are not appropriate to the condition. Some clients electing the less traditional therapy methods have found their therapy claims disallowed as these approaches are not generally well-regarded by "establishment" therapists.

In addition to concerns about the possibility of benefits being denied, many clients are concerned about issues of confidentiality. Although they must give their consent to have information about their therapy released to the peer review committee, if they do not give consent they lose their coverage. Similarly, if their therapists do not provide detailed information about their problems and treatment, the review board is apt to hold up the claim until it does receive such information.

The cost of psychotherapy is deductible as a medical expense on income tax returns when rendered by either medical or non-medical practitioners.

The inclusion of insurance and tax benefits under medical services perpetuates the medical model of psychotherapy. Understandably, as neither clients nor practitioners want to lose out on these benefits, both parties engage in a bit of hypocrisy when claiming them as "medical services." This will continue for as long as psychotherapy benefits are available only under the medical umbrella.

How to Find Names

Several different procedures can be followed to find names of potential therapists in your area. One good way of getting names is from friends and acquaintances who have been in therapy, as they can also give you an advance description of the therapist. Still, therapists are not always the same with every client and there is no guarantee that a friend's favorable experience will be repeated.

Physicians, although frequently used in this capacity, are not apt to be a good referral source. They often belittle psychotherapy, want to treat your problems medically, or try doing psychotherapy themselves. If they do refer, it is likely to be to a psychiatrist even though a therapist from another profession might be more suitable for you. Of course, some physicians do make appropriate referrals, but you should be alert to the possible pitfalls of this source. Psychotherapists, being more knowledgeable about psychotherapy, are a better source for referrals, but they too are inclined to favor practitioners who share a similar therapeutic orientation or come from the same professional background.

Another way of getting a referral is to consult a leading figure in the field who knows many therapists, such as the director of a psychotherapy training institute. That person should be able to make a well-considered referral based on knowledge of both the field and many therapists, graduates as well as students. If such a person is not available to you, or you don't want to pay for a personal consultation, you can still call one or more training institutes and they will probably be happy to give you the names of graduates or refer you to somebody still in training at the institute.

You can call the local professional society for psychiatrists, psychologists, social workers, or psychiatric nurses. They usually give you names of three practitioners in your area and sometimes respond to more specific requests for information about the therapist's services, fees, or years of practice. Names can also be found by consulting directories of the various professional organizations. First decide which professional background comes closest to your philosophical predispositions so you can check the appropriate directory. Psychiatrists are listed in the *American Psychiatric Association Directory*, or in the *Directory of Medical Specialists* if they are certified; psychologists will be found in the *American Psychological Association Directory* and the *National Register of Health Service Providers in Psychology;* and social workers are listed in the membership directory of the National Association of Social Workers or in its *Register of Clinical Social Workers*. The directories, usually available in large public libraries, have a geographical listing where you can first check who lives in the area you want, and then read the biographical entry.

The *Yellow Pages* are primarily useful in providing the names of practitioners in your area, but these names will require further checking. Psychiatrists are not listed separately from "Physicians and Surgeons" and the psychologist and social worker columns do not give the specialty. None of the names are screened for licenses or qualifications, and the lists are not comprehensive because many qualified practitioners do not list themselves in classified telephone books. Psychotherapy clinics are listed under "Clinics" alongside abortion and medical centers and again require further checking on your part.

Of late, there has been a burgeoning of "referral services" in some large cities. These services place ads in the classified sections of various magazines and newspapers under headings such as "Psychotherapy" or "Counseling," or in the *Yellow Pages* under "Clinics." Some referral services were organized by psychotherapy associations as a means of providing the public with a source of qualified practitioners; others are fronts for one or more psychotherapists who are seeking additional clientele. Psychotherapists affiliated with such referral services may or may not be qualified to practice.

Now that advertising one's services is no longer a violation of professional ethics, practitioners have begun to advertise directly in newspapers, in magazines, and even on radio. These persons, too, must be screened because they may or may not be qualified to practice. Most of the people advertising psychotherapy services of one sort or another in the classified section do not include their names. We consider this to be a bad sign. If they are uncomfortable about what they are doing, and have to conceal their identity, it suggests that they should resolve their own problems before trying to help you with yours.

4. Special Issues for Different Groups

ALL PEOPLE enter therapy to alleviate their psychological pain and achieve personality growth, but the specific roads they take to reach these ends are influenced by who they are and the cultural, racial, religious, and sexual values that they bring with them into therapy. Therapists also bring values into therapy that underlie and guide their work. They believe that people have a right to personal freedom, that their individuality should be respected, that they should be responsible for their own lives and choices, and that the role of psychotherapy is to augment their capacity for self-determination and growth. Implied in these basic therapeutic values is respect for the client's cultural heritage and personal values that shape his or her goals and determine the framework in which they are most likely to be achieved.

In addition to basic therapeutic values that are shared, therapists also have personal values that derive from their own heritage. Try as they might to keep a neutral façade, therapists' values will, invariably, permeate their work. To do otherwise is not possible, or even helpful, in that clients benefit most when they are in relationship with a real person rather than with an impersonal technician. If client and therapist share similar backgrounds and value orientations, the chances of their working well together are enhanced. They speak the same language, both literally and figuratively. The therapist is better able to understand and empathize with the client, sensing the most appropriate forms for therapy to take and being attuned to the needs and goals of the client. If client and therapist come from substantially different backgrounds, whether from different age groups, sexual orientations, or cultures, it places greater demands on the therapist, who has to be aware of the client's outlook and be ready to help the client find solutions in ways that are not in the therapist's vocabulary. The therapist must also be more self-aware to be alert to the way his or her personal values and biases might be affecting the therapy.

Large differences between client and therapist also place greater demands on the client. Most therapists are part of the mainstream of society; they tend to be white, middle-aged, middle-class, well-educated, heterosexual men. Clients who come from backgrounds that are out of the mainstream and that are viewed negatively by society may find themselves with therapists who are unable to give up these stereotypes and are therefore also unable to work in a respectful manner with such clients. Minority group members, women, gays, and older people are particularly vulnerable in this regard. They face therapy with a triple burden: in addition to the personal problems that everyone brings to therapy, they have the problem of dealing with various forms of social disapproval and oppression, and the problem of finding a therapist who will not approach them with the same biases. It is likely that members of these groups will encounter special problems in therapy and it is important to keep in mind, if and when that happens, that it is the prejudices of the therapist that are probably to blame.

This chapter deals with some of the special issues that minority people, women, gays, and older persons must face in selecting an appropriate therapist and obtaining appropriate services.

PSYCHOTHERAPY FOR ETHNIC MINORITIES

Although we consider ours a pluralistic society, the different cultural groups that make up that society are, only too often, not allowed full privileges and are looked on askance because they refuse to lose their identities in the melting pot. Ethnic and racial minorities in our country are at a social disadvantage not only because of negative stereotyping but, generally speaking, in terms of education, job opportunities, and economic resources as well. This means that they have more problems to deal with and less ability to obtain needed services. It has been documented that minority people generally receive inferior mental health care, being unable to afford the relatively high fees of trained therapists or not having available trained personnel in the community. They are more likely to be assigned junior rather than senior staff members for therapy, to be diagnosed as having more severe pathology, to receive short-term rather than long-term treatment, and to be provided with medication instead of psychotherapy. Language creates another barrier, as there is a shortage of therapists who can work comfortably in languages other than English. This is especially true of non-Western languages, and the problem of finding a therapist is more acute for the growing Asian population in this country.

In addition to the difficulties involved in locating and paying for appropriate psychotherapy services, minority people must also find therapists who do not harbor racist sentiments. Racist attitudes are so deeply ingrained in our culture that it is very hard for anybody growing up in our society to be free of them, including people from minority groups themselves, who sometimes introject the negative attitudes to which they are subjected. Like others in the society, therapists tend to have ethnic and racial biases. Thus, if you are a member of a minority group, obtaining appropriate psychotherapy services will be more difficult for you than it is for others.

Choosing a Therapist When looking for a psychotherapist, in addition to following the basic guidelines outlined in the previous chapter, you should also explore with a potential therapist his or her attitudes toward your particular ethnic group. If a therapist is uncomfortable in talking about this issue, or flatly denies any prejudice, it may well be that you have touched on a sensitive point and that the therapist is too insecure in his or her attitudes to work with you productively. You can also ask the therapist whether he or she has worked with other individuals from your ethnic or racial group and how familiar he or she is with the experiences and history of your group. A therapist who is out of touch with important aspects of your background is probably not a good bet as he or she would seem to have little interest in keeping up with the needs of the various minority groups that compose and contribute to our culture. On the other hand, it is unreasonable to expect a therapist outside of your group to be fully conversant with your cultural heritage, and if he or she is a good match for you in other respects, that person could become better informed if the two of you work together. It is also unreasonable to expect the therapist to be completely free of racism, even if the therapist is from your own group, but what you can and should expect is that he or she be aware of the tendency to fall prey to such attitudes and be ready to engage in self-examination when working with you.

Research shows that minority group members are more apt than are others to quit therapy after one or two sessions. This is often not because they are less suitable candidates for therapy but because they are uncomfortable with the therapist, who may not be respectful or empathic. If you have concerns about how a therapist behaves with you, bring them up for discussion. You might find, for instance, that the therapist keeps him- or herself too aloof from you. Some therapists maintain a distant attitude with all their clients in the belief that this is the best way to conduct therapy. Others may be aloof with you because they are bigots at heart. Still others may be trying to combat their prejudice by maintaining a respectful distance and avoiding any familiarity that might be experienced as condescension. If you do not relate well to an aloof therapist, and most people do not, none of these therapists would be right for you, except possibly one who falls in the latter case. As such a therapist is aware of his or her bias and working on it, he or she would probably be pleased to have feedback from you and be able to relate more spontaneously.

Monitoring the Therapy It is very unlikely that a therapist would exhibit any overt prejudice while working with you. Prejudice and racist sentiments, when they appear, are usually quite subtle—the therapist may not even be aware of his or her behavior in this regard. A therapist who is unaware of such behavior is likely to attribute your problems primarily to your personal inadequacies and lose sight of the insidious effects of racism on your life. Such a therapist may also be apt to focus primarily on your areas of weakness and not be cognizant of, or work with you on developing, your strengths.

When therapists are aware of their bias and guilty about it, they may try to compensate for the feeling in a variety of ways. A common failing is to underestimate the seriousness of your problems in an attempt to be accepting and noncritical. Another fairly common practice among therapists is to be overaccommodating by working too hard and taking over too much of the therapy, in what is known as the "Great White Father Syndrome." In an attempt to convince you of their good will they may try to overextend themselves for you, but this is a counterproductive attitude in that the purpose of therapy is to help you develop your own resources. A variation on this theme is ingratiating behavior on the part of the therapist, who may be unconsciously seeking to mask negative feelings behind friendly or flattering behavior. Overly friendly and sympathetic therapists represent a special problem in that their behavior may inhibit you from expressing your anger at the underlying condescension you may be experiencing.

Some therapists try to compensate for underlying racist sentiments by attributing all your problems to social oppression. While it is important that the therapist recognize the real problems that you are faced with, it is not helpful to ignore the ways in which you limit your own development, the exploration of which, after all, is the core of therapy. In putting all the blame on society, therapists sometimes unwittingly encourage destructive behavior on the part of clients who have a need to "get back" at society.

Still another manifestation of unrecognized racism on the part of therapists is "color blindness"—the tendency to deny that the client's minority status makes any difference to the therapist or to the client. The issue of ethnic identity is, however, central to all minority people, and avoiding any discussion of it denies a significant part of the client's self-image and reality. The difference in background should be openly acknowledged by both therapist and client and opportunity provided to express and explore the feelings it arouses.

You may find in the course of therapy that your therapist does not always get the gist of what you are saying or may be prone to misinterpret what you are saying. This does not necessarily reflect a racist attitude but may be the result of a communication gap based on different cultural experiences or on language difficulties. The therapist should, of course, be alert to this possibility, but you should not feel hesitant about confronting such issues when the therapist does not seem to be aware of them. It is to be hoped that the therapist will be open to rectifying such miscommunications and becoming more sensitized to them and to your background.

Value Differences All human beings are basically the same in that they have the same developmental needs and follow the same developmental patterns. Nonetheless, there are different ways of living, each of which has its strengths, but also its limitations. In therapy, the job of the therapist is to help clients solve problems in a way that meets their individual needs and respects their cultural perspective and identity. Often the values of therapist and client mesh, or they diverge while remaining within each other's framework. But sometimes they conflict with the result that client and therapist have different views of what is essential for psychological well-being and growth. When this happens, the therapist has an ethical responsibility to present his or her view rather than to conceal it and go along with a pattern he or she considers countertherapeutic. The client may find it impossible to continue with a therapist in such circumstances, or may find that the value clash helps to broaden his or her own perspective. Perhaps a discussion of the differences will even open up new vistas for the therapist. Although it is not the job of the client to educate the therapist, in any genuine human encounter both parties must be open to each other and to the possibilities of change.

Value differences between minority group members and mainstream therapists often involve the role of family relationships. Contemporary middle-class white culture, for example, places a high value on democratic family structure and the early development of independence. On the positive side, this pattern stresses individual autonomy, but on the negative side it leads to alienation and erosion of family ties. Many minority cultures, in contrast, place a high value on authoritarian family structure and family loyalty. On the positive side, this pattern leads to warm and emotionally supportive relationships, but on the negative side to dependency and inhibition of assertiveness. When differences in orientation such as these became an issue in the therapy, therapist and client together have to explore the positive and negative implications of the available choices and decide what is most appropriate to the client.

Value-based differences between minority clients and therapists are apt to intrude in many other areas and have to be confronted by both parties in an atmosphere of mutual understanding and trust. It is condescending and countertherapeutic for a therapist to compromise fundamental therapeutic values to accommodate the client's traditions. For example, it has been suggested that therapists who work with Asian-Americans should meet clients' concerns with status and hierarchy by maintaining professional distance, prominently displaying diplomas, and prefacing interpretations with such phrases as "In my professional judgment." Such an accommodation, however, maintains an authoritarian attitude rather than helping clients adopt a more autonomous stance. Many other value-based conflicts will confront therapists who work with members of ethnic minorities. Consider the following questions, for instance: should a therapist who works with Hispanics question their view that children must not challenge elders, or go along with the cultural convention? Should a therapist accept a black client's habitual lateness because black culture does not have the same regard for clock time as white culture? White therapists will also have to ask themselves if their cultural stress on activity and achievement is in the interest of personal growth or if they cannot learn other, and perhaps more productive, ways of living from their clients.

WOMEN AND FEMINIST THERAPY

One of the most dramatic results of the women's liberation movement has been the opening up of new role options for women. While women before were more or less confined to the home in the role of wife and mother, it has become easier and more acceptable for women to enter the work force, have careers, maintain unmarried relationships, opt not to have children or to have them as single parents, and more. Along with these new choices go the burdens of choice, as well as the burdens of experimenting with uncharted life-styles and of dealing with those segments of society that are still hostile to women's new possibilities. Obviously, a woman contemplating therapy needs a therapist who accepts her new possibilities as legitimate and who is sensitive to the various demands these new choices place upon her. In selecting an appropriate therapist, there are many questions to explore ("Can I trust a male therapist?" "Should I work only with a woman?" "How do

I make sure the therapist is not a sexist?" "What is the difference between therapy and feminist therapy?") and various guidelines to use in evaluating the therapists you meet.

Sex of the Therapist We live in a sexist society that is only slowly evolving and that has long regarded women as the weaker, more passive, more dependent, and less intelligent sex, and as most fit to stay home, have babies, and support their mates in their endeavors. It is very hard for men to give up these attitudes, and even when they are discarded intellectually, many men still cling to them emotionally. But the same goes for women. Many women today still feel they can define themselves only in relation to men and look for stronger men on whom they can lean for emotional as well as financial support. It is difficult to free oneself from age-old stereotyped patterns, and both men and women harbor remnants of the old sexist attitudes. Therapists, too, as members of the culture, are prone to sexist thinking but, presumably, are more aware than others of these tendencies in themselves and more willing to examine these attitudes. A female therapist is more likely to be sympathetic to women's needs and goals than is a male therapist, but there is no guarantee that this will be the case. In selecting a therapist, it is important to screen the therapist on attitudes toward women's issues, whatever the sex of the therapist. If you have found a therapist who seems appropriate in all other regards (see Chapter 3, "How to Pick a Therapist"), probe specifically in the following areas to ascertain whether the therapist is likely to approach you with a sexist bias:

- How does the therapist describe men and women in terms of basic personality and needs? (For example, does the therapist see large differences between the sexes? Are these attributed to biology or to social conditioning? Are women described in stereotypical, passive-dependent ways and men in active-independent ways?)
- What does the therapist think are appropriate role options for women? (For example, does the therapist think mothers of young children should stay at home, that women cannot be fulfilled unless they have children, that some professional or occupational endeavors are unsuitable to women?)
- What is the therapist's position on such issues as abortion, lesbianism, single parenthood? (For example, does the

therapist feel that women have the right to determine their own lives or that they should follow in established patterns?)

- What is the therapist's view of healthy heterosexual relationships? (Should women put needs of the relationship before needs of career, play a seductive sexual role, take sole responsibility for birth control, be in charge of taking care of the home if employed?)

Exploring these questions will help you to determine to what extent the therapist, whether a man or a woman, is bound by cultural stereotypes and unable to help you develop ways of being that are important to you and not in accordance with the traditional mold.

Monitoring the Therapy Despite attempts to screen therapists for sexist attitudes and biases, it is not always possible to do so successfully, in good part because therapists themselves are often unaware of their own prejudices. Because of this, it is important for women to be alert to signs of sexism that may crop up in therapy once it is underway. Look for such typical signs as these:

- In setting therapy goals with you, is the therapist inclined to want you to accept stereotyped sex roles, or is the therapist supportive of your individual goals?
- Does your therapist use such phrases as "penis envy," "masculine protest," "expressing your femininity?" If so, how are these terms defined? Is the therapist critical of your behavior in terms of how "feminine" you are? How does the therapist respond to your questions on this issue?
- Does the therapist use paternalistic language and call you "girl," "sweetie," or similar names?
- Does the therapist use your first name but have you refer to him or her by title?
- Does the therapist behave in inappropriate ways, such as patting you unnecessarily, holding your hand, brushing against you, moving in too close?
- If your therapist is a man, does he respond more positively to you if you wear makeup, or dresses instead of slacks?
- Is the therapist more concerned about your relationships with men and dating behavior than with your work and career goals?

- If you have had forced sexual encounters, either early or recent, does the therapist tend to discount your reports or to attribute the encounters to your behavior?

If any of these signs are present, it is a good idea to bring them up and discuss them. How the therapist reacts to being questioned will be an important indicator of whether the therapy relationship is a productive one for you.

What Is Feminist Therapy? Feminist therapy grew out of the women's liberation movement of the sixties and seventies. Feminists were rightly concerned that psychotherapy could easily work to women's detriment by fostering sexist roles instead of expanding women's options, a danger that loomed larger because most psychotherapists are men, even though most therapy clients are women. Although not all therapy systems ascribe a passive role to women, as does Freudian analysis, for example, many male therapists have gone along with the commonly accepted proposition that a woman's emotional well-being is related to her ability to assume a nurturant, mothering role and to put aside her competitive strivings.

Feminist therapists as a group do not belong to any particular school of psychotherapy or adhere to any one theory. They are agreed, however, on several points: 1) that the therapist-client relationship must be an egalitarian one in order to foster self-respect and autonomy, 2) that the client must be helped to understand the role of society and sexism in shaping her behavior and to not blame herself for problems that she shares with other women, and 3) that therapist and client must recognize the need for social change and the elimination of sexism and sex-role stereotyping.

While the goals of feminist therapy are laudable, they sometimes go beyond the task of therapy. By definition, therapy seeks to bring about change in the individual, whereas feminist therapy's focus is on external conditions as well as internal problems. To the extent that feminist therapy seeks social solutions for its clients, it is not really therapy. Although many women share similar problems, which may also be exacerbated by the social climate in which they live, it takes more than political awareness and social or political action to find solutions for them. Consciousness-raising groups have made a significant contribution to helping women clarify the factors involved in women's oppression, but these groups alone cannot solve the problems of the women who participate in them. The very existence of feminist therapy, as a service apart from consciousness-raising groups, acknowledges this fact. Many practitioners of feminist therapy reflect the confusion about the exact nature of feminist therapy by referring to the women they see as "patients." A woman who is a patient is clearly seen as someone who has a personal problem that requires individual treatment, and for such a person feminist therapy, as a process oriented to social solutions, is not directly applicable.

Feminist therapy assumes that other therapies are adjustment-oriented and based on power relationships. Although that may once have been the case, many therapies today are growth-oriented and focus on developing autonomy rather than adapting to one's circumstances. Adherence to other therapeutic systems does not preclude helping clients to become aware of repressive cultural influences and to muster the courage to confront such barriers to growth. Of course, feminist therapists are more attuned than others to barriers impeding women's growth, but good therapists must be alert to the various environmental pressures faced by all their clients—be they women, minority group members, handicapped, old, or young.

Any woman entering therapy should be sure that her therapist is not a sexist who expects her to conform to existing sex-role stereotypes, but she should also be sure that her therapist does not expect her to conform to any other predetermined roles either. Some feminist therapists, in their desire to ensure that their clients do not lend themselves to oppressive roles, push them instead toward "liberated" roles that may not be authentic for the client. Elizabeth Friar Williams, for instance, says in her book *Notes of a Feminist Therapist* that if a woman cannot "support herself in work that is fun for her and gives her a sense of competence . . . her therapy [is] incomplete," and she encourages women "to stay in therapy until they have found a clear direction in terms of a career." While it is advantageous for women, as well as for men, to be able to support themselves in work that is enjoyable, this is not always feasible or necessarily an important goal. Some people, women and men, because they have other goals of overriding importance, may have to accept that they must stick to their jobs even if the work is not fun and learn not to measure themselves and their worth according to their job satisfaction and status. Some people, women and men, may have to learn how to give up the joys of a satisfying career in order to obtain other joys they may value more, such as those of motherhood or fatherhood. Being a housewife or a househusband does not mean giving up one's independence, financial or otherwise, if two partners can work out ways of sharing their labors and resources. Having a gratifying career is not a goal for everyone, but being free to follow a self-fulfilling path that enables personal growth should be a universal goal.

If you are inclined to work with a feminist, keep in mind that many feminists do not call themselves feminist therapists and that not all feminist therapists may help you toward realizing your particular goals.

GAY AND LESBIAN THERAPY

Homosexuality has a long history, but attitudes toward it vary according to the culture and the times. In our society homosexuality has been viewed as an experience outside normal behavior, and homosexuals have been isolated from the mainstream, being denied specific employment opportunities, prevented from forming legal attachments to their mates, barred from adopting children, and frequently rejected by their families as well. Because of this attitude, therapeutic efforts in the past were primarily directed at trying to change the sexual orientation of homosexuals in order to bring them back into the fold. More recently, largely through the efforts of the gay and lesbian liberation movement, homosexuality is becoming accepted as a legitimate life-style and therapists are starting to direct attention to helping homosexuals maximize their personality development as people, accepting their homosexual orientation.

Criticism of homosexual behavior in our society has been more rampant than in most others, leading many people to develop homophobia—irrational feelings of hatred towards homosexuals. Freud and others have attributed homophobia to a fear of the homosexual tendency that they maintain exists in everyone. Even the mental health establishment is prone to homophobia and, at least until recently, has been in the forefront of keeping these feelings alive. Until 1973, homosexuality was classified by the American Psychiatric Association as a mental illness that, according to specialists in this "sickness," encompassed such traits as "wild self-damaging tendencies," "onslaughts of paranoid ideation," "grossly defective peer-group relatedness," "refusal to acknowledge accepted standards in nonsexual matters," and "general unreliability of a more or less psychotic nature." When the board of trustees of the APA, under pressure from gay activists and after bitter debates within the profession, voted, in that year, to remove homosexuality from its official list of mental disorders, this by no means erased the stigma of homosexuality that the APA had helped to perpetuate among psychiatrists and other mental health workers, not to speak of the public at large and the homosexual population. The negative stereotypes have not only had an impact on heterosexuals but have been largely internalized by homosexuals themselves. A central concern for gay people is how to obtain psychotherapeutic help in repairing damaged self-concepts from a psychotherapeutic community that harbors negative feelings and has not been able to face its homophobia.

Issues for Psychotherapy Gays and lesbians, like heterosexuals, seek treatment for a wide range of emotional problems, but they also have to deal with low self-esteem, feelings of alienation, and the issue of coming out. The stigma of homosexuality usually results in considerable damage to one's self-image. It also results in anger at the rejection by society at large and frequently also by one's family and close associates. Often this anger is projected onto other gay people, interfering with the ability to have close relationships with the very people one is drawn to. Or the anger may be repressed, resulting in feelings of depression, isolation, and powerlessness. Sometimes, these feelings drive gays into other behaviors, such as abusing drugs or alcohol, that further heighten their sense of worthlessness.

An essential task for psychotherapy is to help free the client from the internalized negative social image and develop a positive identity as a homosexual. This involves "coming out." Before clients do come out, they are forced to lead double lives, involving lying, withdrawal, and evasiveness, that make them feel inauthentic and alienated. The first step in coming out, acknowledging homosexuality to oneself, may be as difficult as the other two steps: acknowledging homosexuality to other homosexuals and acknowledging it to everyone else. The latter is a potentially dangerous move that could lead to social oppression, rejection by family and friends, and the attendant stress and anxiety such risk implies.

Choosing a Psychotherapist If you are a gay person considering psychotherapy you, like anyone else, want to find a competent and compatible therapist. But you will have to exercise more caution than other prospective clients because of the widespread homophobia among psychotherapists. Some are open about their feelings and will tell you flat out that they consider homosexuality to be a mental disorder that they can help you, or will try to help you, correct. Others may not be open in their feelings, even to themselves, and may maintain that they accept your life-style when they really regard it as pathological. Only a handful of therapists are free of negative attitudes about homosexuality or able to confront their homophobia in a constructive way that keeps it from interfering in their work with homosexuals. The problem for you is screening therapists on this critical issue.

According to therapists who are themselves homosexual and other therapists who have worked with homosexuals and are not critical of homosexual life-styles, a key screening question for a potential therapist is "What are your views on the origins of homosexuality?" Therapists who view homosexuality as a caused condition whose origins they can pinpoint tend to focus on the prevention and correction of homosexuality, thereby contributing to the internalization of negative self-images rather than focusing on helping clients to come to terms with their sexual identity. You should also inquire how much experience the therapist has had working with gay and lesbian clients and, particularly, whether the therapist has worked on the following issues:

- Coming out;
- Problems of intimacy and relating;
- Self-hatred, both internal and projected;
- Coping without family and social supports;
- Lack of role models.

Another helpful indicator of the therapist's ability to work constructively with you is the extent of that person's general awareness of the gay experience and whether he or she has friends who are gay.

Some homosexuals want only gay therapists, in the belief that only another gay can be truly accepting and helpful. As is the case with other groups that have special needs in therapy, however, sexual orientation in itself is no guarantee of good therapy. A homosexual therapist who is improperly trained and who has not been through therapy might not have worked out his or her own problems sufficiently and, therefore, may not be ready to help you with yours. Also, depending on the particular stage at which a client finds him- or herself, the homosexuality of the therapist can be either an aid or a hindrance. For instance, if a client is in the process of coming out, it is helpful to have a gay therapist as a positive role model who has already been through the experience. However, a client who is unsure about his or her sexual identity may unconsciously experience a homosexual therapist as exerting pressure to declare oneself a homosexual.

The sex of the therapist, regardless of the sexual orientation of the therapist, is an important factor for some homosexual clients. Generally, gays are accepting of either male or female therapists, and some even have a preference for female therapists, but lesbians usually do not want to work with male therapists. This position stems from concern about sexist attitudes in men, which are not restricted to the heterosexual male population. A number of lesbians view their lesbianism as a political rather than a sexual orientation and want to work only with women in accordance with that political stance.

There is some question what effect the professional background of the therapist has on his or her ability to work constructively with gays and lesbians. Research indicates that homophobia is less evident among psychologists than psychiatrists, and most prevalent among social workers. Caution must be exercised, however, in using this as a guideline in choosing a therapist. The data merely suggest the chances of finding an appropriate therapist from one of the three disciplines and does not characterize the individual members of those professions.

Psychotherapy for Gays and Lesbians Versus Gay and Lesbian Therapy Just as the women's liberation movement gave rise to feminist therapy, the gay liberation movement gave rise to gay and lesbian therapy. The contradictions inherent in feminist therapy also pertain to gay therapy in that political and social goals may be confused with therapy goals. Homosexuals of either gender obviously want a therapist who is not antagonistic to their lifestyle and who can maintain a nonjudgmental climate in which clients feel free to work on their problems.

Gay and lesbian therapy, however, also implies, as does feminist therapy, that the therapist must be committed to the concept of full equality for gays and expanded role options for those gays who do not choose to live in the closet. To the extent that the problems facing any particular gay person are social and political, the solutions are also social and political; to the extent that the problems lie in the individual's ability to deal with the social and political climate emotionally, the solutions are to be sought in psychotherapy. As is the case with feminist therapy, there is some confusion inherent in the term "gay and lesbian therapy," and while it is possible to have a therapist who believes in gay liberation, that goal does not fall within the scope of psychotherapy; only individual liberation does.

The AIDS Crisis Because of the AIDS crisis, many therapists who work with homosexuals have taken a strong position against behavior about which they formerly maintained nonjudgmental stands. Promiscuous sexual behavior, which was accepted as part of the life-style of many gays, is now viewed as potentially dangerous and life-threatening, and many therapists feel it is their responsibility to counsel against such behavior.

Those gays who are afflicted with AIDS face tremendous burdens in dealing with the disease and in obtaining psychotherapeutic help. The isolation from society and rejection that gays have been subjected to becomes magnified a millionfold for the AIDS victim. Many do not confide their health problems to anyone because they fear both exposure as gays and being shunned by people who are afraid of AIDS. Those who do acknowledge having AIDS or ARC (AIDS Related Complex) often do find themselves cut off from family, friends, and sometimes lovers. Even therapists who are experienced in working with gay clients may be unwilling to work with AIDS victims, although gay therapists tend to feel that the fears of transmission of the disease are greatly exaggerated. Those who are not worried about catching AIDS may find that they have not had sufficient experience working with people suffering from life-threatening illnesses to be helpful to AIDS victims, or that their own unresolved anxieties about death interfere with their ability to address this issue with a terminally ill client.

Research has indicated that more than 75 percent of the AIDS victims studied attributed responsibility for their health problems to themselves. Therapists experienced in working with these clients feel that they should be encouraged to make positive changes to improve the quality of their lives and to enhance their sense of control and mastery. One common danger for therapists is to interpret clients' positive outlook as denial, and to undermine confidence by projecting their own fears onto clients.

An associated problem is the need for psychotherapy and counseling for the surviving members of gay couples. One of the problems they encounter is that friends often do not allow the survivor sufficient time to grieve as a result of their own need for denial. Survivors who have cared for their lovers during the illness generally develop a heightened fear of contracting AIDS themselves or of transmitting it. They have a hard time relaxing after the death of their lovers, whom they tend to idealize, and often are unable to form new relationships.

Therapists working with AIDS victims and the surviving members of gay couples find it very stressful and generally have a high rate of professional burnout. To help meet the needs of AIDS victims, gay activists are setting up hot lines and support groups. It has been found that surviving members of gay couples who became volunteers in AIDS support groups recover more quickly from their bereavement than those who remain isolated.

PSYCHOTHERAPY FOR OLDER PEOPLE

Every age group has its problems but none more than the older age group. As one gets older, the stresses of living increase while, at the same time, the capacity to deal with them is diminished. Older people have to learn to cope with the loss of many things that sustained them before—their health, occupation, close relatives and friends, the feeling of control they enjoyed while at the "peak" of life, and the respect of society at large. It is no wonder that people in the older age group have the highest incidence of mental health disturbances. Their inner resources, which were adequate to meet their needs before, often prove insufficient in the face of new pressures, or long-standing problems that had been manageable become aggravated given new life circumstances. Despite these increased stresses, older people are less inclined to make use of therapy. When people enter the older age groups they often feel that at their age they should be able to handle their problems without help. Or they may feel that it is "too late" to do anything about their problems. Relatives may also discourage older people from considering therapy, telling them that they are too old to change. Even though people around you may think you are too set in your ways to benefit from therapy, you have greater experience and knowledge to bring to therapy. Whether you can use psychotherapy to advantage will depend more on the attitude you have toward your life than on how old you are.

The Psychological Toll of Growing Old Although older people now constitute a larger percentage of the population than ever before and, as a group, are becoming recognized as an important political and economic factor, on an individual basis their influence is smaller than ever. Society used to value the wisdom and experience of older people and sought to learn from the biographies of those who had experienced more of life, but society now venerates the young instead, and people start writing their autobiographies in their twenties and thirties. With the accent on youth and trendiness, society has begun to develop a denigrating stereotype of the older person that pictures him or her as rigid in attitude, often foolish, and standing in the way of progress. Added to these social attitudes are social policies that make life more difficult for older people. Mandatory retirement forces many capable people out of work, resulting in a decrease in income, interpersonal contacts, and perceived importance. As society defines people in terms of occupation, it is apparent that the "retired" person is a nobody. People who lose their jobs before retirement age still get the short end of the stick in that it becomes increasingly difficult, with each passing year, for them to find employment and financial compensation commensurate with their experience and expertise. Nor does this end the list of problems. As one ages, so do one's contemporaries, and many older people find themselves faced with the deaths of friends and spouses, and erosion of social and familial support systems. Illness and infirmity are much more likely to strike, creating further stress, and lowered income makes it more difficult to meet the new challenges: there is less money available for good medical care, for household help, for entertainment, and so on. This means a forced narrowing of pursuits and a greater disengagement from the world, which also tends to make a person less aware of what is going on and less interesting, and therefore more apt to fulfill the stereotype. Because of the erosion of one's influence, financial resources, and physical stamina, there is often an accompanying loss of self-esteem as well as a tendency toward self-blame for the state of affairs in which one finds oneself. Whatever lingering emotional shortcomings a person has from earlier years become exacerbated under these circumstances. For example, a man with unresolved needs to control others in order to compensate for his feelings of weakness may not have to face this problem while still employed and in a position of influence over others. When these props are removed through forced retirement, however, that person may seek to compensate for feelings of weakness by controlling his grown children instead. Such a response not only is inappropriate but also can alienate him from his family and imperil a much-needed avenue of social contact.

Is Therapy for You? Although there is a commonly held notion that older people are not good candidates for psychotherapy, the reality is otherwise. In a study on psychotherapy effectiveness it was found that older people constituted the group overrepresented by psychotherapeutic success, while college students were over-represented among the failures. Carl Jung preferred working with people "in the second half of life" (to use his term) because his experience demonstrated that they were superior prospects for psychotherapy, having a more inward orientation. While you might be inclined to feel that at your age there is little benefit to be had from psychotherapy and that you are too stuck in your ways, in actuality you have several plusses going for you in psychotherapy that younger people do not, namely a greater sense of urgency in using therapy well and more wisdom and experience to bring to bear in working on your problems. That there is less time before you now than there was when you were thirty or forty does not mean your efforts will be wasted. On the contrary, it may mean that there is even more reason for you to work things out while you still can do so.

Therapy for people in the older age group can be used in a number of ways. It can help you on a short-term basis to cope with crises, and it can help on a more extended basis to reduce self-imposed limitations that make coping with problems of advancing age more difficult than it has to be. Therapy is also help-ful in alleviating disturbing feelings that are especially likely to be experienced by older people, such as anger, grief, depression, and feelings of anxiety, and that are difficult to deal with alone. A supportive relationship with a competent and sympathetic therapist can go a long way in addressing these problems and in encouraging an older person to maintain his or her engagement with life.

Still another use of therapy that some clients find very helpful is conducting a life review. The purpose of a review is to come to terms with life as it has been, accepting its disappointments, recognizing one's achievements, and acknowledging the limits of existence. The purpose of examining the past is not just to look backward to see what you did and did not do, but to look forward to the future and see what you want to do in the time that remains.

Some people find it helpful while in therapy to keep a journal that reconstructs the positive aspects of the past. Each person's life contains many fulfilling experiences as well as frustrating ones and a person can learn from past successes and triumphs as well as from past failures. A journal is also a way to maintain ties and relationships with friends and relatives that you may not be able to see anymore or as often as you like. Photographs, notices about reunions, genealogies, articles about your home town, and other memorabilia all serve to heighten your gratification with time well spent while keeping you actively engaged with the present.

Finding an Appropriate Therapist As one becomes older it becomes more difficult to find a therapist of comparable age and experience and the choice is, therefore, usually restricted to younger therapists. Under these circumstances older people will need assurance that the therapist is not prone to "ageism" but is sensitive to their problems and respectful of them as persons. Not all therapists are prepared to work with older clients. In addition to stereotyped negative attitudes about older people they may also be prone to feel that older people are not suitable psychotherapy prospects.

Many younger therapists prefer not to work with older clients because of their own unresolved anxieties about advancing age and ultimate death. When a therapist who is uncomfortable about issues of aging does work with older clients, he or she is likely to be incompetent as a therapist. Usually such a therapist will inhibit older clients from talking about growing old and dying and offer false optimism about the future. This keeps clients from dealing with central issues and serves only to let the therapist hide from his or her own existential anxiety.

Some therapists express their anxieties about aging by trying to divert clients from a realistic appraisal of their behavior. Instead of helping clients come to terms with mistakes they seek to provide them with "absolution." Such a whitewash is not only off the mark but disrespectful and does not allow the client an opportunity to come to terms with shortcomings or to overcome them, if possible.

One of the advantages of working with a therapist who is not appreciably younger than you are is that there is less tendency toward role confusion. If you start therapy with a younger therapist, you may find yourself relating to that person as you do to your children. The therapist, too, may have a tendency to relate to you as to his or her parents. If the therapist has unresolved problems with regard to parents, this is likely to create difficulties for your therapy. The therapist could, for example, become overly critical of you as a way of working out past hostilities to his or her parents or overly indulgent as a way of expiating past guilt.

If you are an older person who is looking for a therapist, after you find one who meets the basic requirements (see Chapter 3, "How to Pick a Therapist"), check what experience the therapist has had in working with older people, how current he or she is with the psychological literature on adulthood and aging, and what his or her attitudes are about therapy for people of your age.

Sometimes older people find a suitable therapist but are unable to travel to the therapist's office. If this should happen to you, ask the therapist if sessions can be arranged at your home. It is not the standard way of conducting psychotherapy, but there is no reason it could not be done.

Intelligence and Therapy It is a widely held belief that a person's intelligence declines with age and that older people therefore may not have the necessary mental resources to make good use of therapy. This notion is wrong on two counts. First, it is not true that intelligence erodes as one gets older. Certain aspects of intellectual functioning are more susceptible than others and may show a decline, as for instance memory, but other functions remain stable or improve. Research evidence indicates that part of the apparent decline in intellectual ability in older people is a function of lack of adequate stimulation. With loss of jobs, social contacts, and the financial resources for travel, entertainment, and other pursuits, a person does not have the opportunity to use his or her mental faculties and they become rusty. There is also increasing evidence that memory loss in older people is not necessarily a function of aging but is related to other factors, such as dietary insufficiencies, medications taken for physical problems, and the cumulative effects of the ingestion of toxins such as mercury and aluminum. On the positive side, as a person grows older, he or she accumulates greater knowledge and broader experiences on which to reflect. The negative changes in intellect that may occur are as a rule not only quite insignificant but also unrelated to the ability to use psychotherapy. The process of psychotherapy, although it usually takes place on a verbal level, is not essentially an intellectual exercise but an emotional experience. Older people, because of the broader range of their experiences and greater inclination to reflection, may in this sense be more open to psychotherapy than younger, less introspective clients.

The Role of Medication Because of the belief of some psychotherapists that older people are not amenable to psychotherapy there is a greater tendency to treat the symptoms of people in this group with medication. The risks of medical treatment discussed in Chapter 2 are increased for this age group as many of the physical problems encountered among older people are exacerbated by psychoactive medication. The antidepressants, for instance, reduce the blood supply to the brain and are counterindicated if one has high blood pressure or cardiovascular disease. These medications also have side effects that are commonly associated with senility, such as confusion and memory loss. The use of psychoactive medication for older people is also questionable because many people in this group are already on medication for other conditions and the two medications taken together may create further complications.

It is not unusual for symptoms manifested by older people that are often attributed to the aging process to be actually side effects of medication being taken for physical problems. People taking circulatory compounds and diuretics, for example, often suffer from potassium depletion, which shows up in the form of mental confusion and hallucinations. Medication for hypertension can create vascular insufficiency that leads to depression and confusion. Steroids prescribed for arthritis can cause irritability, confusion, and depression. If you have such symptoms—depression, confusion, irritability—and are on medication, it could well be that your symptoms are caused by an inability to tolerate the medication rather than a deterioration in your mental state due to age. Check with your physician about alternative medications you might use, or for dietary regimens that might be instituted to help control your physical symptoms or the side effects of the medication you are taking.

Conducting the First Interview

THE PURPOSE of the first session is for you and the therapist to explore the nature of your problems and to assess the desirability of working together, not to start therapy. When you sense a need for therapy, try to make arrangements for the first session as early as possible. If you wait, the pressure of your needs may become too great to use the screening process to good advantage. Taking the time and effort to make sure you will be in the right therapy setting will pay handsome dividends later on; without that assurance you will not have a valid basis for committing yourself fully to the therapy process.

The "first session" may not be limited to one visit. The term is used to mean all the initial sessions required for you to decide whether a particular therapist is right for you. That may take one, two, or three sessions, sometimes more.

PUTTING THE PHONE TO GOOD USE

Typically, people leave for the first session what should be clarified before scheduling it. When you call for an appointment it is perfectly all right to ask for more than a time and a date. There are several things you want to know before even making an appointment. Unless you are making an appointment for just a single consulting session, the first thing to know is if the therapist has time to see you on a regular basis. Sometimes a therapist will make an appointment to see you and then inform you once you are in the office that his or her schedule is booked up for further appointments. In such an eventuality, you might have to wait for weeks or months before being able to schedule regular appointments. You also want to ask if the therapist has hours available that are manageable for you, otherwise you might not find out until you are in the office that you can start therapy only if you can come at 7:00 A.M. one day and 10:00 P.M. the next. Another important piece of information is the therapist's fee. There is no reason why you should not ask this beforehand and no valid reason why the therapist should not answer. If you cannot afford to continue at a particular fee, there is no sense setting up an appointment in the first place (unless you intend only a single consultation for an opinion or a referral). Some therapists may not want to discuss the fee over the phone because their fee is negotiable, preferring first to find out your financial circumstances. In this case, they can indicate their range of fees.

You can also ask the therapist about his or her qualifications and therapy approach: what kind of training has he or she had, is he or she a Jungian, a gestaltist, a behavior modifier, engaged in individual therapy only or in group therapy as well, and so forth. Feel free to ask any question that is pertinent to the type of service the therapist can provide.

Many therapists will avoid answering your questions on the phone. While there are some questions that do not belong in a phone conversation, those that are relevant to the type of service you can expect to receive should be taken up before you make an office visit. Factual answers to information-seeking questions indicate that the therapist wants to help you make an informed decision on whether or not to contemplate starting therapy with him or her. Refusal to answer may indicate that the therapist feels you do not have a right to the information, or that you are entitled to the information only if you first pay for his or her time. Therapists have a right to refuse to answer questions that do not relate to the services they provide. They also cannot answer questions that require a prior familiarity with you as, for example, whether therapy well be helpful for you or how long it can be expected to take. And, of course, you should keep the amount of time you expect the therapist to spend on the phone with an unknown person to a reasonable limit. If you have questions that the therapist does not have time to answer on the phone or prefers to answer in person, or if you are not comfortable asking those questions on the phone, you might ask if the therapist can see you for a brief personal interview. Such a meeting would provide you with an opportunity to get the information you need and to glean some impressions of the therapist.

When you want to see a psychotherapist, it is important that you make the initial telephone inquiry yourself. You might feel tempted to delegate the task to a spouse or friend if you feel very anxious about it. If someone else calls for you, and the psycho-therapist agrees to make an appointment in this fashion, you and the therapist are starting off on the wrong foot by letting others do for you what you might be able to do on your own. You may want somebody else to arrange the initial appointment because it is that person's idea that you go into therapy. If this is the case, and the therapist allows another person to deputize for you, you and the therapist are agreeing that you should enter therapy against your wish. If at all possible, get on the phone yourself.

When you make an initial telephone inquiry, it is also important that the therapist speak to you directly. It is best to get the an-swers to important questions, such as future availability or fees, from the therapist rather than from a secretary or receptionist. In a clinic or other institutional setting, you will not be able to ar-range an appointment directly with the therapist, but try to obtain the necessary information from the person who handles your call.

SHOULD YOU PAY FOR THE FIRST SESSION?

As a result of the growing consumer movement in psychotherapy, some clients feel that the first "get-acquainted" session should not be billed. Indeed, some therapists now advertise "free consulta-tion." One of the reasons clients are reluctant to pay for the first session, aside from the fact that it becomes costly if one is shop-ping around, is that too often the first session is used to obtain basic information that should be available, without cost, before-hand. As already discussed, we feel that such information as the therapist's qualifications, orientation, fees, and availability to give you the kind of therapy service you need should be provided on the phone or in a brief personal interview before scheduling a regular appointment. Therapists who do not bill for the first session generally choose not to provide this information on the phone and therefore use up part of the first session discussing these issues. For example, in a recent book, *The Heart of Psychotherapy,* the author-therapist says, "The amount per session should be set early, although I don't handle this on the phone . . . I have made it a practice to charge for a first session only if I am going to work with the person. I dislike intensely the experience of seeing someone, deciding that the person ought to go to someone else, and then charging the person for what feels like the experience of rejection. I preface my interview by saying that I am busy, which is true, and probably will use the session to find the right therapist."* To our mind, the first session should be devoted to exploring the client's problems and ways of approaching them, which is rendering a billable professional service. Otherwise, why charge for the first session if a client continues? There does not seem to be any good reason why psychotherapists more than other professionals—physicians, lawyers, teachers—should provide free samples of their work. Some therapists may offer free first sessions because they are uncomfortable with how their first sessions are used, especially if they too are "shopping around" as much as the client, but if it is likely that a therapist will reject a client on monetary grounds or because he or she does not want to fill an hour with somebody found to be unappealing, then it is better not to schedule the appointment in the first place. Other therapists may offer free first sessions to attract more clients into their practice. Whether a first session is billable we think depends mostly on the extent to which it is used to offer a professional assessment of the client's problems and needs in therapy.

MAKING FIRST IMPRESSIONS COUNT

Before you actually start conducting your first interview, you will be getting impressions of the therapist from the physical setting in which he or she is seen. If the therapist works in a clinic, though, these impressions will tell you more about the clinic than the therapist. Clinic offices are decorated by the institution and often therapists are not able to add any personal touches to their offices as many are on staff part-time and share the office with others.

* George Weinberg, *The Heart of Psychotherapy* (New York: St. Martin's Press, 1984), pp. 34–35.

From the furnishings and decorations you can, however, build up some impressions about the clinic's attitude toward its staff and clients, which might have rubbed off on the therapist. Do the furnishings reflect thoughtfulness and caring, or are they rundown and messy, suggesting instead a "don't-care" attitude about the kind of environment you are provided with?

When you see a private practitioner, your first impressions will be more directly revealing, but don't get carried away by appearances. Although a person is reflected in his or her choice of surroundings, some therapists rent furnished office space in professional buildings, share offices and decorate by mutual consent, or sublet offices from other therapists. In these instances office furnishings tend to be nondescript, which does not necessarily mean that the therapist is similarly bland. Some therapists deliberately keep the surroundings neutral and simple. Individuality in decor may indicate that the therapist does not feel it is intrusive if his or her personal tastes are apparent, or that the therapist wants you to notice his or her taste. When an office is decorated in an extreme manner, it becomes obvious that the therapist wants to make a statement about him- or herself. You will have to decide if you feel the furnishings are there to keep you and the therapist comfortable or to impress you.

Take in, but be cautious about how much weight you put on the reading matter in the waiting room and the number of books on the wall in the office. Again, if therapists share a waiting room you do not know who is subscribing to what. You also do not know what may have been left by other clients. The books on the wall could indicate that the therapist is well read, or that he or she wants you to have that impression. Lack of books does not necessarily mean the therapist does not read. He or she may prefer to keep the books at home, or to borrow them from the public library.

Some therapists practice in their homes. If there is a separate office with a private entrance it makes little difference that the space happens to be in a home. In other cases, an office in the therapist's house or apartment may be reached through a common entrance with the family or may even be living quarters of the home, most often the living room. Clients are usually not neutral about such arrangements, and either like the idea a lot or take to it badly. Either reaction bodes difficulties. Those who like the idea usually feel that it brings them close to the therapist, but deriving comfort from an assumed personal relationship with the therapist risks diverting you from the purpose of coming to therapy. If you do not like the idea of seeing a therapist in a home setting, then this is not likely to be a suitable arrangement for you. If you do not have a strong reaction either way, then there is no reason why such an arrangement cannot work out, provided that the personal life of the therapist does not intrude on your time before, during, or after sessions.

Having gleaned some impressions from the physical arrangements, the next step is to enter the office and take a seat. If there is more than one place to sit, the therapist may let you gravitate to the one that suits you best, or invite you to take a particular chair or spot on the couch. A big difference between the comfort of seating for the therapist and client may indicate feelings of the therapist toward the client. On the other hand, a very comfortable chair is important for the therapist, who probably sits in it most of the day. If the therapist sits behind a desk, he or she is creating a distance between you and subtly defining a stance and your relative places in the relationship. The desk helps to foster the impression that you are the object to be studied by the authority; it does not suggest that you are both there mutually to explore each other.

DEFINING YOUR PROBLEMS AND THERAPY GOALS

Once you are seated in the therapist's office, the interviewing process can begin. The therapist may or may not make any comments or ask any questions, but you can start the process by letting the therapist know what your problems are and what you expect from therapy. As you are discussing these issues, you will also be busy evaluating the therapist and getting a sense of your feelings about working with that person. Also, if you have not already done so on the phone, you will need to use this time to find out the terms on which the therapist is offering his or her services and to weigh their acceptability to you. The therapist will be using the first session to explore the nature of your problems, evaluate what you need in the way of therapeutic assistance, and consider if he or she can provide it for you.

The nature of the first interview differs depending on whether you go to a clinic or to a private practitioner. In a clinic, it is conducted by an administrator—sometimes the clinic director, but usually a social worker trained in "intake" procedures. The "intake interview" usually follows a predetermined pattern in which you will be asked to provide information regarding your present situation, original family composition, medical history, sexual history, developmental milestones and, last but not least, your "presenting problem," which means the problem that is bringing you to therapy. The interview is not set up primarily as a means for you and the clinic mutually to explore needs and expectations; rather, it is structured to obtain data from you that will be used to assess your suitability to the clinic, make a diagnosis and treatment plan, and acquaint the therapist with you beforehand. It is not necessary for you to go along sheepishly with the interviewing procedure and answer all questions put to you. If you have reason not to discuss certain issues in an intake interview, feel free to say so. Some clinics will question you on your preferences in therapist assignment but most will assign you to a therapist on a basis of administrative factors rather than therapist-client matching. Whether a clinic does or does not spontaneously give you an opportunity to express your wants, do not hesitate to do so. It may or may not be possible to grant your preferences, but if you do not specify what you want, no attempt can be made.

If you are seeing a private practitioner, make it clear from the start that your purpose in the first session is to explore the possibilities of working together. Despite what the therapist may assume, you are not there to start therapy but to see if there is a basis for starting. After this clarification, the therapist may wait for you to begin or may start the session him- or herself. In that case, a suitable question is "What makes you interested in therapy?" or "What brings you here?" If the therapist does not open the interview you can, by describing your problems and what you want to get from therapy. The therapist will probably ask questions to elucidate the nature of the problem, the way it is experienced, and its origins. Some therapists may ask questions you feel are not relevant to your problem or even avoid the problem as you have presented it, preferring to conduct a standardized interview instead. In this event do not feel coerced into providing all the information requested—give only what you consider appropriate. If the therapist insists on knowing, inquire how giving that information at this particular time will be helpful to you. Provide the information if the answer makes sense but do not accept as an answer simply that the therapist must have all the information requested.

The therapist may suggest during the first interview that you be tested psychologically. This is usually recommended to reveal more about underlying personality and thinking disturbances that may be suggested by but difficult to substantiate through discussion. Unlike a psychiatric evaluation, whose purpose is to provide a diagnosis, a psychological evaluation is intended to provide a broader understanding of how you function and of problem areas of which you may be unaware. The psychological evaluation would probably be based on projective personality tests like the Rorschach test or the Thematic Apperception Test, which present unstructured stimuli (in blots and pictures, respectively) to allow the person's unique characteristics and ways of responding to situations to emerge. Sometimes psychological testing is requested for research purposes as, for example, a study on therapy effectiveness, in which case "before and after" profiles of you would be required. More often than not, the tests used for these purposes are paper-and-pencil tests consisting of various scales measuring traits such as depression, suspiciousness, or anxiety. While these tests may be helpful for research purposes, they are unlikely to be useful to you in your therapy. If psychological testing is requested, find out why and do not feel obliged to go along with the testing unless you are pleased to participate. Also, find out what fees you will be charged, and how the results will be made available to you.

After clarifying the nature of your problem(s) and the expectations you have of therapy, ask the therapist for his or her reactions. What happens in the actual therapy process will, of course, be influenced by what is revealed about you in the course of the therapy itself, but each therapist is going to have some immediate reactions to you and the problems you present, and plans on how to proceed. Ask the therapist to be as specific as possible on these points: does the therapist accept the dimensions of the problem as you outline it or does he or she perceive other difficulties you have not presented? How does the therapist envisage the course of therapy—what is the therapist's feeling about the amount of time that will be needed to approach your goals, and about the most desirable frequency of sessions? Does the therapist want to work with you on a one-to-one basis or have you join a therapy group now or in the future? If this has not been determined before, to what particular school of therapy does the therapist subscribe (psycho-analytic, gestalt, behavior modification), and what approach and methods can you expect in the course of therapy?

If the therapist suggests you join a group instead of or in addition to individual sessions, find out in what ways the therapist thinks it will be helpful. If the idea of a group appeals to you and the rationale is sensible, by all means join. If, however, the idea of a group sounds nonsensical or frightens you, the issue should be explored further.

Some people are afraid to enter groups because of the expectation that the group will be critical of them. Unfortunately, enough people have been exposed to destructive group "therapy" encounters for this possibility not to be taken lightly. Part of the value of the group experience is that it encourages people to express themselves openly. As a result, group members are frequently rewarded by peer approval when they do let themselves go and let their feelings "hang out." In such a climate, the expression of angry feelings is just as appropriate as the expression of any other feelings. Because of this, unassertive people can get hurt in a group if it is not carefully guided in the interests of all. Most therapy groups, however, have a positive orientation, with members who are more interested in giving one another mutual support than in tearing one another down. Of course, some of the fears of joining a group reflect the individual's own fears of being with others in a more open situation. To the extent that this constitutes the core of the resistance to joining a group, the group should be beneficial in that it provides an opportunity to work directly on that fear.

An important aspect of the group is the types of people in it. Before entering a group, you should know something about the others who are going to be in it. Some therapists think this is irrelevant but it is, nonetheless, a very relevant factor because you will get more out of the group if you are compatible with the participants. A good group is usually a varied group, but one varied in terms of sex, marital status, field of work, or interest, rather than in terms of values and basic outlook on life. The nature of the group interaction, the level of psychological sophistication, and the group goals should be appropriate to you.

If the therapist should recommend drug or electroconvulsive therapy either as adjuncts to or as a substitute for psychotherapy, be on guard. As we pointed out in the section on medical treatment in Chapter 2, these procedures entail a much greater risk to both your mental and your physical well-being than psychotherapy. If any mood-affecting drugs, including tranquilizers, are recommended on other than a temporary basis, it is wise to get a second professional opinion. If you consent to such treatment, be sure that you get, or have recently had, a medical checkup to lessen the chances of undesirable side effects.

Some therapists, no matter how you try to define your purpose in the first session, are going to take it for granted that you are there to start therapy. That may be what is happening if the therapist prematurely attempts to gain a detailed case history, interrupts your presentation of the problems you want to work on by focusing on one particular issue, and does not give you the opportunity to ask questions about the therapy. If you sense that a therapist assumes that therapy has begun, it will be necessary for you to let the therapist know that you are still in the process of evaluating that possibility.

During the course of stating your problems, you may find the therapist offering you interpretations of your behavior that are unwarranted on the basis of the information you have presented. This sometimes happens when the therapist wants to impress the client with his or her ability to size up the situation quickly. It is usually the sign of an insecure therapist who needs to show off. It may also be the therapist's way of getting the therapy process started before you have decided that he or she is the person with whom you want to start. While the therapist should provide you with his or her impressions as to the nature of your problem, far-reaching interpretations do not belong in a first interview.

The therapy relationship is grounded on some very concrete conditions, which the therapist may or may not clarify spontaneously. These concern not only the goals toward which you will work and the methods to be used, but also the arrangements under which therapy will be carried out, including appointments, fees, and confidentiality, all of which are discussed in the next chapter. If these issues are not brought up by the therapist, you must raise them on your own. They have to be understood beforehand and be acceptable to you. If you feel that the terms of the therapy relationship are oppressive or unfair, this is bound to interfere with the work that you can do together.

SHARING INFORMATION

If you don't have enough information about the therapist's qualifications, orientation, or personal characteristics before coming to the first session, you can fill in the gaps at that time. Unfortunately, many therapists are defensive on this issue and hide behind various rationalizations to avoid having to give clients direct answers about themselves. One well-known textbook for practitioners suggests that when a client requests specific information, such as how many years the therapist has been practicing, all the client wants is reassurance of the therapist's competence and, therefore, the client has to be told only that the therapist feels competent to work with him or her. Such avoidance of a direct answer expresses an attitude of contempt for the client. The same textbook suggests that, since clients have no basis for evaluating therapist competency, if clients persist in requesting specific information the therapist should comment on the "unusual nature of their behavior," which must have "some underlying meaning": "Perhaps a generalized need to have more information than should be necessary for making decisions is one of their neurotic difficulties, or perhaps they characteristically antagonize people by refusing to take what is said to them at face value, or perhaps they are having second thoughts about continuing in psychotherapy or about their ability to be helped."* Here, the request for pertinent information is turned against the client, who is made to feel there is something wrong with him or her for wanting to know rather than with the therapist for refusing to tell.

If you have strong feelings about any particular characteristic of the therapist, such as sex, age, religion, or his or her personal values, and you sense that they might interfere with your therapy, discuss them with the therapist. You should not start therapy until you are satisfied that you are informed about that particular issue or your concern is put to rest. Here again, as with qualifications, you may run into difficulties getting the information you want. Some therapists feel it is harmful to the therapy to provide any personal information about themselves. (The reasons for this are discussed in Chapter 9, "Feelings Between Client and Therapist.") If the therapist refuses to answer your questions you will have to

* Irving B. Weiner, *Principles of Psychotherapy* (New York: John Wiley, 1975), p. 83.

judge whether the refusal is well-thought-out and based on genuine hesitations related to your particular situation, or based instead on rigid principle, arrogance, or defensiveness.

You and your therapist should have basic values and goals in life that are not too discrepant. When questioned about their values, many therapists will dismiss the question, answering that their values do not enter into their work. If so, they are not very perceptive about what they are doing in the therapy process. The basic values of the therapist cannot help but influence the therapist's approach to you. Clients are often concerned about issues such as homosexuality, politics, women's rights, or drug use. If any such issues are important to you, it is legitimate to ask where the therapist stands. If a therapist responds that he or she thinks you should do whatever you want just so long as it does not hurt others, the therapist is avoiding discussing his or her values. Ultimately you and the therapist will have to come to grips with the value questions you are raising; it is better sooner than later.

A therapist who does not want to answer questions about him- or herself shows an inappropriate defensiveness and a lack of respect for you that does not augur well for a productive therapeutic relationship. Further, if the therapist implies that there is something wrong with you for asking such questions, you have come to the wrong office and had better start looking again.

ANALYZING THE THERAPIST

In the course of discussing your problems and asking the therapist questions you will be able to start forming impressions about the therapist. Are you getting positive "vibes"? Is the therapist a person you respect and someone with whom you feel comfortable? Do you like the therapist, and does the feeling seem to be mutual?

Do you think the therapist can help you? Does the therapist accept your right to ask questions or discourage your inquiries? Do your questions lead to satisfying interactions and a furthering of understanding? Does the therapist make you feel that what you have to say is important, or does he or she take a patronizing air with you? Does the therapist talk to you in a way that is meaningful to you?

Does the therapist seem to have the characteristics necessary for successful psychotherapy? Is the therapist sensitive and able to understand you, does he or she seem to be concerned about you, and does he or she strike you as a genuine person free of defensive affectations?

Do you trust what the therapist says, or is the therapist trying to impress you with professional jargon, forced friendliness, or exaggerated promises of a "cure"?

Is the therapist free of signs such as nervous tics, strained voice, or awkward mannerisms suggesting excessive tensions, inadequate self-control, or other personal problems? Smoking (discussed in Chapter 7, "Sore Spots") also falls into this category.

To answer these questions, take stock of your observations and immediate reactions to the therapist. Do not be afraid to trust your impressions; your feelings are the best guide available to you. If, from your experience with the therapist, you sense that he or she is genuine, responsive, warm, and able to understand you, most likely that person is genuine, responsive, warm, and able to understand you. If you sense that the therapist is abrupt, cold, and disrespectful, he or she probably is abrupt, cold, and disrespectful. Do not dismiss any feelings you have about the therapist. If some are not clear, explore them in subsequent sessions.

YOUR END-OF-SESSION OPTIONS

When you have finished the first session you may or may not want to schedule another. Remember that it is up to you to ask or not to ask for another appointment. Do not let the therapist take this choice away from you. Several options are open to you:

- If your impressions about the therapist are so clearly negative that you are sure you do not want to continue with that person, do not hesitate to tell the therapist that you do not want to come back. Feel free to say why if you want to.
- If your feelings about the therapist are mixed and you are not sure whether or not you want to return, tell the therapist about your uncertainty and that you will phone again if you want to continue. You may find that given some time to reflect about the therapist you will be able to reach a decision. Or you might want to interview another therapist and see if you come away feeling better about your prospects.
- If your feelings about the therapist are positive but you need more time to discuss all that is important in making a

decision, tell the therapist that you would like more time to explore the possibilities with him or her and set up another appointment.

- If your feelings about the therapist are clearly positive, and you definitely want to start therapy, set up a schedule of appointments and consider yourself on the way.

Sometimes therapists or clients arrange for a "trial period" of therapy. A trial period means that although both parties agree to work together, the relationship is considered to be tentative until experience shows that both parties can work productively together.

Should the therapist tell you that you have to make an on-the-spot decision about continuing if you want to have hours open for you, do not feel pressured into going along when you still have doubts. Such pressure in itself constitutes a lack of sensitivity to your legitimate concerns.

CHECKLIST FOR FIRST SESSION

- Did the therapist make it easy for you to explain your problems and reasons for coming to therapy? Does he or she seem to understand what you were talking about? Do you feel comfortable with the therapist?
- Are you and the therapist in general agreement on problem areas and expectations for the therapy? Is his or her concept of therapy compatible with yours?
- If the therapist wants to include medication, do you agree and are you taking proper safeguards?
- Does the therapist have a "therapeutic" personality: competent, sincere, and responsive? Is he or she free of obvious signs indicating excessive nervousness or emotional disturbance?
- Did you check the therapist's qualifications, training, experience, personal therapy, credentials?
- Did the therapist answer your questions, whether about you or the therapist, adequately?
- Did you work out contractual issues, including time and fees, to your satisfaction?

6   *The Therapy Agreement*

THERAPY IS a relationship between two people in which each has certain legitimate expectations of the other and obligations to the other. Clients usually know that they are supposed to show up for sessions, present material for therapy, and pay for each session. But clients are vague about what else therapists expect from them and what they can and should expect from therapists. They are not clear about how they and the therapist will work together, what methods the therapist will use, and more important, if their work together is oriented toward the client's goals. Therapists, on the other hand, do have goals and operating procedures in mind, but they usually do not clarify them for the client. A therapy agreement based on mutual consent offers protection to both you and the therapist. By clarifying the conditions of therapy, an agreement reduces the chances of the therapy relationship going on the rocks and it can even offer some legal protection should that ever become necessary. You and the therapist can work meaningfully together only if you agree beforehand on the goals, methods, and arrangements of the therapy.

An agreement also establishes the principle of mutual accountability as the basis of the therapeutic relationship. It places you in a responsible role in the therapy relationship from the outset by recognizing that you and the therapist must define the goals and conditions of therapy together. If at a later date either of you finds the terms of your agreement cumbersome, it will be easier to change them because the process of reaching mutually acceptable conditions has already been established.

Discussing the terms of your therapy relationship before you start therapy makes it more likely that you will come to a suitable agreement. After you start, your emotional investment in the therapy will reduce your freedom to negotiate. Not only do you want an agreement, but the process of discussing it is an excellent way of learning at an early point how well you and the therapist can work together.

There are three major areas in which you want to spell out your rights and obligations: the goals toward which you will work, the methods that will be used, and the arrangements under which the therapy will be carried out.

AGREEING ON GOALS AND METHODS

Unless you have stated what your goals and objectives are in coming to therapy, and unless the therapist agrees to work with you toward these goals, you may find the therapy running into difficulties later on. It often happens that a client comes to therapy with limited goals and that the therapist pushes the client to work toward more rewarding objectives. In such a case, although the therapist is working toward what he or she conceives as in the client's best interests, this private agenda may not coincide with the client's self-perceived problems. A therapist should certainly let a client know if he or she thinks a particular set of goals is restrictive, but he or she has the obligation to work toward the goals the client has set. If the therapist feels that these goals are not legitimate or inclusive enough, the therapist has the responsibility to explain this, and if the client still does not agree, the therapist should not work with that particular person.

While the basis of working together is agreement on what is being worked toward, this does not mean that either the client or the therapist cannot suggest a change in goals at any given point. Both parties are free to bring up the question of goals when they think it is called for. If the goals are then modified, it represents a change in the agreement because it is done with the explicit understanding of both parties.

Before starting therapy you will want to know what methods the therapist is likely to use. Do not consider yourself obligated to engage in any type of behavior that you do not find acceptable or to accept any later innovations that you have not agreed on. It is desirable to have a clear statement in the agreement on all issues that are important to you. The most common areas of concern about methods are:

- Will your therapy be essentially a verbal process, or does the therapist want to introduce any acting or body techniques? Does he or she insist on your following through with such techniques?
- Does the therapist want you to use a chair, or the couch, or is that choice open to you?
- Does the therapist expect you to join a group now or at some later time? Does the therapist have a group you can join if you should want to, or will he or she help you find a group?
- Does the therapist expect you to see anyone else, such as a physician for a medical checkup or a psychologist for diagnostic evaluation?
- What is the therapist's attitude towards medication? Will he or she want you to use medication if you become very anxious or depressed, or to avoid such medication? If you do not agree with the therapist on the role of medication in psychotherapy, will the therapist respect your choice or insist that you follow his or her position?
- Does the therapist want to interview other members of your family? Will the therapist do so if you should make such a request? Is the therapist willing to work with other members of your family if you want to augment your personal therapy with marital or family therapy?

It is not possible to specify in advance the host of techniques that may be desirable during the course of your therapy; nor is it necessary. However, you should have a fairly clear idea of how you will be expected to work with your therapist and find these procedures agreeable.

As with goals, it may become desirable to change the ways of working in your therapy at some point. For instance, a particular method previously not considered may become appropriate later on because you have become more open or because the therapist has acquired a new skill. Sometimes a change in goals calls for a change in method: for example, if the focus of therapy moves from the broad goal of insight development to the specific goal of becoming more assertive, a shift from emphasis on nondirective techniques such as free association to more active encounter techniques would be in order. An agreement does not preclude such changes. It can always be amended and, in fact, helps to clarify the changes that you want.

DURATION OF THERAPY AND REVIEW

While it is impossible to specify exactly how long your therapy will take, an agreement can specify the length of time you and the therapist want to work together before reviewing, and possibly renegotiating, the terms of your agreement.

The length of time agreed upon may depend on your goals, how long the therapy is expected to take, and your degree of confidence in the therapist. As a general rule, an agreement should be for a period of not less than three months and not more than a year. A period shorter than three months is usually not a sufficient amount of time in which to get much accomplished, and a period of more than a year does not automatically provide for periodic review of the therapy relationship. Though many therapies will last for more than one year, the one-year agreement can be renewed as often as desirable. You will need to discuss with the therapist if he or she is willing to work on a specified short-term basis, if that is what you want, or on an indefinite time basis with annual renewal of your agreement.

It is a good idea to discuss the duration of therapy with the therapist even though it cannot be specified in the agreement. The only meaningful way to estimate duration is in terms of what you hope to accomplish within the therapy process. The time required depends also on your accessibility to the therapy process and how hard you work at it. The more open you are to your feelings and the more determined you are, the faster your therapy will move along. Similarly, the therapist's capabilities and compatability with you will influence how long therapy will take. Some people feel that the more active therapies cut down the length of time required for the therapy process, but there is no evidence that they do. There is, however, some indication that therapists who are talkative and energetic have shorter therapies than therapists who are taciturn. Getting an estimate from the therapist of how long the therapy will probably take not only helps you decide on a suitable time period for your agreement, but orients you to the work ahead.

FEES AND APPOINTMENT SCHEDULE

Ideally, you will have established the therapist's or clinic's fees beforehand. If for any reason you have not, you will want to determine the fee right away and decide if it is a reasonable sum for you to pay.

You also need to think about the fee in relation to frequency of sessions. If the therapist feels that the number should be increased at a later point, this should be clarified from the start since it is important in determining whether it is economically feasible for you to pay for therapy under those conditions. What does the therapist consider the optimum number of weekly sessions for you to be? Does the therapist want to start once a week and then increase the frequency later? Will the therapist work with you on a once-a-week basis because that is all you can afford, even though he or she prefers to see you more frequently? Will the therapist want to increase the number of sessions if you can afford it at some later time?

There are no clear guidelines on how often sessions should be scheduled to produce the best results. Generally, the more ambitious the goals, the greater the change you desire, the more frequent the sessions should be. More frequent sessions permit greater intensity of feelings and thereby help to bring about significant change in you. Research suggests that clients who are so defensive that they find it hard to become involved in therapy on a once-a-week basis can make better progress if the session frequency is increased. There are important individual differences here; some clients move along faster in therapy on a once-a-week basis than others who go two or more times per week. There is also no clear relationship between the frequency of sessions and the total duration of the therapy process. While clients often expect that a greater frequency of sessions will mean they can finish the therapy sooner, it can happen instead that it prolongs the therapy because the additional visits allow the client to broaden the original therapy goals. The limited research that is available suggests that once-a-week sessions are a necessary minimum for a meaningful psychotherapy process. Most therapists consider once a week a minimum for supportive therapy, and twice a week a minimum for therapy aimed at personality changes based on a deeper understanding of yourself.

Another issue concerning fees is the manner in which the therapist wants to be paid—at each session, weekly, or monthly. Does the therapist or clinic qualify under your insurance coverage? Will the therapist fill out your insurance forms? Will the therapist fill them out during sessions or at a different time? Will there be a charge for filling out your forms? Some clinics bill clients for preparing such statements.

What is the therapist's policy about sessions you miss? Will the therapist automatically bill you for all missed sessions? Will the therapist bill you for absences that are your choice (going on vacation) but not bill you for those that are unavoidable (being in the hospital)? If the therapist bills you for all missed sessions, will makeup sessions be offered? Therapist practices with regard to missed appointments vary widely, but there is less rigidity now about charging for missed sessions than there was in the past. Independent practitioners tend to be more amenable to arranging for makeups than therapists in clinics, who usually have to adhere more closely to standardized procedures. Theoretically "orthodox" practitioners are more apt to charge for missed sessions than adherents of the new approaches that have a greater spirit of flexibility built into them. While there is some rationale in consistently charging for missed sessions (see Chapter 7, "Sore Spots"), a therapist who does so without offering makeups and regardless of the circumstances indicates a rigidity of attitude that may interfere with his or her ability to be sensitive to you.

What time is available for your appointments? Is this time convenient for you? Are alternative times available for makeup sessions, or is the offer to permit makeup sessions an empty gesture?

How long will your "hour" be? Most sessions are for a fixed time of forty-five or fifty minutes, but a few therapists leave the time indeterminate and end the session whenever they choose to. There is no definitive research on the relative effectiveness of different length sessions. The forty-five-to-fifty-minute hour was settled into on an empirical basis, working out well for clients' needs and being a convenient way for therapists to divide their time, allowing for a client every hour with a short break in between. Although there are occasions when a fixed time will not seem enough, or other occasions when it will seem too long, knowing the time allotted to you for each session helps you to use it more constructively. You can gauge yourself accordingly and, if you do not utilize your time to good advantage, it can make your resistance to working at therapy more apparent. Some clients use the time as a way of "testing" the therapist's concern for them. They will leave important material for the end of the session to manipulate the therapist into extending the time for them. Some clients feel "cut off" when the therapist announces the end of the session and interpret this as a lack of interest in them. If you recognize that the time has been prearranged, it will help you separate your concerns about the therapist's regard for you from the realities of your arrangement. Many clients leave it to the therapist to announce the end of the hour, seemingly oblivious to the amount of time they have left. It is one of the obligations of the client to the therapist to recognize the limits of the session and not to ask for more than has been agreed upon.

One of the difficulties in making financial arrangements is the current unstable economic climate, which sometimes makes it questionable how long a client will be able to pay a particular fee and how long a therapist can continue to charge a particular fee. Although the financial part of your agreement may have been negotiated in good faith, changing conditions might make it impossible for either one of you to keep to its terms. Some therapists are willing to reduce their fees when a client runs into financial difficulties, such as a loss of job, but it is unreasonable to expect a therapist to work for an extended time at a fee considerably below the usual one. Although it is unfortunate, a client's inability to continue to pay for sessions may mean that the therapy relationship will have to end. Another problem occurs if the therapist wants to raise fees because of cost-of-living increases. It is also unreasonable to expect a therapist to keep the fee constant when his or her expenses of conducting a practice go up markedly. In the last year or two, for example, there have been substantial increases in professional rents and the cost of malpractice insurance. If the probability of a fee increase looms on the horizon, it can be specified in advance that the agreement will be valid for only a limited period of time, at which point the fee may be renegotiated within limits that have been specified beforehand.

Many therapists, especially those who determine their fee according to your financial status, want to raise their fee when there is a substantial increase in your income. Raising the fee makes sense if it had previously been lowered to accommodate your financial circumstances, but not if it is raised beyond the therapist's usual range. How much money you have does not determine what the therapist's services are worth. If the therapist is no longer satisfied with the fee previously set just because you come into more money, that becomes a problem for the therapist to work out.

AVAILABILITY OF THE THERAPIST

When starting out in therapy, clients take for granted that the therapist will be available for them as long as they want. This assumption often turns out to be false. Because of their training functions, clinics and psychotherapy centers have a large turnover of therapists. Many stay at a clinic for only one or two years to meet training requirements and then leave for other jobs or to start private practice. That makes it a good idea to check beforehand how long the therapist intends to remain on staff. Some therapists at clinics will be able to continue seeing a client after they leave for private practice. However, in such instances, the therapist may want a fee increase. Other therapists are bound by contractual agreement not to take clients with them when they leave.

Although private practitioners are more likely to be available for extended periods, they too move, accept part-time appointments, or change office locations, any of which can influence their availability to you. It is always wise to ask the therapist if he or she expects to remain at the same location for the foreseeable future and to have the same hours open for you. While no one can be expected to make firm commitments into the far future, some therapists might be planning changes of one sort or another that would affect you, but that they might not mention if you do not raise the question. For example, if you were to arrange for lunch-hour appointments that you can just squeeze in at the present office location, and the therapist is planning to move the office to the other side of town, you will not be able to continue therapy as planned. Similarly, if a therapist is contemplating a part-time teaching appointment and will no longer have your afternoon hours open, you had better know about this in advance.

Also check on the therapist's vacation schedule. Some therapists take one to three months time off in the summer, which may be longer than you want to go without regular sessions.

It is also a good idea to ask about how often the therapist expects to cancel sessions because of other professional commitments. Some therapists give lectures at symposiums, therapy technique demonstrations, or such, and they interrupt their regularly scheduled client appointments to meet these commitments. If this is acceptable to you, fine, but if not, you should inquire beforehand whether such interruptions are likely to occur.

Another aspect of availability, which becomes important if you are in a crisis situation when you enter therapy, is the amount of extra time the therapist has to see you at other than your specified sessions. Will the therapist try to see you on an emergency basis? Does the therapist feel it is more beneficial for therapy to hold tightly to the set schedule and thereby not to be available for extra sessions?

Will the therapist speak to you on the phone if you have a problem that you feel cannot wait for the next session? Telephone conversations can be a touchy issue between therapist and client. Some therapists will discuss crises on the phone but others feel the phone is an inappropriate medium for working on a problem. The rationale for these attitudes is discussed in Chapter 7, "Sore Spots."

TERMINATION ARRANGEMENTS

One of the areas to be clarified in advance is the conditions under which you, or the therapist, may terminate your agreement. If you feel that the therapy is not working out and that you are not making progress toward your goals, you should have the right to terminate the agreement. However, you have an obligation to notify the therapist beforehand and to discuss the basis of your dissatisfaction. What if the therapist feels the client is not working at the therapy and that it is fruitless to continue working with that person—does the therapist have the right to terminate after giving prior notice and discussing his or her dissatisfactions? If a therapist feels that the therapy is stymied, the question of termination should be brought up and discussed. But if the client still wants to continue therapy, the therapist has an obligation to try to continue working with the client and to give the client a reasonable time in which to come to grips with the problem. Of course, if the client should not live up to his or her obligations, for example, by refusing to pay for services the therapist has the right to terminate. Some therapists use the threat of termination as a way of making clients comply with new conditions. Having an agreement of specified duration and specified working arrangements makes it less likely that a therapist will try to threaten you in this way. However, if this should still happen, it is better that you terminate since such a coercive relationship will not be productive for you.

CONFIDENTIALITY AND RECORDS

Professional ethics require the therapist to keep confidential all that transpires between the two of you. Under no circumstances should a therapist provide any information about you, written or oral, without your written permission to do so. However, violations do occur so it is best not to take confidentiality for granted and to spell out guarantees in your agreement.

Most therapists feel free to present your "case" at professional meetings or in journal articles without requesting permission, provided that your name and other identifying data are deleted. However, it is up to you to determine whether any material about you may be presented and, if so, what details should be deleted to protect your anonymity. Sometimes others will request information about you from the therapist at your or their behest. You might, for example, ask your therapist to provide case history material to another professional in conjunction with a consultation, or an insurance company may request information about your therapy to determine if you qualify for reimbursement. If you do authorize a release, have it specify what information is to be provided and to whom. While most therapists will not send out such information without your authorization, many do not want to show you what they did transmit. They might rationalize their behavior, saying that you will be unable to understand the material properly, or that it would be harmful for you to see it at that particular time. It is arrogant for a therapist to assume that you are not "ready" to handle what he or she tells others about you. If there is any question about your ability to understand a communication, it behooves the therapist to explain it in a way that you can grasp.

It is common practice in clinics to discuss cases for supervisory and training purposes. This is usually in the client's as well as the therapist's interest. But you should know if and when your therapy is discussed and you might want to know with whom. As mentioned earlier, you also will want to find out who has access to your file. At clinics associated with hospitals, clients are sometimes asked to attend a case seminar where the staff members can see and hear the "case" in person. At these case presentations various people will feel free to question you and observe your reactions, but usually you will be invited to leave without getting the benefit of learning firsthand their impressions of you and your problems. You are under no compulsion to participate at such a seminar, and should not let yourself be pressured into doing so. If a therapist does try to pressure you to participate, he or she is putting personal interests above yours.

Sometimes therapists make tape recordings or take notes during sessions. These may be used to discuss the progress of your therapy with a supervisor, or only for the therapist's purposes for lectures, records, or books. In either case, it is up to you to decide if you want to allow it. Some therapists have taped sessions without the client's awareness. This should not be tolerated.

Several aspects of confidentiality are removed from the therapist's discretion. One is a situation in which information might be requested by a court in conjunction with legal proceedings. For example, a therapist might be asked to testify about your mental condition or moral character in reference to your competence to obtain or retain custody of a child or to administer estates. Another situation could be your accountability under law for criminal acts. The degree of protection offered you would depend somewhat on the extent to which the concept of privileged information is recognized for the profession of the particular therapist you see. Confidentiality accorded to psychologists is the broadest and was initially defined to equal that of the legal profession and protect all communications between the psychologist and the client. Psychiatrists, who practice under the confidentiality provisions for physicians, cannot offer as broad protection. The confidentiality provisions for physicians state that the practitioner shall not communicate without the patient's permission any information relevant to the disorder for which the patient consulted the physician, but information not relevant to the disorder is not protected. Psychiatrists are trying to broaden this protection but the courts to date have not been willing to extend it. Depending on locality, professionals may be required by law to report automatically certain types of information, particularly any incident of child abuse whether verified or not and any threat of violence made against an individual. Child abuse is to be reported to appropriate state or municipal authorities but threats against a person are to be reported directly to the person so threatened as well as to the police.

A FORMAL CONTRACT?

Most contracts between clients and therapists are in the nature of oral agreements, but some people have recommended more formal contracts. A few years ago, the Public Citizen's Health Research Group based in Washington suggested that the agreement between therapist and client be specified in written form. The Health Research Group has developed a sample contract, which they offer for use as a model by all clients going into therapy. It includes the following major elements: the name of each party, the date of beginning and end of the agreement, the length of each session, the goals toward which the therapy will be directed, the cost of sessions and time of payment, the services to be provided by the therapist, provisions for terminating and canceling sessions, provisions for renegotiation of contract, provisions for changing therapy goals, acceptance of lack of guarantees for attaining therapy goals but statement of good faith, and access of client to records and client control of access by others.

There is a good deal of resistance among therapists to making formal contracts. The Health Research Group found this resistance stronger among psychiatrists than other practitioners, perhaps because it is contrary to the traditional doctor-patient relationship, which places all power in the doctor's hands. Regardless of professional identification, many therapists rely on the doctor role for their own sense of security and, therefore, are hesitant to accord their clients equal footing. Some therapists object to formal contracts because they see them as having a limiting influence on the therapy; others may fear greater susceptibility to malpractice charges or to legal suits. Still, it is important that you come to an understanding with the therapist, whether it is written or oral, formal or informal. If you find that you cannot make suitable arrangements for the course of the therapy relationship, there is very little hope that it will be a productive therapy.

7 *Sore Spots*

ALTHOUGH YOUR arrangements with the therapist should be spelled out at the start, unforeseen situations do crop up later on, some of which can be quite bothersome. These problem areas generally stem from a lack of understanding on your part, or the therapist's part, or both, of the rationale involved in various therapy arrangements.

MISSED SESSIONS

One recurrent point of tension is the policy of charging for missed sessions. If you wake up late and miss a session, it is easy to see your responsibility in missing it and you probably won't mind paying for the session. But what if you break a leg and obviously can't get to the office because you're in traction? On top of your medical expenses, why should you have to pay the therapist when he or she knows you can't make it? Or suppose you were caught in a traffic jam, stuck in an elevator, or attending a funeral. Is the therapist right to charge you under such circumstances?

There probably isn't any one correct attitude toward the various situations that may arise, but it is important that you and the therapist are in basic accord on the issues involved. If you resent his or her approach, it will be a constant bone of contention between you and will hamper a productive relationship. Different attitudes toward money are not necessarily something that can be "worked through." Of course, it just might happen that you are the type of person who always has to have something to fight about, and having a therapist whom you can always accuse of greed might be a perfect situation as far as you and your problems are concerned. But more frequently, disagreements about payment reflect differences in basic attitudes that make for incompatibility.

When the issue of payment for missed sessions arises, most clients automatically resent the idea that they should pay. Many agree to pay anyway just because they think this is the way it is in the field. A few admit some right of the therapist to charge them, but pay up resentfully, feeling that the therapist is more concerned about the fee than about them. Why should a therapist receive a fee for sessions when he or she does not work? In answering this question, clients generally use other professional situations as models, most frequently drawing an analogy between the therapist and physician or dentist.

What happens when you have an appointment with a physician? If you come on time, chances are you will be kept in the waiting room anywhere from a half hour to an hour or more waiting for the physician who, invariably, was delayed at the hospital. The physician will see you when he or she has time, regardless of the time originally set for your appointment. If you call up to cancel an appointment, you are usually not charged. You did not really have a specific time reserved for you in the first place and if you do not show up it does not upset the physician's schedule. By contrast, your therapist keeps a specific hour open which is a time for you and no one else. You will not be kept waiting except, perhaps, once in a while for five minutes or so, in which case extra time will usually be added at the end of your session. If you call to cancel, your absence is decidedly marked. For the time of your appointment, your therapist sits in the office with no other clients going in and out of the door. Of course, he or she might use the time to make phone calls or read magazines, but the fact remains that a specific time has been set aside for you and you are not there to fill it.

The analogy to dentists is a little more apt, though still not quite up to the mark. Your dentist probably will set aside a certain time for you and, if you should cancel, be left sterilizing the instruments or making phone calls. Dentists often do charge a cancellation fee but, more important, clients are very unlikely to cancel dental appointments, wanting to get them over with quickly. In fact, a dental appointment is the type of situation for which clients are tempted to cancel psychotherapy appointments. Psychotherapy appointments are regular and are experienced with less urgency; if a client misses a therapy session, he or she is often content to wait for the next regularly scheduled session. When a person cancels a dental appointment, he or she usually wants to schedule an alternative time right away. Another difference between the dental and psychotherapy situations is that dentists are more likely to fill canceled sessions with other clients, while a psychotherapist's canceled session can rarely be put to remunerative use.

When we look at therapy as an educative process, and take schools and tuition payment as a model, the parallels seem much closer. If you sign up for a course you know that the class will meet x times a week, and that you pay full tuition regardless of whether you miss any classes. If, for any reason, you miss a class, you work harder to make up for lost time. So it is in therapy. Your therapist signs on with you for a course to open up your ways of thinking and experiencing. Class meets regularly once or twice a week, or however frequently specified, and is open for you to attend whether you can make it or not. The time is reserved for you, and if you do not show up it is lost both for you and for the therapist. Just as a private tutor or school will bill you for a stipulated number of lessons whether or not you attend, psychotherapists also expect to be paid for prearranged time.

Although there is a good rationale for the practice of paying fees for missed sessions, there is little need for adhering to this practice rigidly. Some therapists make strict rules to avoid misunderstandings and the hassles that result from these, others because they do not take clients' needs into account. It is important that clients recognize their obligation to pay for scheduled sessions, but it is also reasonable to provide some flexibility for canceling or changing sessions. The client and therapist should discuss the conditions under which a session can be canceled without the client being charged for it. Some therapists apply a "twenty-four-hour-notice" rule, and bill for all sessions canceled without such prior notification, regardless of the reason the client does not come. This policy recognizes that even though a client may cancel for unavoidable reasons, the therapist should not bear the burden for the client. The client's obligation to respect the therapist's time is not reduced by such situations. When notice to cancel is given earlier than twenty-four hours before the session, the reasons for such cancellation become relevant to the decision about billing. If a client cancels for unavoidable reasons, and the therapist can arrange a makeup session, there is little rationale for charging. But if cancellations are made irresponsibly, there is little rationale not to charge. Financial obligation for missed sessions also helps to reduce habitual cancellations that stem from resistance (see Chapter 10).

It is important that there be reciprocity between therapist and client about rights in canceling sessions. For example, if the therapist wants to be free to cancel sessions to attend professional meetings, he or she should respect the client's right to cancel for reasons of comparable importance. The therapist should not assume prerogatives that he or she is not willing to accord to the client.

A frequent practice is to offer a makeup session when a client cancels for an unavoidable reason such as illness or an important business meeting. While the therapist's desire to maintain income may be part of the reason for the prevalence of this practice, there are others that relate to the therapy itself. If sessions are not made up, there can be an interruption in the flow of the therapy, which hampers progress. This can be especially pronounced when the therapy sessions are scheduled less frequently as, for example, once a week, where a two-week lapse between sessions can create a break in the process. Another important reason for a makeup session is to preclude an uncommitted attitude toward therapy. But when the therapist insists on making up a session missed by the client, the therapist should also be prepared to offer makeup sessions when he or she cancels the session. When the therapist cancels, the client has a right to know why the therapist is canceling.

Some therapists do not charge for canceled sessions if they can fill the time with another client. The rationale for this practice is solely income protection for the therapist. It leaves the client with a sense of uncertainty, not knowing beforehand if he or she has to pay and having to rely entirely on the therapist's honesty.

CHANGES IN APPOINTMENTS

Once you have arranged your therapy hours, both you and the therapist expect that they will be maintained. However, something might happen that makes it impossible for you to keep that schedule—a change in jobs gets you off work too late or cuts into your lunch-hour appointment, you have to be home earlier because your kids get out of school earlier, or whatever. Under such circumstances, you will want to work out more convenient hours, but the therapist may not be able to accommodate you. This does not necessarily mean that the therapist is rigid, or inconsiderate. Usually, changing your hours means changing someone else's hours as well, and a therapist is not free to offer you new times if his or her other clients are unable or unwilling to change their schedules. For the same reason, you may find your therapist asking you one day if you can switch your appointments around. Sometimes clients resent being asked to make changes, feeling they are being put out to accommodate someone else. Of course, you do not have to make a change or inconvenience yourself, but you might want to help someone out if you can. Other clients may try to accommodate themselves to you in the future, although they are no more bound to do so than you are.

Therapists may also ask you to switch your appointments around to accommodate themselves. Many therapists have part-time teaching appointments or consultantships that change from year to year. The therapist has an obligation to check with you beforehand about your schedule rather than just expecting you to make changes to meet his or her needs. When asking you to make a change the therapist should tell you the reasons for it. He or she should not try to intimidate you into altering your schedule or threaten to terminate if you cannot arrange new times.

A related problem is the timing of individual sessions. Sometimes a therapist may run overtime with a previous client and keep you waiting. This can anger clients who feel they are being used for another's convenience—which is so. Clients tend to be touchy about this when they are concerned that the therapist does not really care about them, or if they think the therapist likes other clients more. If a therapist keeps you waiting, the lost time is usually made up at the end of your session. If this is not convenient for you because you have to race off to another appointment or back to work, the therapist should make up the lost time when it is convenient for you. The therapist should not presume on your time and make a habit of keeping you waiting and extending your appointment. Occasional incursions may be warranted, just as your time may run over into someone else's, but if this becomes a pattern, the therapist is being inconsiderate and treating his or her time as more valuable than yours.

The therapist is not the only one who is late for sessions. Sometimes clients show up late too. Habitual lateness is often a sign of resistance, anger toward the therapist, or a way of testing the therapist, but people can be late for a variety of reasons beyond their control: traffic tie-up, accident, and so on. When you show up late for a session, regardless of the reason, the situation is analogous to your missing a session without notice. No matter how unforeseen the circumstances, you cannot expect the therapist to have time to extend your session accordingly. It is an unfortunate happenstance of life, which may occasionally befall you as it does the therapist and other people.

VACATION SCHEDULES

Therapists generally encourage clients to take vacations when they do. This creates less disruption in the therapy process and in the therapist's practice. Some therapists charge for clients' vacation time if it is taken outside of the therapist's vacation. Some have even charged for whole summers if the client was away, for example, to study in a foreign country. The practice of charging for vacations originated when summer was the usual time for taking vacations. Therapists worked for the duration of the school year, from September to June, July, or August, and expected their clients to conform to this schedule. With the changes in vacation patterns brought on by the jet age, including the popularity of winter, spring, and autumn vacations, it has become less realistic for therapists to expect clients to take their vacations only in summer months. Although there is good reason for clients to try to coordinate their vacation schedule with the therapist's, for a therapist to insist on this is to ignore the legitimate needs of the client to take a vacation when it is best for him or her to do so. If we grant the client as much right as the therapist to take a vacation when he or she wants, there seems to be no justification in billing for vacation time that falls outside the therapist's vacation schedule. The right of the client to take a vacation without paying for missed sessions should not be abused to the point of the client's taking off for excessive amounts of time. Barring that, in our view the client is entitled to "separate but equal" vacation time.

Naturally the client has the right to be away from the therapy for an extended period of time, but not with the expectation that the therapist must be available on the same terms afterward. The therapist cannot be expected to guarantee the time for a client who chooses to interrupt the therapy unless the client reserves that time by paying for it.

PHONE CALLS AND EMERGENCIES

There may be times when you want to talk to your therapist before your next session because of a crisis that has come up or because you feel especially bad. Even if the therapist is willing to arrange an earlier session, you feel you just cannot wait till then and have to get some help right away. Is it appropriate for you to call the therapist at such times and what can you expect from him or her?

If your need is urgent, then by all means call. In our opinion, the therapist should discuss urgent problems with you on the phone, though not all therapists will agree with this. Some will object on theoretical grounds, considering such phone calls as an indulgence in feelings that should be contained. Others feel that since they are paid on the basis of time, telephone calls constitute an abuse of their services. This could be a consideration if a client makes a habit out of such calls, but most clients call rarely and do so only if they have no other recourse.

It can happen that clients use telephone calls and crises as a way to test the therapist's concern for them. In such cases the problem, although real, is usually not so critical that it cannot wait for a day or two. A client may know this, but call anyway just to see how the therapist reacts or to get reassurance that the problem is not that catastrophic. It is a good idea, if you want to phone, to ask yourself first if you really need help or just want to test the therapist.

Though a therapist should be available to discuss a crisis over the phone, the client has to recognize that the phone may be an inappropriate medium in such a situation. Phone calls can help, but they are not a replacement for direct personal communication. A therapist might be reluctant to talk with you at length over the phone and insist instead that you come for a session. If the therapist is willing to make time available for you outside of his or her normal working hours, the additional session is usually offered in your interest rather than as an excuse for cutting short phone contact.

You will have to indicate just how urgent your need is and not cry "wolf." But if the therapist is not there for you at a critical moment, you may need a new therapist.

Phone Calls from Others

A frequent source of annoyance for clients is the therapist's taking phone calls during a session. Since the client is, in effect, buying a certain amount of time, there is justification for being annoyed at any encroachments on that time, but the realities of life sometimes necessitate interruptions. The therapist, like anyone else, needs to be available by phone not only because of those infrequent professional emergencies but for personal emergencies as well. Granted the legitimacy of telephone accessibility, the therapist should nonetheless keep calls brief and, whenever possible, cut the call short and phone back on his or her own time.

The annoyance of interruptions can be lessened by expressing it and by making up the lost time. Many therapists overlook these time losses, making their clients rightfully more angry. It often happens, though, that clients will be angry even when the therapist does make up the time because they resent other people or other problems intruding into their sessions. While this is an understandable reaction, it is an unreasonable demand. On the other hand, the therapist should recognize that a crisis of the client during the session is every bit as pressing as one that may be coming in on the telephone line and be prepared to let the phone go unanswered when the disruptions would be harmful to the client. The incoming call, as well as the client in session, may have to wait at certain times.

Smoking or Nonsmoking?

It used to be that therapists objected to clients smoking on the ground that it allays anxieties that otherwise could be profitably worked on during a session. Nowadays many therapists want to dissuade clients from smoking during sessions as well as at other times because it is a health hazard.

Occasionally therapists tend to forget that clients may also have feelings about the therapist smoking. Nonsmokers may resent being subjected to the smoke created by therapists, and smokers as well as nonsmokers may be bothered by excessive smoking as a sign of lack of control on the therapist's part. If the therapist's smoking bothers you, we feel that you have a right to ask the therapist not to smoke; he or she should be able to go for forty-five to fifty minutes without a cigarette.

If either client or therapist has strong feelings about smoking, that should be discussed at the very start. The therapist can set his or her working conditions and you have a right to reject them, as well as vice versa, but, one hopes, smoking will not be an issue on which you and the therapist cannot accommodate each other. In light of the harmful effects of smoking, it seems prudent to us to favor the needs of the nonsmoker.

NOTE TAKING AND RECORDING

Many therapists take notes or tape record sessions. Some ask for the client's permission and others take it for granted. If you have feelings about your therapist taking notes or recording your sessions, be sure to discuss them. The therapist does not have the right to take your consent for granted. Some clients feel that it is a violation of their privacy and others find it distracting or disruptive of the interaction. Still others feel that it shows a lack of concern on the part of the therapist in that he or she cannot remember the important things unless they are written down or taped. Note taking and tape recording can serve a variety of purposes and the therapist should clarify what these are. Records to enable the therapist to keep track of your work together are in both your interests. Records for research, seminars, or books may be only in the therapist's interest. If the therapist needs notes to keep on top of the process or for record keeping, the therapist should not let the note taking intrude on the interaction and preferably do it after the session is over. If the therapist keeps notes or records for his or her own purposes, that, too, can be done after the session, and there is little reason for you to put up with it if it disturbs you.

WHAT TO CALL EACH OTHER

The way you and the therapist address each other says a lot about the kind of relationship you have. Usually client and therapist start off addressing each other formally by last name, with the client using the therapist's professional title, if any. Many therapists prefer the formality and prestige of being called by their title. After working together for a while, therapists usually start to call clients by their first name. This informality arises naturally for therapists out of the personal contact they have with their clients. It is not disrespectful unless the therapist uses the more familiar first name without a corresponding feeling of closeness to the person. Then it represents a condescending familiarity and will be experienced as a put-down.

Some therapists start right off on a first-name basis to undercut the social distance implied in using last names, inviting clients to call them by first name, too. Occasionally clients will start off calling the therapist by his or her first name on their own initiative, but for most that form of familiarity does not express a genuine feeling of closeness. Most clients see their therapist as an authority figure and feel more comfortable using his or her last name (or avoiding using a name altogether) until such a time as they can experience the relationship on a more equal level. Some therapists always call clients by their last names, even after years of work together. Considering today's informal customs, clients can also become resentful of this if they feel it shows a lack of warmth. The therapist may be too reserved or bound to the professional role to become more personal.

Sometimes a therapist wants to be addressed by title and last name while calling clients by first name. We feel this sets up an inappropriate disparity between the two. Any person, therapists included, can ask to be addressed formally, but then that person has the obligation to address others on the same level. If a therapist thinks it is proper to call you by a first name there is no justification for insisting that he or she be called by last name and title.

SMALL TALK

Usually both client and therapist enjoy a bit of personal banter. Such encounters are a pleasant diversion and helpful in getting to know each other. It is natural to be interested in each other: where are you going on vacation, how did you like the ballet last night, did you read about so and so in the news, et cetera. The danger comes if such exchanges alter the mood with which you come to therapy. For example, pleasant chitchat could divert you from experiencing an angry or anxious feeling that you wanted to work on in the session. Also, sometimes such talk begins to revolve more and more around topics of exclusive interest to the therapist. For example, a therapist may, in asking about how you enjoyed your vacation, get carried away and start asking for various details about the trip, the scenery, the hotels, the restaurants. Or the therapist may pursue his or her interest in hot tips from a business client, or for political gossip from a journalist client, or for the "dirt" on the social set. Clients tend to go along and answer questions because they are anxious to please the therapist, but after a while they will become resentful if the therapist is using their time in a way that is not productive for them. They may feel the therapist should not ask irrelevant questions during the session, although they would be glad to answer such questions afterward—when they are usually not asked. It is unfortunate if a therapist lets his or her interests intrude into your session in this way, and it is even more unfortunate if you allow this to continue. If you need to curb the therapist too much, the question of whose needs are being served by the therapy arises.

CHANGING TECHNIQUES

A therapist may, seemingly out of the blue, ask you to make a change in your way of working together. He or she may want you to switch from the chair to the couch, to join a therapy group, to do body exercises, or to go on a weekend workshop. A suggestion like that might be made because the therapist feels that it has become appropriate at that particular point in your therapy, because he or she has just become acquainted with or trained in that technique, or because he or she now feels free to ask you without your kicking up a fuss. Whatever the reason, the change has to make sense to you. Discuss the reasons the change is being suggested, air whatever questions or doubts you have about it, and then see how you feel about it. You may, after discussion, think it's a great idea, you may be skeptical but willing to give it a whirl, or you may be completely turned off to the idea. Whatever your reaction, it is your decision whether to go along with any changes in therapy that were not agreed upon at the outset of therapy.

AVOIDING QUESTIONS

Often clients want to know how the therapist feels about a particular issue, his or her reactions to experiences brought up, or something about the therapist him- or herself. These may be questions such as "What is your attitude toward abortion?" "How do you feel about my decision not to go home?" or "Have you ever been married?" As we discussed before (in Chapter 3, "How to Pick a Therapist"), many therapists avoid answering questions like these even though they are relevant to the therapy process, and sometimes such questions are turned against the client, with the implication that there is something wrong about asking them.

Some therapists do not want to answer these questions because they believe that doing so is detrimental to the therapy. They think that the more neutral the therapist remains, the more the client will reveal about him- or herself. Being important figures in a client's life, therapists are bound to be influential even without wanting to be so. But these considerations do not make it necessary for a therapist to hide his or her attitudes or to pretend a neutral stance. In our view, when you feel that it is important for you to know how a therapist feels about an issue, you should bring up the question. Of course you must explore the reasons why you want to know: do you have doubts about what you are doing and need reassurance, are you afraid the therapist might not approve of what you are doing, or do you want to check your own attitudes against those of someone you trust and respect? Once you know what is at stake for you in determining the therapist's attitudes, and once you have examined your own attitudes on that subject, there is little reason why the therapist should feel constrained about telling you how he or she feels. In fact, it can be very helpful for you to learn how to deal with attitudes of important others that may diverge from yours, without suspending your own judgment.

Besides questions about attitudes, clients also ask therapists questions for clarification and explanation: "Do you see anything else in that dream?" "Why do I feel so anxious?" "Why did you ask me that?" Many therapists also avoid answering these questions on the grounds that doing so allows the client to shirk his or her own therapeutic work. Sometimes clients use questions in this way, and then it is best for the therapist to delay answering to encourage the client to take the initiative. At other times, a point of clarification from the therapist can help a client move on to a deeper consideration of a therapeutic issue. Therapists have to use their clinical judgment about when it seems better to answer a client's question and when it seems better to delay answering.

SOCIAL INTERACTION

As client and therapist work together and develop closer feelings toward each other, clients sometimes want to extend the relationship outside the office. It is not unusual for clients to want their therapists to come to events marking a milestone in their life, especially since they are often related to work done in therapy. For example, the therapist may be invited to the client's wedding, to the opening of the new shop or the client's art show. Sometimes therapists are invited to other personal occasions such as a cocktail party or dinner. Is it all right to invite your therapist and is there any good reason why he or she should not accept?

Despite your friendly and warm feelings toward each other, the psychotherapy relationship is not the same as a friendship. First of all, it is not a mutual relationship. In therapy, the client's needs are always uppermost and the therapist has the responsibility to defer to them. Friendships are built on greater mutuality, on freer give and take. Friendships also differ in that they are multifaceted, whereas therapy relationships are primarily oriented toward the client's problems and growth. The therapist, because of the nature of the relationship and needs of the client, is subject to restraints and formal commitments that do not exist in friendships. To have friendlike social contact with clients, the therapist has to step in and out of roles and for this reason many prefer to stick to the therapist role, at least until the therapy is terminated.

Therapists will accept or reject your invitations depending on their conception of their role as therapist, their flexibility in dealing with different roles, their feelings about you and how important the events are to you, and their own attitudes about the particular event. A therapist should accept your invitation only if he or she really wants to attend, but may sometimes reject an invitation even if he or she wants to attend. You should extend an invitation only if you really want the therapist to come. Some clients feel obligated to invite their therapists to important occasions and others invite them only as a test. Often clients feel uncomfortable when their therapist does accept the invitation because the therapist's presence makes the client self-conscious and ill at ease. Invite your therapist if you genuinely want him or her there, but also be prepared to discuss your reasons for the invitation as well as the therapist's reasons for accepting or declining it.

Similar issues arise in connection with asking for favors from the therapist—letters of reference, letters of excuse, the loan of a book, and so forth. While the therapist must keep your needs uppermost within therapy, this obligation does not extend to matters outside it. Clients generally feel rejected if the therapist does not want to go along with the request, but a refusal is sometimes appropriate and not always a rejection. Of course, the therapist should discuss his or her reasons for refusal with you if he or she cannot go along.

8 *Making Therapy Work*

WHAT ACTUALLY happens in therapy? What do you do, what does the therapist do? According to the old stereotype, all you have to do is talk and the therapist listens. But a lot more goes on in therapy than that. True, you will have to do a lot of talking since you—your feelings, your attitudes, and your way of being—are what the therapy is all about. The burden rests on you to make yourself known as fully as possible by providing the material for you and the therapist to work on. That work, however, is a constant interchange of effort, a constant back and forth.

The therapy sessions usually start with you bringing up something you want to talk about. This can be anything that's on your mind at the time: an argument you had with the bus driver coming to therapy, a dream you had last night, feelings about your mother, or something left unresolved from the last session. Often sessions center on current problems, and talking about them provides relief as well as bringing out underlying therapeutic issues. Whatever you talk about, your job is to be as honest and straightforward as you can be. Try not to hold back any thoughts or feelings because of embarrassment; you have to let your feelings out to learn to accept them and become a whole person.

The therapist's job is to help you express yourself by providing you with a relationship that allows you to open up and experience the threatening feelings you block off. He or she leads you to new routes to awareness—free association, dream interpretation, role playing, body exercises, and other techniques—and helps you use them to get in touch with yourself. The therapist doesn't just sit there but listens and observes carefully to help you discover what he or she learns and utilize this knowledge to overcome the barriers you experience. By mirroring what you say or how you say it, he or she can make you aware of aspects of yourself that ordinarily slip by you. The therapist calls your attention to feelings and attitudes that may be emotionally loaded by emphasizing them when you gloss over them. He or she notes sudden changes in your behavior ("You became so animated talking about your father. What were you feeling then?") and helps you examine inconsistencies in your behavior that suggest conflict ("Last time you were optimistic but today you seem down in the mouth. What is going on?"). The therapist helps you grasp connections between your feelings and behavior ("Look how tightly your hands are clenched—you started clenching them when you started talking about your mother"). The therapist also makes you more aware by calling your attention to what you don't do or don't say ("Last week all you talked about was your upcoming interview with your boss, but today you haven't said a word about it. I wonder why"). Through the supportive interaction with the therapist, through dialogues and confrontations, you will learn new ways of experiencing, be exposed to new perspectives, and be encouraged to try new alternatives in responding to life's problems.

Clients often think that explanations of their behavior will be the answer to their problems. This idea makes it difficult to understand why the therapist makes them work at developing insights on their own when seemingly he or she has the answer all along. Insight alone is not enough; it is a precondition for changing your feelings and behavior. Moreover, insight cannot be given to you but has to be actively acquired. The lack of insight does not stem from insufficient knowledge but from emotional forces that resist that knowledge. Only through a change in your readiness to face that knowledge, an increase in your confidence that you can take it, can the insight occur. While the therapist can lead you to that knowledge and encourage you, it will become meaningful only through your active acceptance.

Things that are hard to face are usually accepted only gradually. Acceptance comes about by repeatedly going over the same issue, though often from different perspectives, to build up the tolerance and courage to act on it. This process, called "working through," is often a difficult aspect of therapy and the point at which many people want to quit. They become disillusioned that the initial insight did not lead to change and that the major job of doing something about themselves still lies ahead.

Therapy is bound to be a bumpy road with times of fast movement, times of no progress, and times of plateaus. Undoubtedly you will feel antagonistic to the therapy at times. Being prepared for these feelings and knowing what to do in therapy is the best antidote for times of discouragement. Approach therapy as openly as possible and work with those techniques that seem the most natural to you.

TALKING

Psychotherapy has been called the "talking cure," and talking is still the basic component of most psychotherapies. As it is a process of exploration of oneself, only you, the client, can provide the material. It is up to you to present as much information as possible, to lay open the thoughts, fears, expectations, fantasies, anxieties, and feelings that constitute your existence. To do this, talking is usually the most direct approach. Talking is not only a medium of communication but a help in and of itself. It stimulates thinking, evokes feelings, and allays anxieties. Often in the process of verbalizing feelings and identifying them one learns how to deal with them more productively. Talking is the point at which psychotherapy begins and the way in which problems will be expressed, goals set, and the conditions arranged for the therapeutic relationship.

The beginning sessions of psychotherapy are usually tinged with anxiety about starting out and finding the right therapist but, in another sense, these sessions are easier because there are clear issues to bring up. After the first few sessions, in which the major problems and reasons for seeking therapy are outlined, some clients suddenly find that they don't know what to talk about. Should they go into detail about their childhood histories, talk about anything that comes into their heads, or sit back and wait for the therapist to ask questions?

The course you take may be influenced by the psychotherapy approach and practitioner you have chosen. Some therapists will be more directive, some less so. Some will want to concentrate on childhood and some on contemporary events, and some will want to observe what you will do. Still, there are some guidelines you can follow in bringing up material.

Talk about what seems most meaningful to you at the time. If several issues are pressing all at once, the particular one you pick is not all that important. The goal is to develop deeper understanding of your way of living. This awareness can come through talking about anything and everything that matters to you.

Talk about yourself in a direct way rather than as an outsider who is describing you. The more concretely you talk about your experiences and the more alive you can make them in the sessions, the greater the possibilities of understanding what is going on. For example, instead of summarizing your reactions to generalized situations ("When I am at large gatherings I feel insecure"), talk about what it was actually like when you were in such a situation ("When I was at the party I got this terrible feeling in my stomach and felt I was going to throw up every time someone spoke to me").

When you talk about events in your life describe how you, not others, experience them. Instead of focusing on the reactions of others ("When I had lunch with my mother she thought the food was awful and the service was dreadful and she didn't enjoy it at all"), relate your reactions ("When I had lunch with my mother she made me feel bad because she was critical of everything that was happening and I had the feeling she wanted to put me down").

Try to talk about things as what they are rather than as what they are not. For example, "I feel like crying" rather than "I am not happy," or "I feel I could kill you" rather than "I do not want to talk to you."

Emphasize your feelings about a situation, not just the details of what happened to you. For example, instead of talking about events happening around you ("My boss came in and told me I would have to prepare a whole new report that night to be ready for the 9:00 A.M. meeting"), talk about how you feel when these things happen ("When my boss came in and told me what I would have to do, I got so angry I could feel my face getting hot, but I just couldn't get any answer out of my throat").

Say things as you think them. Do not polish your thoughts for the therapist or put them into polite language or quiet tones. Let them come out as you experience them. For example let the therapist know that "When you sit there looking so goddamn smug, I could punch you in the nose," rather than telling him or her that "You have such an odd look on your face."

Try to be as open as possible and let your thoughts and feelings emerge even if they are embarrassing or shameful to you. If those are the feelings that are hanging you up, those are the feelings you must deal with. The more you express them the less hold they will have over you, and the less horrible they will seem.

If you feel "stuck" and at a loss for words, try then to describe that experience as well. "I don't know what to talk about. My mind is a blank. It makes me feel very uncomfortable. You must find me dull." If you get too upset in a session, the therapist is there to help you. "I just feel awful. Say something to me."

PAST OR PRESENT?

Most therapies begin and end with talk about the present. After all, it is current problems that bring a person into therapy and it is one's capacity to deal with them that means it's time to stop therapy. Nevertheless, reconstructing events of the past can often be an important element of therapy. It is not so much the events themselves that are critical, but the meaning extracted from these events. The past is important insofar as it gives rise to certain attitudes about yourself and your possibilities in life. When these attitudes become set and are not changed by present experiences, understanding the past can help you understand your present reactions.

Clients vary in their attitudes toward discussing past experiences. Some, because of earlier trauma, are stuck in the past. They cannot move on until the events of the past are re-experienced in a way that allows them to gain perspective on and defuse the troubling emotions. For these people, dealing with the past is an essential part of therapy. Other clients want to deal only with current issues and resist attempts to focus on the past. People interested in the "here and now" may feel it is a waste of time to bother with the "there and then." A refusal to look at past events or feelings about early figures in one's life sometimes masks a defensive posture and fear of stirring up painful echoes. Or it can be akin to the demand for "relevance" of the last student generation in its attempts to throw history out of the curriculum and replace it with contemporary social studies. Relevance cannot be determined in a vacuum: one must first get an overview before deciding what is meaningful and what is not. But when a client feels that such an endeavor has outlived its usefulness, there is no point in continuing such a course just because the therapist wants to fill the gaps. Covering the past, if done as an automatic exercise, can become a waste of time and divert therapeutic energies from more meaningful pursuits.

REMEMBERING YOUR THOUGHTS

Sometimes clients in therapy want to bring up all sorts of thoughts, memories, or feelings at their next therapy session only to find, when they get there, that they have forgotten everything but the memory of having something to talk about. This happens when you have "resistance" to bringing up certain material in the therapy sessions, or when the anxiety around the thought is so great it becomes uncomfortable to keep it in mind. Thoughts also get lost naturally when your mind is occupied with other aspects of daily living. Having to remember things to do for the job, or what to buy for supper, or letters to write, can take your attention away from the seemingly less pressing problems of your inner self.

There are some simple ways to help you keep track of those thoughts which pop in and out of your head. One is to keep a pad with you and to jot down thoughts or memories you don't want to lose. Just the act of putting them on paper tends to make them stick more, but once they are written down you do not have to rely on your memory. Some people find it helpful to keep a diary when they start therapy for much the same reason. They can go over the day's events and cull from it feelings and experiences that were especially meaningful. A diary can also help you in the process of self-analysis, if it is used not only as a record of events but as a distillation of the experiences as well.

LISTENING

Practically everyone has heard the joke about the therapist who, in answer to a question about whether it doesn't upset him to hear people relate their troubles all day long, responds, "Who listens?" It is not only therapists, however, who have trouble listening, but clients too. While many clients feel that their therapists do not talk enough, as if more input from the therapist would more quickly solve their problems, it also happens that when therapists do talk, clients sometimes do not hear what is said.

Clients can tune out what a therapist is saying for a variety of reasons—a need to control the session, annoyance at being interrupted, a need to reject the therapist—but the most common reason is defensiveness. When critical issues are being discussed that make the client uncomfortable or anxious, clients learn to listen through a self-protective screen. Because of this screen, the therapist may make a point repeatedly, yet it may be heard only partially or not at all, although sometimes an initially "unheard" remark may have an impact later. Clients are not always emotionally ready to hear what is being said and for that reason therapists may defer interpretations if they feel the timing is premature, or repeat an interpretation later when they feel the time is ripe. For example, a client had been complaining in therapy about the lack of intimacy with his grown children, lamenting that although they phone him regularly they never really tell him anything. As he recounted these conversations, the therapist pointed out that when his sons do relate personal information, he does not welcome the news but offers criticism, suggesting his sons might have done better. The client did not hear what the therapist was saying and responded that he always tried to help his sons. One day, after the client repeated a particularly frustrating phone conversation, and the therapist told him again that he was pushing his sons away by his overly critical and destructive behavior, the client, with a look of surprise, said, "Why didn't you tell me that before?" The "telling" that suddenly became apparent was actually a culmination of repeated working over of the same material, which the client could only hear when he was really listening.

A frequently used way of not listening to the therapist is by avoiding the gist of what is being said, focusing instead on the manner in which it is said. A client might notice a mistake in the therapist's grammar and interrupt to correct it, or just silently put down the therapist for making the mistake, thereby shifting attention from the material that is being discussed. A similar maneuver to avoid dealing with difficult material is to quibble with the words that the therapist is using to describe a feeling or thought. If the words are not entirely accurate or descriptive, the client can then more easily dismiss the thought being expressed. When you are listening to the therapist and feel impatient, angry, or in other ways critical of how things are being said, these feelings may be cluing you in to your own areas of vulnerability rather than to the therapist's inadequacies.

It could be, of course, that your difficulty in listening stems from the emotional tone in which the therapist talks to you. Is the therapist too critical of you or putting you down? Is the therapist being insensitive and reflecting an inability to listen to you? Or is the therapist bringing up issues that make you uncomfortable and that you would rather not face? In the absence of a pattern of condescending or critical behavior on the part of the therapist, chances are that your discomfort at what is being said has more to do with you than with the therapist. Further guidelines on sorting out these issues are presented in Chapter 10, "Resistance or Incompatibility."

SILENCE

Some people cannot tolerate silence. When they are alone they use the radio or television to fill in the emptiness with sound and when they are with another person they need the assurance of constant conversation. People who are uncomfortable with silence can find it more discomforting in a psychotherapy session, which they expect to be all talk, and they may regard such silence as a waste of time and money. Does silence in a psychotherapy session mean that the therapy is getting nowhere, or can it also be useful?

Silence, like talk, can be used both constructively and destructively. The value of the silence will depend on how you experience and use it. Silence is necessary to search for or reflect on memories, ideas, or feelings. Sometimes silence follows an outpouring of emotions, when time is needed to integrate the feelings that have just been experienced. Therapists will generally not interrupt a period of silence if they think you are using that time to experience yourself more deeply.

Sometimes therapists ask clients to be silent for a while because too much talking can be a way of occupying time with irrelevant material. If there are uncomfortable issues to discuss, or feelings that cause embarrassment, excessive talking can be a way of avoiding coming to grips with these feelings. If the therapist senses that you are using talk as a defense against opening up, he or she might ask you to be silent to rid your mind of smoke screens that are keeping you from coming closer to what is really bothering you.

Silence can also indicate a lack of communication between you and the therapist. If you feel uncomfortable or angry with the therapist, you are more apt to clam up and feel further resentment if he or she does not attempt to break through the silence. Often the client sits waiting for the therapist to speak or to inquire about the meaning of the silence. In part, it is up to the therapist to sense the quality of the silence and the purpose to which it is being put. However, if you are not talking because of discomfort with the therapist based on his or her insensitivity to you, the task of breaking that silence falls on your shoulders.

Therapists have been accused of using silence as a retreat of their own. Clients sometimes feel, especially if they are not face to face with the therapist, that the therapist is unconcerned when silent or using that time to daydream. This can very well be the case. If so, there will usually be other signs of the therapist's lack of interest in you as well, such as lack of attention to what you are saying or inability to remember important facts about you. More often than not, an inexperienced therapist will talk too much rather than too little. The neophyte therapist can also be uncomfortable with silent phases, fearing that they reflect his or her inadequacy as a therapist rather than a legitimate space for experiencing on the part of the client.

FREE ASSOCIATION

Freud's "basic rule" in psychoanalysis was that the client must say everything that comes into his or her head no matter how trivial, unpleasant, or irrelevant it seemed. This process is known as free association. Rather than trying to relate thoughts in an organized way, the client was instructed just to let thoughts and feelings come as they would and to be "absolutely honest" in reporting everything that came to mind. Freud likened free association to looking through a railway window and reporting to a fellow passenger the changing views outside.

The idea behind free association is that if you follow the spontaneous trend of your thoughts and feelings rather than try to organize them consciously, sooner or later important feelings and memories that have been blocked off will surface, providing the material for therapy. A client may, for example, ramble on in an associative stream about movies seen, popcorn eaten, gum wrappers on the floor, disgust with fellow movie patrons, anger at society and its filth, annoyance with spouse for making the house dirty, and a memory from youth of coming home to a filthy house presided over by a sloppily attired mother. In this stream of thought, it eventually becomes apparent that the client feels hostility toward the spouse and mother and that he or she finds it difficult to confront the issue directly. Evoking such thoughts, in addition to creating awareness of repressed feelings, helps to discharge unpleasant emotions in the process.

While orthodox Freudian therapists still use free association as the basic tool, the technique does not have primacy among therapists of other persuasions. People are psychologically more sophisticated than they were in Freud's day and more capable of zeroing in on their problems. Many therapists view free association as a process that consumes unnecessary time, and some feel that the associations are often detached journalistic recountings, which do not have enough emotional impact for the client. What matters is not just the relating of all thoughts and memories but the re-experiencing of these memories in an emotionally meaningful way. Free association is not always genuinely free and clients can hide their feelings behind an associative stream of sterile facts and details. Since most clients enter therapy because they are in some way blocked off from their feelings, they cannot engage in genuine free association. It is only after they have made some therapeutic progress that they are truly able to free-associate and re-experience the emotions that have been blocked off.

Many clients find it more meaningful to focus on their problems directly and to use free association when they are blocked and have run out of things to say. While it is difficult to free-associate in a genuine way at the outset of therapy, using the technique does encourage you to open pathways to hidden feelings and to recapture the immediacy of past experiences. If you feel that you have run dry of things to talk about or that you have already covered everything and all that is left is to repeat yourself, you might productively try free association at that point. If, however, you find that the process is not suited to you, if you find yourself unable to let thoughts and feelings flow in a genuine way, do not force yourself into free association as a primary method on a prolonged basis.

THE COUCH VERSUS THE CHAIR

The couch, originally introduced by Freud as an aid to the free association process, has become an integral part of the psychoanalytic mystique. Reducing stimulation from without by reclining in a room with subdued light fosters the flow of ideas and feelings from within. To the extent that the therapy is modeled after the psychoanalytic process and geared to a full exploration of your feelings, the couch can be a potentially useful tool. However, if your therapy is geared more to specific and immediate problems, you will probably find it easier to work on them sitting up. As a gestural process, sitting up conveys a stance of active engagement. It is a posture in which you are accustomed to think and communicate. Lying down is a passive stance associated with dreaming, fantasizing, and letting oneself be engulfed by more basic feeling processes. The posture you assume should suit the type of process your therapy is aimed at eliciting.

Since many psychotherapists practice both problem-oriented and "uncovering" psychotherapy, many offices are equipped with both chair and couch. In the initial sessions, when you are still getting to know each other, it is more suitable to sit up facing the therapist. Once your goals and ways of working together are defined, the issue of couch versus chair will more naturally settle itself. If a therapist should insist that you use one or the other, and you are uncomfortable with that choice, feel free to talk about it and to discuss your preference. While the couch can be helpful in the associative process, there is no magic in the couch and you should not feel coerced into using it.

DREAMS

Dreams have long been recognized as representing a unique aspect of human awareness and dream interpretation has figured importantly in many ancient cultures. Freud, who regarded dreams as the "royal road to the unconscious," helped to reintroduce the modern world to the psychological significance of dreams and made dream interpretation a cornerstone of psychoanalytic technique. In a dream state, a person is open to moods and feelings that are often shunted aside or overshadowed while awake; using dreams in therapy helps to broaden awareness and clarify underlying emotional patterns that otherwise might not be recognized by the dreamer.

When people start therapy, they are often unaware of having any dreams. Since research has indicated that people dream all the time, the lack of dreams seems to relate to the inability to recall them in a waking state. If you are unaware of having dreams or forget your dreams between the time of waking and the therapy session, you can probably get yourself into the habit of remembering them. When you go to bed, tell yourself that you would like to dream and when you do wake up from a dream think about it right away to let it get ingrained in your mind before drowsing off again. Keeping a pad near the bed to jot down notes on the dream as you awaken will help. Some people even keep a tape recorder near the bed and repeat the dream onto the tape as soon as they wake up. After you play it back to yourself, you will find it easier to remember the dream.

Interpreting dreams is not a difficult or mysterious process. It requires only a receptive attitude and practice in associating to the various dream elements to derive their meaning. In telling your dreams to your therapist, report them as you would any other experience. The more you recapture the dream, not just the various scenes but the feelings they aroused in you, the more you will have to work with. After re-experiencing the dream by relating it, you might get a spontaneous grasp of what the dream is saying. If not, go back over the dream, associating to the various elements in it. What do the dream situations bring to mind, and of what do the particular dream objects—schoolroom, hotel, lake, people, or whatever—remind you? If the people are unfamiliar, do any memories come to you as you think about them? If they are familiar, try to explore the situations in which you knew them and your feelings about them. Try to relate the feelings you experienced in the dream to the activities and situations within the dream. In what other situations have you had those feelings? Sometimes reconstructing what happened on the day of the dream helps capture its meaning: what did you do, what feelings did you have, and are those feelings or events somehow related to the dream? When you have uncovered this additional material, going over the dream again may help you to understand its meaning. Then your input can help the therapist help you analyze the dream as he or she adds other perceptions and associations.

The role of dreams in your therapy will vary according to the therapist's theoretical predilections. Some do not work with dreams at all and those who do have different approaches to dream interpretation. According to Freudian theory, dreams express the unconscious wishes that the dreamer cannot own up to in a waking state. The dreamer, alert to the possibility that these forbidden desires might break through, "censors" the dream so that the final dream product is a statement of the repressed wish in disguised form. The actual dream (its "manifest content") is a distorted statement of the actual wish ("the latent content"). To understand the dream, one must cut through the distortions and discover the true latent meaning. This is accomplished by interpreting the symbolism in dreams. Dream objects are not seen as meaningful in themselves but as representing other objects. For example, objects with elongated shapes, snakes, tall buildings, pencils, rifles, and so on, are assumed by Freudian therapists to be phallic symbols when they occur in dreams. The dreamer is then seen as making some statement of penis envy, fear of castration, or something pertaining to phallic strivings. Similarly, receptaclelike dream objects such as pocketbooks, bathtubs, and sugar bowls, are assumed to be symbols of the vagina and again expressive of the dreamer's sexual desire. Therapists of other theoretical persuasions take the dream images more at face value. They maintain that while snakes, buildings, and rifles do bear some structural similarity to one another and to a penis, such an approach to dream material does not deal with the question of why one dreamer dreams of the penis, another of the snake, another of the building, and still another of the rifle. A snake, like a penis, is made of living tissue, but a building is a lifeless edifice, while a rifle is not only lifeless but life negating. While the Freudian approach views dream images as a secret code in which each dream object stands for something else, other approaches view the dream images as having meaning in their own right. A cigar, which a Freudian therapist would probably also interpret as a phallic symbol because of its shape, is seen by other therapists as a cigar. The meaning of a cigar, however, is very encompassing. A cigar not only has a certain shape but it is made of tobacco, has a heavy odor that many find offensive, is usually smoked by men and often associated with smug, successful, or macho-type men who may throw their masculinity around. If you dream of a cigar you are dreaming of all elements combined as well as of some personal associations of your own. The phallic element is just one of many and may not be particularly pertinent to you.

Because dream events are often so odd and deviate so much from usual waking-state experiences, people often feel at a loss in trying to make sense out of them. Remember, though, it is your dream and you made it up, so it is well within your understanding. The major difference between your thoughts and feelings when awake and when asleep is the language you use. During the day you communicate in words, but when asleep you communicate in visual images. In interpreting your dreams, focus on what messages are contained in those images, each of which is rich in meanings that are available to you.

Because understanding clients' feelings about the therapist is very important in therapy and clients do not always feel free to acknowledge their feelings about the therapist, therapists often look for hidden signs of clients' involvement with them in dreams. If a client has a dream about a teacher it is possible, of course, that the dream is making a statement not only about the teacher but also about the therapist insofar as he or she is also teacherlike. But it also happens that therapists see themselves in dreams with little cause. The following dream interpretation, from Walter Bonime's *The Clinical Use of Dreams,* illustrates this tendency. The client had been working on her fears of the therapist's becoming really friendly with her, as it was so difficult for her to relate to people. At one session she reported acting inappropriately with people, being silly, destructive, and behaving "like an ass." As she said this she recalled a dream: she is in a nice house set in a very nice park, but inhabited by a crazy woman—wild and unreasonable. The crazy woman is very hostile to her. The client wants to stay but is afraid of the crazy woman. The therapist's interpretation of the dream was that the crazy woman was himself because the client was afraid of accepting him as a friend and because his office was on Park Avenue—the park in the dream. Overlooked in this interpretation was that the memory of the dream was triggered by the client's recognition that she is destructive and acts "like an ass." She acts, in fact, much like the crazy woman in the dream. If the focus is put on what the client is feeling, it becomes more reasonable to interpret the crazy woman as representing the crazy part of the client, her silly destructive ways, of which she is becoming aware but from which she cannot yet break. The house seems to be the client's house, where she would like to live if she could make peace with the silly part of herself who also lives there. For the therapist to assume that it is his house because of his association of a park with Park Avenue, he must also ignore the client's dream experience of the park as a park, not as a concrete strip. To insert himself into the dream, the therapist forces the dream contents to fit his interpretation and loses track of what the client is saying about herself.

An important guideline in working with dreams is that the interpretation must make sense to you. Do not accept a therapist's interpretation as valid just on his or her say-so. It must not only be meaningful to the therapist, but meaningful to you. If you feel uneasy about an interpretation because it misses the point or does not seem true to your feelings, accepting it on the therapist's authority is doing yourself a disservice.

Dreams, like everything else in life, have meanings on different levels. Therefore, dream content can be interpreted correctly in different ways. Suppose a man dreams after starting therapy that he is at the movies watching a film. That dream might be reflecting the dreamer's interest in projecting his own life on a screen for observation now that he has entered therapy, or the dream might be reflecting on the way the dreamer lives—as an observer who sits on the sidelines and watches the activities of other people. Yet another possibility is that the dream reflects the dreamer's need to relate to people according to a predetermined script because of fear of more spontaneous engagement. Any one of these interpretations might be correct, or all of them together. To get the most out of a dream, don't stop analyzing it as soon as you have an insight but look for meaning on as many levels as possible.

When you have a dream in therapy it is of immediate help in expanding your awareness of what is going on at the time, but it also has benefits for the future. Sometimes an old dream will pop up weeks or months later during a therapy session when new insights suddenly enrich your previous understanding of the dream. Keeping a record of your dreams can also help by documenting your progress in therapy. As you move along from one level to another and start to enlarge your possibilities your dreams will reflect this. For example, a woman who dreamed only of inanimate objects when she first came to therapy found her dream contents changing to incorporate various forms of life as she herself became less an object to be manipulated by others and, thereby, a more alive person.

THERAPEUTIC EXERCISES AND STRATEGIES

A host of exercises and therapeutic strategies, originally developed as therapy technique systems in themselves, have become incorporated into the more traditional psychotherapies as adjuncts to the basic talking process. These techniques have been borrowed from psychodrama, gestalt therapy, behavior modification, paradoxical psychotherapy, and other systems with the idea that, although not sufficient in themselves, they are useful in broadening awareness or in providing clients with immediate help in coping with various problems.

Role playing is a widely used technique and is practiced in many variations as an aid in helping clients deal with persons and situations that are perplexing or anxiety provoking. For example, if a woman client feels she is being exploited by her husband but is afraid to tell him off, she might role play this situation, with the therapist taking the part of the husband. By engaging the client in this interaction in as realistic a way as possible, the therapist brings the client closer to experiencing what is causing her anxiety and she gains the opportunity to practice ways of dealing with it. One variation of this technique is role reversal, in which the client takes the role of the other person with the therapist taking the role of the client. In the example above, the wife would take her husband's part and the therapist the wife's. In this situation, the client can experience how her behavior triggers responses in her husband and she can learn alternative approaches to her husband from the therapist's behavior. Role playing facilitates coming to grips with anticipated situations by putting the client in closer touch with the feelings aroused in both parties and by offering an opportunity to explore and practice various modes of behavior. A gestalt therapy variation on role playing has the client enact conflicting roles or aspects of him- or herself. The client, playing out the "top-dog" part of him- or herself—the bullying self-righteous conscience—sits in one chair yelling at that other part of him- or herself in the empty chair to "shape up" or "do better." The client then switches to the other, "underdog" chair to play out his or her submissive but tricky self who defies the top-dog aspect: "Please, give me another chance, you don't let me live!" In this way the client discharges stored-up feelings and becomes aware of his or her inner conflicts.

Exercises have been designed to heighten awareness of many

common problem areas. For instance, some exercises are specifically directed at developing assertiveness. By letting the client behave in a dramatically assertive way, these exercises enable him or her to experience directly both the bodily and the emotional components of this mode of behavior. In a typical exercise, the client stands up, feet apart, and says in firm clear tones, "Me," while striking the chest. Clients who have difficulty in self-assertion initially find such an exercise embarrassing and difficult to do, but while doing it they gradually become comfortable and build up competence in this behavior. As such exercises become spontaneous, the client at the same time assimilates the experience of self-assertion. In a similar way, other exercises direct themselves to particular trouble spots. Some try to help the client release stored-up feelings of anger. The client beats on a pillow more and more vigorously while giving vent to the angry feeling: "I hate you, I hate you." Although the activity may seem artificial at the outset, when it is continued the client becomes emotionally engaged and the experience can become very real. The exercise not only lets out anger but also helps clients lose their fears of their own aggressive feelings. Other exercises are directed at developing feelings of trust. The client, with his or her back to the therapist, falls backward into the therapist's arms. In this situation, the client's feelings of trust or distrust for the therapist are very clearly experienced, and practicing "letting go" in the fall at the same time affirms the client's ability to trust the therapist.

Another group of exercises tries to broaden the client's awareness both of the world of objects and of him- or herself as a physical being. An awareness exercise might direct the client to make up sentences stating what he or she is aware of at a particular moment as, for example, "Now I am aware of . . . how the words on this page stare up at me." "At this moment I am aware of . . . the itchiness of the chair covering." Some exercises focus on sharpening the client's contact with the environment. The client shifts attention from one object to another, noticing and verbalizing emotions: "I like this but not that part of it," "I don't like that," "This I hate." A body awareness exercise might have the client lie down with eyes closed and focus on the sensations of the body: How does the body feel, what are the points of tension, how can the body shift and reduce the tension? While becoming aware of bodily sensations such as "a pain in my neck" or "a weight on my chest," the client also tries to become aware of the intertwined feelings: "Who is giving me a pain in the neck? What is weighing me down?" and so forth. Other body exercises direct the client to emotional awareness of different body postures. Clients take various positions—submissive, assertive, angry, aggressive, and so forth—and direct their awareness to the feelings these bodily expressions evoke. Or the client can be directed to focus on a particular function of the body: "Feel yourself breathing. Feel the air going into your nose, down through your windpipe, into your lungs. Feel the rib cage expand, the chest expand. Feel the muscles relaxing, the breath exhaling." Breathing exercises are also frequently used as a means of relaxing and of controlling anxiety.

Imagination exercises focus on areas of insecurity or conflict. They require the client to imagine being in such situations and to try to capture the feelings. For example, the client might be instructed to imagine swimming nude in a pool with his or her father. The therapist then asks, "How would you feel, what would you say, what would your father say?" Or the client is asked to imagine standing next to his or her father. "Lean over and whisper something in your father's ear. What did you say? How do you feel? What does he reply?" In guided fantasy exercises, the therapist leads the client in the fantasy by offering support along the way. "Are you frightened, do you want someone with you, would you like to go on, can you do it by yourself?" When the client has successfully grappled with the problems in the fantasy and no longer feels troubled, the therapist lets the client leave the fantasy situation.

Behavior therapy techniques can also be incorporated into the therapy to help clients overcome problems involving either their own habits or interpersonal situations. For example, if one of your problems is running short on time and being disorganized or unable to accomplish all that you feel you should, you can try to work out, with the therapist's help, a reasonable schedule of tasks to set yourself in a given period. Or if one of your problems involves money, you might try working out a reasonable budget for a certain period. In the process of working on the practical aspects of a problem you might also find yourself becoming more able to come to grips with its emotional aspects. As you make entries into your budget or cross tasks off on your schedule, you can also try to focus on the feelings involved in doing so: how does it make you feel when you are spending more money than you should, and when you are spending what you consider reasonable? Similar processes can be worked out with problems involving another person. For example, when two people who live together irritate each other in little ways, each person can draw up a list of behaviors disliked in the other, and the list can be used as the basis of a compromise. Disliked behaviors can be "traded off" against each other. Tallies can be kept of the disliked behavior, and appropriate "penalties" charged against the offender—such as contributing an extra dollar to the joint account or washing the dishes twice in a row. These devices, while not getting at the root of the problem, can help to allay undue distress while therapy works at trying to deal with the source.

Some techniques are more in the nature of therapist strategies to evoke feelings and awareness in the client. One technique is for the therapist to mirror the client's behavior in an exaggerated way—to highlight certain aspects of a client's behavior. For example, if a client is stuck in the feeling that he or she has no alternative but to do the bidding of others and complains "I have so little time for me because I have to take care of Jim, meet my mother at the airport, balance the bank statement, et cetera, et cetera," the therapist might repeat these statements while assuming the martyr position of a person on a cross. Such caricatures of client behavior can convey to the client an immediate awareness of what he or she is doing, although there is a risk that this may be done in a mocking fashion. Another strategy for the therapist is to unexpectedly agree with the client when he or she expresses attitudes that are basically untrue but which he or she is unwilling to relinquish. While the client is prone to repeat these attitudes to him- or herself and to others, their falsity can become apparent when they are expressed about the client by someone else. For example, a client who hides behind an attitude of inferiority may tell the therapist, "I know why I wasn't invited to the party. I'm really kind of boring and I don't have much to offer. The others are so much brighter, they've been around, they're scintillating, but I'm dullsville." When the therapist agrees with the client, "You're right. Why should they want you at the party—you're dull and uninteresting while the others are scintillating and exciting," the client, in anger at this characterization, may be able to detach him- or herself from such self-defeating attitudes.

Therapists vary in their inclination to use and skill in using available techniques. If your therapist tries to engage you in any, it is a good idea to be experimental and see if the exercises can be helpful to you. If suited to your temperament, the various techniques can help the therapy to progress at a more rapid pace. Most clients have found, however, that while these exercises can get you out of a rut or push you along, they are not a substitute for talking and working through.

Using the Interaction

Therapy sessions encompass much more than talking about outside events. They are also a live interaction that will provide much of the material for therapy (as discussed in Chapter 9, "Feelings Between Client and Therapist"). As you work with the therapist, you are going to have feelings about what the therapist says, does, or asks. You will find yourself feeling pleased, annoyed, hurt, admired, or rejected. You will find yourself wondering, "What does he or she think of me?" "Why is he or she so quiet?" "What is he or she thinking now?" Or you might ask yourself, "How come he or she ended the session so abruptly?" "Why does he or she always interrupt me when the time is up even when I'm in the middle of a sentence?"

Whatever your feelings and regardless of whether they seem irrational, embarrassing, or insignificant, do not keep them bottled up inside. How you react to the therapist and what you do with your feelings are as much a part of you as the way you behave outside therapy. Although you will probably find it difficult at first, learn to use your sessions to discuss what is going on between you when that is what you are feeling most strongly about. The therapist is another person in your life with whom you want to establish a relationship that is meaningful to you, and you have to be able to work it out with the therapist as well as with anybody else. Indeed, the therapist should provide the atmosphere that makes it easy for you to express yourself spontaneously: to confront, to question, to complain, to appreciate, to admire, to love.

Decision Making

Clients are often uncertain whether they should ask their therapists for advice on problems such as splitting up a relationship, getting married, leaving or taking a job. Since many clients come to therapy because they are insecure and have difficulty making decisions, the temptation to ask for advice is great. The uncertainty is often compounded by the variety of therapist responses: some are eager to give advice, some do it reluctantly, and some refuse to give it altogether.

If one of your problems is that it is difficult for you to make decisions, that's certainly an area you want to work on. Psychotherapy can help you discover and work through the feelings that hinder your making decisions, but your ability to make them is undermined whenever the therapist makes a decision for you. That does not mean the therapist cannot help you in the decision-making process. He or she can help expand your awareness of what's at stake in the decision, help clarify the possibilities, and support you in facing the consequences of whatever decision you do make.

A common area in which people have difficulty making decisions is commitment to relationships. For example, a man or woman may be involved in a relationship in which the partner wants to get married. The client finds it impossible to make a decision to marry or to separate: he or she has real doubts about the potential of the relationship, but there is also much anxiety about living alone or the ability to form a new relationship. Overwhelmed by the conflict or the fear of living with the consequences of either outcome, the client wants the therapist to make the decision. In so doing, the client is asking that the therapist take the responsibility for making the choice. What the client needs is not a decision, but encouragement to take the risk involved in making one. Once the decision has been made, the client can, of course, expect continued support from the therapist in carrying through and meeting the consequences, or in reexamining the choice, if need be.

CHANGING LIFE PATTERNS WHILE IN THERAPY

You may want to, or have to, make some major changes in your life while you are in therapy. Some therapists discourage their clients from doing so, fearing that feelings stirred up in therapy that may still be unresolved will influence the change that is made. While this possibility should always be considered, life cannot be held in abeyance because you are in therapy. You have probably undertaken therapy to help you lead a more productive life; to stop living and remain static is not the way to find fulfillment. On the other hand, that you are in therapy does not mean you should force changes on yourself. Sometimes people feel that it is a good idea to make a major change earlier than they might have just because they are in therapy on the grounds that if the move does not work out they have support in dealing with the consequences. Major changes, whether in or out of therapy, should be made with sufficient time, if possible, to weigh the alternatives and to assess the feelings involved. Changing your life-style while in therapy should be helpful rather than harmful, since the therapist can help clarify your feelings and weigh different possibilities.

PACING THE THERAPY

As was discussed in Chapter 6, "The Therapy Agreement," there might be times when you want to increase or decrease the frequency of your therapy sessions. If you started therapy tentatively on a once-a-week basis, you may find that this spacing of sessions does not allow you to get into things deeply enough and that your sessions are over before you have even begun to say what you wanted to say. You may find that though such limited visits worked well in the past, now that you have gotten into a particularly troubling aspect of your feelings you need more frequent contacts to work them through. Or you might want to increase the number of sessions if you are going through a particularly difficult period caused by external stress such as a death in the family, the loss of a job, a serious health problem, or some other crisis. You may also want to increase your therapy sessions for less sound reasons. The desire for more frequent contact can actually be a desire to have the therapist take over and care for you more. Similarly, the therapist might want you to come more often to fulfill his or her needs rather than yours—becoming closer, making you more dependent, or augmenting his or her income.

Decreasing the frequency of sessions may also be called for at times. If you increased the number of your sessions to work on a particular crisis it will probably make sense to fall back into the usual tempo once the crisis is resolved. Sometimes practical issues such as a change in your work schedule or financial circumstances require you to reduce the number of your sessions. Sometimes people decrease the frequency of sessions when they feel more capable of handling problems on their own as a prelude to termination. On the negative side, decreasing the frequency may be a way of expressing anger at the therapist. You may think of coming less often if you are upset with the therapist and do not want to deal with these feelings. That is a way of giving the therapist a "slap" while at the same time protecting you from "having it out." Similarly, a therapist may suggest reducing the frequency of sessions because he or she is angry with you. The idea of reducing the frequency of sessions may occur to both of you when you feel that the therapy is getting nowhere as a way out of looking at the real problem.

Because increasing and decreasing the frequency of sessions can be in your best interest or your worst, it is important that any desire to do so, whether emanating from you or from the therapist, be carefully examined before it is accepted as a change in your contract.

REASSESSING YOUR GOALS

Clients and therapists are usually conscientious about setting goals at the start of therapy but inclined to forget about them soon after. As you get involved in therapy, you will probably find yourself a very interesting subject and may also find it easy to go far afield from your original objectives. Your digression may not become apparent unless you and the therapist periodically assess your progress. Every so often, at intervals you can stipulate, but probably at least once a year in a long-term process, you and the therapist can sum up what you have accomplished and what still remains to be done in light of your original goals.

It may, of course, be perfectly sensible to change your goals as a result of what you have learned or accomplished in therapy. You may want to set your sights higher, direct them to more specific goals, or just reaffirm the original goals. For instance, a former goal of "becoming more independent of my mother" might be expanded to "establishing a firmer sense of myself." Or a vaguer goal such as "feeling less anxious and insecure" may become the more specific "overcoming my performance anxiety and desensitizing myself to criticism." But when you change your goals, it should be a conscious process and not just something into which you drifted. The more you and the therapist are aware of and convinced about the merit of what you are working toward, the better you will both be able to work. Having clear objectives helps to keep therapy from becoming an interminable affair.

TALKING ABOUT YOUR THERAPY WITH OTHERS

Some therapists advise their clients not to talk about the therapy with anyone other than themselves. The idea behind this is that feelings might get watered down or attitudes changed by discussing them with others, making them less available for exploration in therapy. While there is merit in the position that it is always best to express your feelings directly to the person involved, a policy of restricting your freedom to talk about therapy outside the office represents a danger in its exclusivity. It also reflects a bit of grandiosity on the part of the therapist and a low opinion of you if it implies that other people are incapable of helping you to resolve these issues and that you will be unable or unwilling to bring them up once they have been talked over with someone else. Your therapy relationship must be open for inspection as much as any other relationship in your life. Of course, talking to others should not be a substitute for, or avoidance of, dealing directly with the therapist. Even though the therapist-client interaction is the core of the process, psychotherapy is not limited to the office and anything that helps you to expand your awareness is beneficial and should be encouraged.

It is very important that you let the therapist know what you do say about the therapy to others. This is not so that he or she can keep tabs on you, but to make sure that you do not avoid bringing up your feelings about therapy with the therapist. If you do, then something is wrong. The therapist may be intimidating you, or you may be angry at the therapist and trying to make him or her feel bad by not sharing important feelings with him or her that you do with others, or perhaps there are other reasons. Although you should feel free to discuss your problems with whomever you want, you must examine what is going on if your therapist is one of the people with whom you don't want to talk about your problems.

Sometimes therapists don't want you to talk with others about any issues that you should discuss with the therapist, such as unresolved feelings involved in decisions, dreams, et cetera. You might want to talk about these things because your sessions have not given you enough opportunity to explore your feelings or because you value someone else's views. Again, talking out feelings with others can dilute your experiences in therapy sessions, but the stricture to save these discussions for the therapist is not necessarily in your best interest.

EXTRACURRICULAR STUDIES

Some therapists have an injunction not only against talking about your therapy with others but also against engaging in other therapy-related activities while you are in therapy, such as reading about therapy, taking courses in therapy, or participating in workshops. This injunction is based on the notion that such outside influences might confuse you, suggest things to you that are incorrect, or dilute your therapy. Though these possibilities exist, this attitude shows very little respect for you because it concludes that the overall effect of your getting additional knowledge will be more harmful than useful.

When you are in therapy you might be stimulated more than ever to read about therapy and learn all that you can about it. The more you read, the more you know, and the more possibilities you expose yourself to, the better. If your new knowledge raises questions or brings up doubts, that's useful too. Therapy, of all endeavors, should not teach you to avoid life because life may create difficulties.

PHASES IN THERAPY

Typical therapy experiences are made up of different phases and changing moods. At the beginning of therapy, if you've made a good choice, you usually feel relieved. You have gotten over the initial hurdle of finding a therapist and are now with someone who gives you a willing ear on which to unburden yourself. Very likely you will get immediate help from the therapist in overcoming some of the most pressing difficulties you face at the time. But, as the therapy goes along, you start to realize that progress is not so quick or simple as you had hoped. The therapist doesn't seem to do anything concrete for you to make the problems go away. You begin to realize that you have a big job to do and that it is going to be tedious work. At times you will make progress and feel elated, but much of the time you will find yourself unable to move forward, and will feel discouraged. Sometimes you may even have the feeling of being worse off than before. This happens when problems and troublesome feelings you successfully warded off before begin to emerge in therapy. As you open up to these feelings they often seem to rush at you and make you panicky about your ability to control them. Even if you do not go through periods of disorganization brought on by a lowering of your defenses, you may become more disillusioned with the way you are. The status quo will no longer be acceptable to you because being in therapy makes you expect more of yourself and more out of life.

One of the more difficult aspects of therapy to accept is that progress is so unsteady. You wish for a constant rate of improvement and growth but instead find a hilly road with ups, downs, and long level stretches. Working hard does not always yield immediate payoffs, and finding out what is causing a problem does not mean that you are going to be able to shake it off. You will find yourself going over the same material again and again but each reworking, while seemingly repetitious, gives you the opportunity to develop new perspectives until problems gradually dissolve.

The ups and downs in therapy will be easier for you to live with if you have realistic expectations of what therapy is like. Typically, progress leads to anticipation of rapid changes, which is inevitably followed by disappointment. Change comes in spurts and patches, and sometimes coalesces when you least expect it.

9 Feelings Between Client and Therapist

As THERAPY involves you in a close relationship with the therapist it is likely that you will develop strong feelings about him or her. These feelings become as much a part of therapy as the other feelings you bring in from the outside. Recognizing and understanding them is a key element of most therapies.

Positive feelings toward the therapist are a precondition for success. Unless you feel good about the therapist you will not be able to open up fully and feel safe in revealing yourself. Once the therapist demonstrates that your trust in him or her is warranted, your positive feelings will be reinforced. But your feelings are more than a barometer of client-therapist match: they can be the crux of therapy. The more you tune in to your feelings as you experience them in the interaction, the more alive you are in therapy; and the more you engage emotionally, the better able you and the therapist will be to come to know you as you really are. How you react when you are with the therapist is as much a reflection of your personality as are your feelings and reactions to others. By being open to the emotional interchange between you and the therapist, you will learn as much, if not more, about yourself as you will by exploring your feelings in other situations. Your encounters with others can only be explored secondhand in therapy, but your encounter with the therapist is immediate and potentially of greater value.

THE NATURE OF THE THERAPEUTIC RELATIONSHIP

The therapeutic relationship is structured in a way that facilitates your coming in touch with and expressing feelings. Compared to other close relationships, the therapy relationship is unique in that it is not based on mutuality of obligations. In therapy the client's emotional needs always come first and constitute the prime focus of the relationship. This creates a sheltered situation in which you can more safely express yourself. Being free from fear of rebuke and from having to deal with the therapist's needs gives you the space you need to experience yourself as you really are. It is easier for you to let yourself feel anger if you do not have to worry about the therapist's counterhostility, or for you to feel tenderness if you do not have to worry about the therapist's taking advantage of it. The therapy relationship has been compared to the parent-child relationship in that both are concerned with creating an environment for growth aimed at helping the individual become autonomous. However, parent-child relationships are fraught with hidden agendas, with the parent's acceptance of the child only too often based on the child's ability to satisfy the parent's needs. The therapist, in contrast, must be prepared to make an unconditional commitment to the client and respect the client for who he or she is and is striving to become. Of course therapists, like other people, are rarely perfect, and it is unreasonable to expect that any therapist will always be able to keep his or her own needs in check and maintain that affectionate detachment necessary for good therapy. This is one reason a constant examination of your feelings toward the therapist and the therapist's feelings toward you is so essential.

Clients often say that the therapy relationship is not a "real" one. This is true in the sense that the therapist's professional role limits his or her personal involvement in order to protect the client from feeling impelled to respond to the therapist's needs. Nevertheless, the therapy relationship is real in the sense of two people having genuine feelings about each other that grow out of what takes place between them.

Therapy systems differ in their understanding of the nature and role of client-therapist feelings, but virtually all agree on their importance. Freud used the word "transference" to describe the feelings of the client for the therapist. It was his belief that people carry around unresolved feelings toward early adult figures in their lives that are then transferred onto other important people. Thus the client relates to the therapist as if the therapist were the mother or the father, and examining the transference feelings enables the client and therapist to gain insight into the client's feelings about the parents. Sullivan introduced the term "parataxic distortion" to explain the feelings of the client for the therapist: the client distorts his or her perceptions of the therapist and others based on inappropriate generalizations from prior interpersonal experiences, with early experiences serving to mold the way people are perceived in later life. The existentialists maintain that the client-therapist relationship is a genuine relationship, not a transference phenomenon, even though distorted ways of perceiving may limit the manner in which the client can relate to the therapist. The way your therapist understands the nature of your feelings about him or her is going to have an important influence on the therapy process. If the therapist thinks that your feelings are only reenactments of past feelings toward your parents, the therapist is not going to be inclined to examine his or her role in bringing out certain feelings in you. If the therapist recognizes that you are engaged in a genuine relationship with him or her, even though you may tend to distort, the therapist will be more willing to acknowledge personal responsibility for bringing out reactions in you. While there is a tendency to perceive others in terms of one's preconceptions, one also reacts to the realities of the situation and may accurately perceive a therapist to be aloof, loving, or hostile, not because of one's mother, but because of the therapist. It is important to keep in mind that a tendency to misperceive your therapist's behavior and attitude toward you does not mean you cannot also have correct perceptions. Your feelings about the therapist will be a product of both the attitudes you bring in and the attitudes your therapist presents.

YOUR FEELINGS ABOUT THE THERAPIST

Because of elements common to all therapy relationships, clients' feelings about their therapists tend to fall into certain patterns. During the early stages of therapy, assuming you have made a good choice of therapist, you will probably be very impressed with your therapist. While you came in confused, the therapist seems to be very clearheaded and insightful. He or she may quickly be able to highlight things that have been bothering you for ages and help you put your problems in a new perspective. You become impressed with how knowing your therapist is, and assign an omniscience to the therapist that he or she does not possess. Because the therapist has been able to broaden your understanding, it is easy to believe, and you will want to believe, that the therapist knows everything and can help you with everything. The more faith you have in this idealized therapist whom you are creating, the more optimistic you will feel about the therapy. You may start to fantasize that the therapist is a perfect person. If he or she is so knowing about people, his or her personal life must run smoothly and everything the therapist does must be wonderful. Unfortunately, few people are so perfect but, even more unfortunately, many therapists find it necessary to maintain your admiration of them in this way and try to encourage rather than clarify such distortions on your part. It is necessary that you respect and like your therapist, but the therapist's ability to help you understand yourself does not make him or her a superbeing. Also remember that reliance on the wisdom and expertise of a marvelous therapist is not the road to success: it is not the therapist's understanding of you that is important but the therapist's ability to help you understand yourself.

The tendency to idealize the therapist also makes it natural for you to want the reassurance of knowing that this wonderful person admires you. Do not be surprised if you find yourself courting the attentions of your therapist and trying to get him or her to take a more personal interest in you. If, for example, you have started to take more care dressing whenever you have a psychotherapy appointment, or you arrive a little earlier for your sessions, it may be that you want the therapist to take more notice of you. Perhaps your interests take a slightly different turn than they did before and, surprisingly, in the direction where you think the therapist's interests lie. If the therapist has his or her own paintings on the wall, perhaps lately you have been talking in your sessions of all those art shows you want to visit. Or maybe you have been tracking down the therapist's publications and talking about them in your sessions. It is also possible that you, like many others, will start feeling sexual interest in the therapist that you want to have reciprocated. Knowing that the therapist finds you sexually attractive is a way of knowing that you are admired. If the therapist does not respond to you with the admiration and interest you want, you may find yourself feeling hurt or rejected, and come to experience the therapist as cold and aloof. You may even start to wonder why you ever thought this uncaring person was no nice. Whatever feelings do occur, try to look at them in the perspective of your situation. Knowing that it is not unusual to feel rejected under these circumstances will help you to sort out whether your feelings are coming from unrealistic expectations or from truly callous behavior on the part of the therapist.

Unrealistic admiration of the therapist can lead to negative feelings in other ways as well. Often, when the client has built the therapist up into some godlike figure, he or she is bound to feel betrayed when the therapist turns out to be less than divine. If you do not expect perfection and the therapist does not pretend to it, you will both be better able to recognize and deal with therapist shortcomings if and when they intrude.

The exclusive focus on client needs in therapy facilitates wishful fantasies about the therapist. Because the therapist is always there for the client and does not withdraw acceptance, some clients imagine that they have found the idealized parent or lover. They try to use the therapy relationship as a substitute for other, less "perfect" relationships and become disappointed, perhaps even angry, when the therapist does not make their fantasies come true. Therapy cannot replace the missing relationships in one's life, but understanding the need to use therapy in this way can help to make possible more meaningful relations with others.

Although you will tend to look at your therapist from a typical client perspective, you will also find yourself looking at your therapist from a very personal perspective that is influenced by your particular experiences with people and the types of behavior you have come to expect from them. If you think that people find you uninteresting, chances are you will be looking for signs in the therapist that he or she is bored with what you are talking about. You might, for example, interpret a blank look as an expression of lack of interest. Or you might notice a yawn that would go unseen by another client. This, of course, does not mean that it is not possible for your therapist to be bored and uninterested in you. It does suggest that if you see your therapist acting toward you in ways that you see everybody else acting toward you, the reason may lie in your tendency to focus on such behavior rather than on the therapist's true feelings about you. An important part of therapy is learning to separate your beliefs about the attitudes of others from attitudes that are really there. This is what is known as "working out the transference feelings," although it could more aptly be called learning to perceive in broader perspective. Since you are inclined to relate to the therapist in the same way that you relate to other people, your feelings about the therapist are very important to bring up in the therapy sessions. From these exchanges you can learn the ways in which unrealistic perceptions restrict you in relationships with others. As you will also have realistic perceptions of the therapist, the ways in which you may be misinterpreting must be clear to you. You should not accept a therapist's statement that your perceptions are distorted if this cannot be demonstrated to you in some tangible way. Either the therapist is incorrect, or he or she has not done a proper job of helping you understand.

Some people feel more strongly about their therapists than others. This relates partly to the type of person you are, partly to the type of person the therapist is, and partly to the intensity of the psychotherapy process. If you are generally an emotionally reactive person you will probably find yourself feeling intensely about the therapist as well. If you are reserved in your feelings it is likely that you will be that way toward your therapist. Similarly, different degrees of emotionality on the part of the therapist will modify your responses. The place therapy has in your life is also important. When you are deep into therapy, have frequent sessions, and find yourself focusing your life on the therapy sessions, you are going to become more involved with your therapist than a person for whom therapy plays a peripheral role.

When people compare notes about their therapists, it often happens that a client may feel disappointed to learn that others have very intense relationships with their therapists while they do not, or that others are "wild" about their therapists while they experience him or her neutrally. There is no "proper" way to feel toward your therapist and the feelings that do emerge result from the combination of you, the therapist, and the goals you set. Intense positive feelings about the therapist are no guarantee of good or better therapy. Positive feelings as well as negative feelings are restricting for you if they arise out of a need to see the therapist in a particular way and to maintain a set view of the world. You want to be open in therapy to experience the therapist as he or she is, not as you would prefer to have him or her. To be open to the therapist and to his or her flaws and limitations is basically a more positive experience than to be blindly swept away by unrealistic admiration or hate. Try to evaluate your therapy relationship in terms of its meaningfulness to you, not according to what your friends are experiencing.

THE THERAPIST'S FEELINGS ABOUT YOU

According to the traditional schools of thought, therapists are supposed to be impersonal and anonymous. The reason for the dictum that therapists should not reveal personal feelings or personal information about themselves is that the less the client knows about the therapist, the more easily one can observe distortions in the client's perceptions about the therapist; whatever is imputed to the therapist is then clearly a product of the client's feelings. Many therapists have come to recognize that they are not just a blank screen or mirror for the client but a living person who exudes feelings and sentiments even when just sitting quietly. A therapist cannot avoid an emotional relationship with a client, only deny it. Even aloofness is a form of emotional relationship. Since research has shown that successful psychotherapy depends on a genuine, warm, and empathic therapist, it is hardly in keeping with psychotherapeutic goals to have a therapist who remains detached and indifferent. All therapists have feelings about their clients. Mature therapists are aware of their feelings and can keep them from interfering with their genuine concern for the clients; immature therapists either deny the existence of their feelings or put them above the needs of the client.

Therapists also tend to react to clients in the same way that they react to people at large. Therapists who are generally overbearing are also apt to be overbearing with clients. Therapists who are generally unsure of themselves as people will also be more sensitive to a challenge from a client. Therapists who are generally more comfortable with women will be more comfortable with women clients. Therapists who are very nurturing like dependent clients, while therapists who are authoritarian like submissive clients. You cannot expect a therapist not to have personal predilections, but you can expect a therapist to be aware of these feelings rather than to deny them and risk their coming to expression in an uncontrolled and possibly destructive way.

In addition to therapists' idiosyncratic feelings about clients, there are some fairly typical feelings that therapists hold toward clients. Therapists, like other people, tend to like clients who they feel like them. Hostility in clients produces anxiety and hostility in the therapist, which often causes defensive behavior. Therapists will try to pacify, withdraw from, react with counterhostility to, or "court" clients whom they perceive as having a negative attitude toward them. Less competent therapists have more negative attitudes toward clients than competent therapists. Therapists tend to be less effective when the problems experienced by their clients are similar to their own problems. Therapists' feelings toward clients can also vary day by day. Research bears out that when the therapist is feeling good, he or she will be warmer, more genuine, and more effective with the client than when feeling bad or beset by personal problems. The effects of transient moods of the therapist cannot be eliminated but they can be recognized rather than erroneously attributed to other aspects of the therapy.

There is a tendency among therapists to admit to their feelings but to put the burden of these feelings onto the client. That is, the therapist will talk about his or her feelings with the client but ask what it is about the client that produces these particular feelings in the therapist. Looking to the client's problems to understand the therapist's reactions is a valid and often fruitful technique but it can deny the therapist's role in the feelings he or she experiences. For example, if the therapist is sarcastic with the client, the therapist may ask, "What about this client makes me so hostile?" rather than putting the question, just as pertinently, "What about me makes me respond to this client in such a hostile way?" Because therapy is a relationship between two people, the therapist must ask both questions together.

One of the most problematic aspects of therapists' feelings for clients involves sexual feelings. In their need to gain approval and acceptance by the therapist, clients may become sexually seductive. Sometimes therapists see clients who are openly eager for sexual relations as a form of reassurance that the therapist is interested in them. To complicate the situation further, many clients come to therapy with sexual problems and seek therapeutic help in becoming more sexually responsive. The therapist then finds him- or herself sought after as a sex teacher and sexual object combined. Many therapists are themselves sexually attracted to a client and find it easy to rationalize their own sexual interest as a reaction to projected seduction, even when there is no sexual seductiveness on the part of the client. Since the majority of therapists are men, and the majority of clients are women, usually younger, the classic pattern of older admired man becoming sexually involved with younger admiring woman is often reenacted. The gossip about professors and their young female students or physicians and their young female patients finds its counterpart in tales about therapists and their young women clients. While there are no statistics on the extent of sexual intimacy between therapist and client, it has been openly acknowledged by many women clients, and some therapists—for example, Martin Shepard in *The Love Treatment*—used to profess a belief that such sexual encounters might be beneficial. There is good reason to believe that many more therapists engage in sexual intercourse with their clients than are willing to admit it: while within the therapy they may promote such activity as being in the client's best interest, they are quick to deny to anyone outside that they have engaged in sexual activities, thereby belying their own statements to the client. In the past, the profession of psychotherapy itself did not help much in defending female clients from such behavior on the part of male therapists. Just as in cases of rape, there was a tendency among psychotherapists to hold the woman client responsible for sexual activity between her and the therapist, attributing it to her needs or seductiveness. This attitude has changed considerably of late, but the practice of sex with clients continues. Although it is widely condemned, some therapists still tend to excuse the behavior of their fellow practitioners. A recent article in the professional literature* referred to the "dual vulnerability of both patient and therapist" and recommended a "troubled therapist service" to "diminish the abuse, and salvage both the damaged patient and the distressed therapist."

In her book *Women and Madness,* Phyllis Chesler reports on a variety of interviews conducted with women who had sexual relationships with their therapists, most with unhappy consequences. Subsequent research studies have found that sexual intimacies

---

* Seymour L. Zelen, "Sexualization of Therapeutic Relationships: The Dual Vulnerability of Patient and Therapist," *Psychotherapy* vol. 22, no. 2 (Summer 1985), pp. 178–185.

within therapy leave women with lower self-esteem than when they began therapy, and with heightened sexual difficulties. While it is understandable that sexual attraction between client and therapist can blossom in the intimate atmosphere of a therapy relationship, once the relationship becomes one of sexual intimacy it can no longer be a professional relationship. Undoubtedly contact with a warm and loving sexual partner can be therapeutic, but it is not psychotherapy. If a client and therapist have such strong feeling and attraction for each other, it is time to terminate their therapy contract. Perhaps the most abusive aspect of sexual relations between psychotherapist and client is the practice of charging for "sessions." In such circumstances, it would seem that whatever professionalism is left would be more aptly termed prostitution than psychotherapy.

10

Resistance or Incompatibility?

WHEN YOUR therapy is moving along well, you will probably feel very positive about it. Therapy seems great when you are getting tangible help with disturbing problems or when you are caught up in the excitement of growing and changing.

Negative feelings about therapy are more significant and harder to track down. Negative feelings arise not only when the therapy is not working but, paradoxically, also when the therapy is working. It is easy to understand why you would feel antagonistic to therapy when something is going wrong. But why would you feel that way when it is going right? When therapy works, it means that you are uncovering and dealing with unpleasant aspects of your existence. It also means that you are coming face to face with alternative ways of living that both beckon and make you despair. While everybody who is committed to therapy wants to change, when therapy brings you to the point where the possibility of change becomes real, strong pulls emerge from within to keep you the way you are. Long-standing life-styles cannot be given up, even if they have caused much suffering, without the anxiety of losing the familiar and the fear of confronting the unknown. Abandoning old patterns of existence when you are not sure that you can make it any other way is a frightening prospect. When therapy brings you to this point, you may want to run from it. Because the idea that one stands in the way of one's own attempts to change is very difficult to accept, most clients attempt to prevent having to acknowledge it by fighting the therapy. This blocking of therapy to avoid its impact is called "resistance."

You cannot have successful therapy without feeling resistant at times. Resistance is a sign that therapy has brought you up against something important. Feelings of resistance are disturbing to both client and therapist. They make the client feel guilty and the therapist feel frustrated. But these feelings are not to be condemned or shunted to the side. Understanding the fear that is creating the resistance can be the key to permitting you to face it and go on.

Because negative feelings about therapy can arise when the therapy is working as well as when it is not, it is important that you determine where such feelings are coming from. If you start to feel annoyed with therapy or angry at the therapist, you will start wondering: "Is it all my problem or is there something wrong with the therapist? Am I resisting or do I have a legitimate complaint?" These doubts can become very problematic and need to be ironed out with the therapist. Unfortunately, many clients don't have the wherewithal to bring up critical feelings; that's why they're in therapy. Those who can brave it out and talk about their doubts aren't always successful in clarifying their feelings, for they frequently meet with the pat phrase, "You're resisting." The therapist may point out that focusing on therapist inadequacies is a way of avoiding looking at the client's own inadequacies, or that the client characteristically reacts in an accusing and hostile manner when getting close to someone. While most therapists are very quick to see the client's resistance to continuing therapy, many are much slower to explore their own role in client dissatisfaction. Clients do resist therapy but it also happens that therapists can be unsuitable or just plain incompetent. A good therapist recognizes that when a client raises questions about the therapist's competence, more may be at stake than resistance. It should be obvious to the therapist, as it is to the client, that something is going on that needs to be explored. Only a defensive therapist will take such questions as a personal threat or view them primarily as a vehicle for the client's aggression. Trying to hurt the therapist and get in a couple of good licks is a popular game among clients, but a competent therapist will seek to explore with the client what is at the root of this need to hurt the therapist, and often it is something that the therapist has done or said. For a therapist to admit to his or her role in arousing the client's anger is not necessarily to attest to incompetency; if he or she has made an error in judgment, it remains to be seen whether it is of such magnitude that it will interfere with the future productivity of the therapeutic relationship.

When clients become distressed about shortcomings in their therapy and are intimidated about discussing these feelings openly with the therapist, they frequently try to clarify such problems with friends. This also tends to be labeled as a form of resistance. Freud originally formulated the view that any outside discussion of the therapy was an indication of resistance, and this view is still held by some therapists. Justification for such a view exists only if the client does not bring these issues up for discussion with the therapist.

Since the question of resistance is a crucial one and since many therapists are touchy when you question the therapy, below are some guidelines to help you distinguish between negative feelings stemming from resistance and negative feelings stemming from shortcomings in the therapist.

SIGNS OF RESISTANCE

If you find yourself falling into the following types of situations, you may well be dealing with resistance.

- Everything in the therapy was going alone fine, but then suddenly it seems to turn sour.
- You've been with several therapists and find yourself repeatedly coming up with the same kinds of dissatisfactions.
- The dissatisfactions with the therapist are similar to those with other important people in your life.
- Sudden attitude changes occur toward things affecting the therapy, such as finding the therapy is costing you too much time or money, or becoming convinced that therapy doesn't really work.
- The press of other activities makes you cancel or forget your therapy appointments.
- You keep the therapist in the dark about relevant issues in your life.
- You start thinking about terminating therapy long before you had originally planned.

- There's nothing specific you dislike about your therapist but you have an overwhelming impulse to flee.

While your wanting to quit therapy is the most blatant way that resistance expresses itself, these other reactions are indirect ways of withdrawing from the therapy. If you are not aware of any resistance on your part but your therapist tells you that you are being resistant, do not reject such a suggestion out of hand. Your therapist should be prepared to discuss with you the behavior on which his or her view is based, and the explanation should be plausible to you.

SIGNS OF INCOMPATIBILITY

Since the bias in the therapist's attitude tends to be toward interpretations of resistance rather than acknowledgment of realistic discontent, it is helpful to have as well some basis on which to evaluate your therapist's role in making you unhappy with therapy. Certain types of behavior on the part of the therapist suggest that your negativism is being caused by an unsuitable therapist rather than by your resistance to the therapy process. Clear and direct feelings that the therapy is not being helpful are more likely to be indicators of questionable therapy than are indirect feelings of which you are less aware. Here are some situations that suggest that the fault lies with the therapist or therapeutic relationship rather than with you:

- The therapist is not your type of person. Therapy is difficult enough without burdening it further with a lack of rapport. If you and your therapist were not meant for each other, it may be futile to try to stay together. Sometimes you feel right from the beginning that you don't make a good pair, sometimes that doesn't strike you until later. Maybe you sense the therapist is ungenuine and stereotyped. Maybe he or she is pretentious and stuffy—throwing big words around, or trying to impress you with his or her important clients. Perhaps the therapist is just plain dull and limited—he or she can't understand a literary allusion, thinks a madrigal chorus is a rock group and that *Playgirl* is a magazine for liberated women. Perhaps the therapist has other qualities that turn you off and make you wonder about how well he or she is put together: obesity, chain smoking, nervous twitches, very fussy or overly casual dress, bleached hair, and so forth. Whatever the complaint, if you're on different wave lengths you'll both have trouble tuning in clearly to each other's messages.

- There is a value conflict. Very often, barriers to therapy are created by a divergence in basic values between you and the therapist. Mutual respect for each other's ethics, style of life, and future goals, whether in or out of therapy, is a prerequisite for a productive relationship. The therapist may be too conventional in outlook and frown on your search for new ways to fulfill yourself, or he or she may indiscriminately swing with each new fad while you are looking for more meaningful and lasting experiences. Perhaps the therapist is a sexist who belittles your struggle to establish your sense of self-worth as a woman. Or perhaps the therapist feels your radical politics are nothing more than an adolescent rebellion. If you don't accept the therapist's values, or feel that he or she pooh-poohs yours, you'll have a tough time making a go of it.

- Your therapist is a cold fish. If you experience the therapist as too cold or aloof, you may not be receiving the kind of emotional warmth that is needed for relationships aimed at personal growth. While the purpose of therapy is not to provide you with a new friendship, a friendly and responsive atmosphere helps you mobilize your strengths. A therapist may try to mask an inability to extend him- or herself to you by labeling his or her behavior as professional distance. Such emotional detachment may not, however, be serving your interests as much as the therapist's defenses.

- Your therapist is a "star." It is very exciting to be "in" with a therapist who has flair, who sparkles, and who exudes "personality" and charm. Such magnetism can easily turn into hero worship, however, and become overpowering. While it is easy to get started with a very expressive therapist, and to become fascinated by his or her charisma, in the long run such an influence can be stifling. An intense, personal relationship with such a therapist can rob you of your autonomy and, perhaps more dangerously, your objectivity about what is going on. Some therapists exist as a type of guru and feed on the admiration of their cultists. Excessive devotion to the therapist subverts the quest to find power and value within yourself.

- Your therapist is hung up on unimportant areas. If the therapist repeatedly encourages you to discuss issues that don't seem particularly relevant to you it may be because his or her needs are overshadowing yours. Sometimes a therapist may spend much of the session pressing you for details of your childhood, a dream, or a personal encounter. Or the therapist may want details on a party, a play, or some other event you may feel is not important. In these cases, the value of such probes may be only in feeding a therapist's need for theory confirmation, or for gossip or vicarious excitement. If you feel your therapeutic time could be spent to better advantage, it probably could.

- Your therapist is hung up on you. You might sense that your therapist is overly involved in you personally rather than as a client. He or she may be jealous of your other interests or relationships and become critical of your attempts to move out into the world. In extreme cases, a therapist's needs get played out in more active abuses of clients such as inducing a client to have sex with him or her under the guise of liberating the client's blocked ability to love, be intimate, or have orgasms. To maintain control of a client, some therapists threaten dire consequences if you want to leave the relationship: "You'll become an alcoholic again"; "You'll fall apart." The main threat is, however, remaining locked into such a manipulative relationship.

- Your therapy is in a rut. If you find your sessions becoming increasingly uneventful and face them as another chore to be gotten through, something is wrong. Perhaps you are both tired, bored, or disillusioned, and the therapist is unable to find a different approach to which you can respond. Perhaps your therapist feels that your problems are so ingrained that he or she sets the goals too low. For example, the therapist may regard you as so basically passive and unresponsive that he or she doesn't try hard enough. Conversely, perhaps you have advanced to a level of feeling that places greater demands for emotional intensity on your therapist and he or she may lack the emotional competence to face up to your newfound strengths and independence. While the therapist was adequate before, he or she may no longer measure up to the job and back off from the confrontation you seek.

- You feel down on yourself after therapy sessions. If you leave sessions feeling depressed and more displeased with yourself than before, this sense of dissatisfaction may be coming from an inadequacy in your therapy. As in any other relationship, there is always a possibility that the interaction with the therapist may be inherently damaging rather than constructive. Your bad feelings may stem from disappointments with the therapy or the way you are allowing yourself to be treated within therapy. Of course, many depressive feelings that emerge in sessions have nothing to do with the therapist, and may even reflect the problem that brought you to therapy in the first place. But you should distinguish between those downs that brought you into the therapy, and those that you take away from it.

- You feel forced into a mold. Another way the therapist's needs can intrude into therapy is by his or her encouraging you to react and respond in ways that do not seem right for you. Therapists often feel that they know best, and see their role as getting you to accept this. The therapist's need to maintain control over you and to preserve status as the authority may push you into uncomfortable corners. For example, the therapist may expect you to be compliant and cooperative as a sign of your "adjustment." Refusal to accept an interpretation about yourself becomes a sign of your "resistance." Arguing the point with the therapist becomes further proof of your guilt (by revealing the depth of your resistance). Your need for independence is seen as negativism toward the therapist. Acquiescence on your part, while ostensibly for your benefit, may really be working against you.

- You both behave in destructive ways. Sometimes therapy becomes an unending series of senseless arguments, blame-throwing sessions, or attempts to tear down each other's sense of self-respect. If the destructiveness cannot be resolved, it indicates a failure in the relationship. Such blaming and accusing often stem from a disillusionment of client with therapist or vice versa. If either one has unrealistic expectations of the other (which should not have been allowed to flourish in the first place), failure for them to materialize leads to frustration and anger. Like the child who finds the idealized parent is really weak, or the parent who finds the unrealistically appraised child is not a genius, the disillusioned client or therapist can find frustrated expectations turning into deep resentment.

- Your therapist is inconsiderate or selfish. Many clients feel annoyed at certain ways the therapist acts or at certain things he or she does, but accept these as occurring naturally in any therapy. Inconsiderate behavior, however, not only is unnecessary but should not be tolerated. While occasional lapses can be overlooked in a therapist as in anybody else, repeated occurrences should not be accepted. Some frequent abuses clients needlessly take for granted are: cutting sessions short, changing or not keeping appointments, reading mail or falling asleep (yes, this really happens), rigid refusal to discuss a problem on the telephone, inflexibility in charging for missed hours, lack of concern for your immediate problems (job demands, family needs, sickness) that interfere with maintaining regular therapy appointments, or unreasonable demands on you in terms of fees or time of appointments. Also to be questioned are objectionable personality traits that repeatedly manifest themselves, such as excitability, belligerence, defensiveness, argumentativeness, sarcasm, lack of patience or sense of humor. Your therapist should, at the very least, be able to treat you with the ordinary respect and courtesy due another human being.

- Your therapist won't discuss your doubts. One indication that therapy is not working out is a therapist's refusal to discuss your doubts about the therapy. If you should bring up any of the above points, or want to talk about any other doubts or discontents and the therapist refuses to do so, then his or her adequacy as a therapist is suspect. Some therapists may let you ramble on, but then become very defensive and/or accusing. Perhaps most telling of all, some therapists may angrily reject you, telling you, "If you don't like it here get out!" If that should happen, it is probably the best advice the therapist has ever given you.

You can, and should, discuss these issues with your therapist, but if such discussions get you nowhere, you are still left with the job of deciding what is causing your displeasure with therapy. Sometimes an outside opinion is useful. You can go to another therapist to consult about your quandaries but here, too, you must be on guard against biases. Some therapists are prone to see the therapist as always in the right, while others are happy to help you find fault with your therapist because that gives them a sense of superiority over their colleagues. Other biases might exist about the particular type of therapy you are in or about the professional training of your therapist (whether medical or psychological). More recently, the gender of the therapist has become an issue, with some female therapists decrying the sexist influence of male therapists on female clients. Of course there are therapists who will be able to help you clarify your feelings and the issues involved without biases clouding the picture. The point is, it is just as important that you exercise discretion in choosing a consultant and accepting his or her interpretations as it is when you choose a therapist. You might also try discussing your problem with an informed friend. Getting feedback from a person you respect who has no vested interest in the situation may help you clarify your feelings and reformulate your own thinking.

Ultimately you, and only you, have to be the one to decide whether you and your therapist are incompatible. Don't be afraid to listen to your own feelings and use your own judgment; if you sense that things are going wrong, you are probably right.

INCOMPATIBILITY IN GROUPS

Just as major disparities between client and therapist can create an unproductive relationship, major differences among group therapy members in terms of basic values and orientations can also prove disruptive. While it is usually helpful to have variety in a group, it is not conducive to constructive efforts when there are strong antagonisms and very divergent outlooks. If you are a single person, for example, or recently separated, you will not find it useful to work in a group with others who think preserving marriage is the highest calling in life. If you feel that a group is condescending because you are the only one without a college education, it does not necessarily follow that you have to stay and work this feeling through. It could very well be that it is a snobbish group and you should not burden yourself with it when you could get more out of a group experience with other people. Similarly, if you feel that the other group members are unsophisticated and insensitive, this does not necessarily mean that you are a snob. It may indicate instead that you would benefit more from a group experience in which the other members were more tuned in to you and your way of thinking. Your time in the group should not be spent fighting the others but working with them, and whatever facilitates supportive interaction is going to make for a productive group experience.

If you are critical of the group, ask yourself if your criticisms are valid or defensive. You might not get much help from the group in evaluating your feelings because the group exerts pressure on its members to belong. The therapist will probably ask you to express your criticisms to the group, and you should do that if you possibly can. But if you can't confront the group, do not let your difficulty in asserting yourself keep you bound to a group that is not useful to you. By the same token, if you are in a group that starts to shrink and you and the other group members feel that there are not enough participants, you are not bound to continue attending the group. When the group is no longer productive it should be disbanded. The therapist should suggest the dissolution of the group when it begins to fizzle, but if he or she is negligent in this respect the group members have to bring up the issue of dissolution themselves.

11 *Terminating Therapy*

How DO you know when it's time to stop therapy? The obvious answer is that you terminate when you reach your goals. The problem with this answer is that few people have goals that are so specific. If you do come to therapy to overcome a particular symptom or problem, then knowing when to terminate is relatively easy. But if you come to therapy because you want to grow and become freer as a person, then the decision becomes more difficult because there is no clear ending to personal development. The decision to terminate therapy in that case is based not on reaching a perfect solution to your problems but in having developed the ability to keep growing and searching on your own.

WHEN IT IS TIME TO STOP

The realization that you are ready to terminate therapy comes about gradually. A variety of changes take place in you that, after a while, add up to the feeling that you are ready to go it alone. No two people experience this the same way, but some typical changes are being more open to feelings, appreciating the good things about yourself, becoming able to see things more clearly, and having a greater sense of confidence. You become able to let go of past hurts and realize that future satisfying relationships are possible and attainable. You feel ready to embrace life more fully and tolerate the anxieties that are part of an open encounter with life. With the assimilation of these gains, the principle of diminishing returns sets in: you realize that the burdens of therapy, the time, effort, and money involved, are starting to outweigh the benefits.

As you begin to change and feel your own power, you will also start to notice changes in the relationship between you and the therapist. The therapist will become more and more like any other person to you. You will be able to recognize your therapist for what he or she is and not approach him or her with awe or with unrealistic expectations. You will be able to accept his or her limitations without feeling angry or betrayed. You will find it easier to confront the therapist, you will be able to tell the therapist when you think he or she is wrong, and you will be able to disagree without questioning yourself first or worrying about the consequences. You will find that you have become more genuinely active in your sessions and have taken on more and more the role of the therapist. You will look less for guidance, realize there is less work to do, and find time to share more information and laughter. You will be able to think of the idea of separation without becoming panicky and wondering what will become of you. Finally, you will start feeling somewhat restless in coming to therapy and wonder if it isn't time to quit.

How to Terminate

Termination is not a specific act, but the last phase of therapy. The first aspect of termination is to clarify your reasons for wanting to terminate and to explore for resistance as well as for positive indicators. While some clients are prone to wait for the therapist to suggest that it is time to terminate, it is really up to you to know when you are ready. In fact, the therapist may wait for you to bring up this issue as a sign that you really are ready to leave.

Sometimes the client wants to terminate and finds that the therapist disputes his or her readiness to do so. This creates a difficult situation for the client, who then has to gain the therapist's approval, leave without it, or stay in therapy without being committed to doing so. If you feel you are ready to terminate and the therapist disagrees, it is up to the therapist to point out and discuss with you the reasons why. Since resistance is an inevitable phenomenon in psychotherapy, it often happens that clients have a desire to flee when they come face to face with more difficult problems. The therapist's function is to help you clarify your need to terminate at that particular point and to present in a straightforward manner what he or she considers the drawbacks to termination. Some therapists, if they have very strong feelings about a client's termination, either because they fear that it may be dangerous for the client or because of their own needs, try to persuade the client to remain in therapy. Sometimes a therapist may even arouse a client's anxieties by predicting a relapse as a result of terminating. Although the therapist may be correct in his or her predictions or reasons, he or she should not try to force you into staying any more than he or she should make any other decisions for you. The therapist's responsibility is to clarify what is involved in your decisions, but he or she must leave them up to you. When you and the therapist remain at odds, and you find it difficult to evaluate the situation, it is a good idea to consult another therapist.

Once you have reached a decision to terminate—with, one hopes, the therapist's concurrence—set up a time so that your remaining work can be done with a specific end date in sight. Part of the ending period is used for reviewing and integrating what has gone on in therapy. It is helpful to tie up the loose ends and know where you are, where you want to go, and the resources you have to rely on. During this period you will want to do as much of the therapeutic work as possible, not only because you are ready to be your own therapist, but to help you experience that power in yourself. The therapist's role during termination is not so much to be a therapist as to make sure that you become aware of any tendency to leave that job to someone else.

Setting aside a specific time for termination also has the advantage of getting you and the therapist used to the idea of separation. When your termination date is fixed and you both know you are winding up, it helps you become accustomed to the idea of no longer having the relationship.

TERMINATION ANXIETY

If you have qualms about your decision to terminate you may suddenly find new problems or experience old problems with an urgency you did not have before. While you can pinpoint new areas you still want to work on, your final sessions are not the time to start that work. Termination is a time for integrating what has been accomplished, not for opening up new problem areas, except for those brought up by the termination process itself. When you have terminated, you may find that the problems about which you suddenly became anxious do not seem as awesome as they did before and that your temporary panic has dissipated.

Even though you may be comfortable about a decision to terminate, once that decision is made anxiety about termination can still set in. This is apt to occur when there has been a productive and close relationship with the therapist, because the impending loss is then a significant one. Termination anxiety is especially likely if previous leave-takings in your life were unsatisfactory and if the residual feelings from those separations were either not adequately dealt with in the therapy, or not a focus of therapy. The therapist, too, might be prone to termination anxiety and unready to give up the relationship with you because of his or her own psychological shortcomings, as we will discuss in the section on delayed termination, or because your anxiety about termination makes the therapist feel guilty for not having helped you sufficiently to work through those feelings earlier.

It is important to recognize such possible reactions to termination for what they are. For you, they provide an opportunity to work on those issues before ending therapy, and for the therapist, they enable him or her to guide your termination to a good conclusion. If termination anxiety is not recognized it is likely to lead to various defensive maneuvers that could spoil the ending of therapy. One common reaction is to deny the importance of the therapy relationship, causing both client and therapist to feel rejected. Or one of you may make light of the termination and thereby not provide enough time to explore and work through termination issues. Another reaction is to become angry and to blame each other for having fallen short of the therapy goals in some way. Still another is to withdraw from engaging each other emotionally in the ending sessions, creating a shallow termination that leaves both parties feeling empty.

PREMATURE TERMINATION

People often stop therapy before they have reached their goals or have approximated the possible benefits. Such premature terminations may be brought on by either the client or the therapist. Premature client terminations occur for a variety of reasons, some good and some bad. As was discussed in Chapter 10 ("Resistance or Incompatibility?"), sometimes you have to terminate therapy because it is unproductive or destructive. You might also want to terminate prematurely when you are in productive therapy because of resistance to change, and guidelines for assessing such resistance have already been given. Sometimes, when people are afraid of what the therapy may uncover, they find that they suddenly lose their symptoms and start to feel fine. This "flight into health" occurs because the person finds it easier to relinquish a particular symptom than to relinquish the defensive system on which it is based. In such a situation, the flight into health is rarely permanent and symptoms or distress usually reappear in short order. Some people terminate prematurely because they despair of ever being helped and they just give up even trying. Both extreme despair and a flight into health, while evidencing the client's resistance to change, also indicate that the client does not have enough faith or trust in the therapist to help him or her through the struggle. Conversely, another reason for premature termination is the unwillingness to let another person be helpful. People who find it difficult to enter therapy because they are afraid of becoming dependent on the therapist are apt to terminate prematurely to nip the possibility of such dependence in the bud. They want to make sure that they can manage everything on their own and do not like to acknowledge the need for others. Some clients terminate prematurely as soon as they have made some tangible progress. They are not dissatisfied with the therapy; rather, their gains make them overly optimistic and they leave therapy out of elation at what they have accomplished, but before they have gotten fully into it.

Premature terminations fostered by the therapist are similarly motivated by good and bad reasons. Sometimes a therapist will suggest early termination because he or she feels realistically unable to help the client any longer. The therapist may feel that his or her particular way of working is no longer suited to the client's needs or temperament or that he or she just does not know how to meet the client's needs. In such a case the therapist might suggest that the client terminate their relationship and continue therapy with someone else. Although such a suggestion is apt to be experienced as a rejection by clients, it is offered in their best interest. A therapist might also suggest a temporary break in therapy to give a client time off to assimilate what has been going on and to consolidate gains. In this case, the termination is also suggested in the interest of the client.

It also happens that therapists encourage termination because of their own needs. A therapist might start to feel very uncomfortable with a client whose progress is slow because that makes the therapist feel inadequate. The therapist may then exaggerate signs of progress to convince him- or herself and the client that the therapy has been successful and suggest termination before the client is ready. Therapists may also terminate prematurely because they basically don't like a client and just don't want to work with him or her any longer. It could be that the therapist did not realize the extent of this dislike at the outset of therapy or that he or she needed to fill the time and decided to put up with the client until a "better" one came along. If a client, or the client's problem, is experienced by a therapist as very threatening and the therapist is not able to tolerate these anxieties, the therapist might suggest termination, using a variety of excuses. Even if a client does not upset the therapist, but the relationship just does not satisfy his or her needs, the therapist may want to replace that client with another who is more readily accessible to his or her influence or more admiring. Sometimes therapists terminate prematurely for reasons unrelated to therapy: they want time off to write a book, to see a higher-paying client, to cut down their hours, or any one of a number of personal reasons. When clients are rejected for such reasons, therapists rarely acknowledge them and try to put the responsibility for ending therapy on the client by suggesting the client is unmotivated, too resistant, or "not a candidate for psychotherapy." Such a rejection does not reflect on you. Although it is painful, you must keep in mind that it comes from the therapist's problems rather than from yours.

DELAYED TERMINATION

As with premature termination, termination may be delayed by either the client or the therapist for a variety of reasons. Clients delay termination when they are unduly afraid they cannot make it without the therapist's help. Sometimes, even after they become aware of the desire to leave, they suddenly revert to unproductive patterns of behavior as a way of convincing both themselves and the therapist that they are not yet ready to go. Clients also become addicted to therapy, afraid to face life without their weekly "fix." When termination is delayed for such reasons, it is usually because the client's dependency needs or the therapist's need to maintain control have not been worked out. It is very hard to terminate if you are getting the message from the therapist that he or she feels you have not attained sufficient strength to be on your own. Some persons, while realizing they are ready to leave therapy and able to handle the problems they came in with, fear that they may not have the resources to deal with new problems that arise. In such a case, it is up to the therapist to help the client make the break, with the understanding that it is always possible to come back and resume therapy if and when necessary.

Occasionally therapy is prolonged because of side benefits. If a client has been using therapy as a way to obtain special indulgences from others ("What do you expect from me—you know I'm in therapy"), he or she may be unwilling to give up these secondary gains. In such a case, this need to garner attention or make excuses is itself a problem that the therapy could still profitably work out.

Some clients delay bringing up termination because they are afraid of offending the therapist. Therapists sometimes do feel rejected if a client wants to leave. The therapist may feel guilty that the client will leave before the therapist has "finished the job" or because he or she is afraid that the client wants to leave because the therapist has not been effective enough. Although you may be correct in expecting that your therapist will be upset with your leaving, this is no reason to delay terminating. You have to leave when you are ready: you are not in therapy to work out the therapist's problems.

Therapists may also try to delay termination. A therapist may want to hold on to a client because that person has some particular quality that is attractive. For instance, quite a few clients come from glamorous worlds—the theater, broadcasting, politics, publishing—since generally these are the people with enough money to pay for therapy. For many a therapist whose private world is rather drab by comparison, having a relationship with such a worldly figure becomes a vicarious route to participating in the exciting goings-on. Such a client may also be the therapist's entree to other prominent clients. Therapists have a tendency to evaluate their status according to the status of their clients, so that letting an "important" client go can mean a loss of personal prestige as well.

One of the most obvious reasons for keeping a client in therapy longer than desirable is financial. On the average, a client who comes twice a week represents a fee of about $7,000 a year. If there isn't another client on the waiting list, that's a big chunk of income walking out the door. If the therapist is open and responsible, he or she will face it and not let it stand in the way of indicated termination. But if such monetary anxieties are not recognized, the therapist might doggedly insist that the client stay in therapy, without looking at why the client wants to leave, since that would necessitate dealing with his or her own concern over the money.

A therapist may also be unwilling to let a client go because of his or her positive involvement and personal growth needs. A client, to a therapist, represents a great deal of time and effort. A therapist gets involved in a client's progress as a writer gets involved with a manuscript, a chemist with an experiment, or a mathematician with a complex equation. Once a therapist gets drawn into the client's problems and into the client as a problem, it is difficult to let go for the simple reason that people don't like to leave engrossing work half done. There is a drive for completion, a drive for resolution, a desire to polish things and to create something whole and beautiful. Any therapist with any degree of involvement with his or her clients is apt to feel that his or her work is being taken away without a chance to finish up if the client leaves too soon. When a therapist is engaged in a client's therapy to the point where his or her own growth processes are stimulated, giving up the relationship also means losing that avenue for the therapist's own development.

Still another reason a therapist may want to keep a client in therapy are the feelings he or she develops for the client over time. When a therapist becomes genuinely fond of a client, it is natural that he or she doesn't want to lose the relationship. When such a person leaves, the therapist loses more than just another client.

Perhaps the most common reason for delaying termination involves both client and therapist. Each may experience a sense of loss and sadness at having to end a relationship that has been intense and meaningful. Unable to bring themselves to part, client and therapist drag out the therapy even though there is nothing much to be accomplished any longer. When these feelings of affection and mutual unwillingness to sever ties are openly acknowledged, the separation becomes easier to bear. Facing these feelings and being able to live with the loss is, in a way, the ultimate test of the therapy.

UNPLANNED TERMINATION

Sometimes, even though you might not want to, you have to terminate therapy for reasons extraneous to the therapy. This might be necessitated by a sudden drop in your income, a move to a new location, a long-term illness. When you find that you can no longer come to therapy, it is a good idea to explore with the therapist the factors involved. Even though external events occur that make it difficult to continue, sometimes clients use these happenings as a way of leaving therapy when they do not want to face their own resistance to continuing. For example, if a loss of a job means you cannot pay your fee, do you announce your intention to quit before discussing the possibilities of a lowered fee with the therapist? Or, if you have to relocate, are you looking into the possibilities of a therapist at your new location? While you are free to quit for any reason you want, make sure that you are aware of your real reasons for doing so and not hiding them from yourself.

When you have to terminate for reasons beyond your control, you may experience this as a real loss. Perhaps the break will be temporary. In the meantime you can try to continue on your own, exploring your feelings and being more open with yourself. Perhaps you can continue to have intermittent contact with your therapist, if not in person, by mail.

Therapists may also terminate the therapy for reasons external to the therapy. In such instances clients always feel rejected and, in fact, they are since the therapist is saying that other things in life are more important than continuing the relationship with the client. The therapist should be prepared to tell you why he or she has to terminate and to give you advance notice. Since you might have strong feelings about the therapist's leaving, he or she should make sure that you have the opportunity to express them fully. If you request help, the therapist should be prepared to suggest a replacement.

In unplanned terminations, as well as in planned ones, it is a good idea to use the last sessions to tie up loose ends by summing up work done and work remaining.

Chronic or Interminable Therapy

It is difficult to decide when to terminate therapy even when you sense you have made progress and are close to becoming the kind of person you want to be. But knowing whether to terminate when you have been dragging on in therapy for years without satisfactory progress is even more difficult. How long should therapy go on? Some people accept therapy as a part of their lives and become chronic clients: they may have put in ten or twenty years in therapy and are prepared to keep going even with no end in sight. Others put in many years but are troubled that they keep going and going. If a person feels he or she needs continued therapy, is it a good idea to keep it up indefinitely?

In part, the feeling that therapy drags on comes about from a false expectation that it should make rapid changes in a person's life. Many personal growth systems promise transformations in weeks or even weekends, and so the prospect of years of therapy seems a bit much by contrast. Yet to change one's way of life, to relinquish ingrained patterns, to search the depths of one's soul, and to learn new ways of being must take time. There are no miracle cures. Sometimes people seemingly change overnight, and certain experiences do have profound effects. When such sudden changes do occur, it is usually because the groundwork has already been laid for change. Years of therapy may appear to have no effect, but a concentrated growth seminar afterward may produce wonders because the soil was fertile. Thus "interminability" in therapy is often a product of faulty expectations.

Of course, it may happen that therapy drags on unduly. In some instances clients use never-ending therapy narcissistically, seeking to establish their complexity and specialness by virtue of the time required for the therapist to come to understand and know them. Although such clients could use therapy in order to come to terms with their poor self-image, the therapist should not allow interminable therapy to serve the needs for self-embellishment but confront those needs head-on. In such a confrontation, the therapist may have to insist on termination if the client wants to prolong therapy for ultimately self-defeating reasons.

Some clients who are stuck in the past and exceptionally resistant to change move at a frustratingly slow pace, making little progress over the years. Because of severe early deprivations and resentments, such clients just cannot give up the immature demand that life owes them something and has to make it up to them. They persistently reject taking responsibility for themselves and seek in therapy a way to balance the ledger rather than a way to close the account books. In such a situation there is serious question whether a person should continue in therapy indefinitely. After one has put in years working on the therapy and the results remain uncertain, there comes a point when one should terminate, ready or not. Staying in therapy may serve to strengthen the expectation that the pains and problems of living can be taken over by others. It may well be that venturing forth without supports will help one to build on what has been accomplished. Despite the fear of going it alone, everybody sooner or later has to take the chance. This does not mean that one cannot look for help again, but first one should try it alone. If a person finds it necessary to reenter therapy, that is always open to him or her and new types of therapeutic experiences should be considered as possibly offering broader avenues for movement and change. Chronic clienthood not only saps the client's incentive to dare life on his or her own but also tends to sap the therapist's vitality or ability to work creatively with the client. If a client progresses slowly the therapist also finds little room to grow and may lose the feeling of challenge necessary for good therapy. Despite the therapist's guilt at "abandoning" a client who wants to continue on and on, it is usually the best solution.

Occasionally clients linger on indefinitely in therapy because of a continued need for external support when more appropriate sources are not available. For example, adolescents who come to therapy with behavior problems frequently find, once they get these sorted out, that there are no adult figures or other sources available for continued guidance. In such a case, the therapist, unwilling to leave the client in the lurch, takes on the role of guidance counselor and surrogate parent, and the so-called therapy becomes a long-range affair. Similar situations can occur with disadvantaged persons who face a paucity of support services, with persons of limited inner resources who need continual guidance to function in a complex society, and with persons who through unusual circumstances find that there is no one available to serve as friend or companion. Though the therapist can provide tangible help for these persons, such help is not psychotherapy. It is difficult for a therapist to refuse a client in need, but it is questionable whether a therapist should offer his or her services in such a setting. Offering guidance and companionship under the guise of therapy maintains the fiction that the client's problems stem from self-imposed limitations, whereas in reality they stem from shortcomings in the environment. Therapy should not obscure the truth; its ultimate job is to encourage people to face the truth of their situation and to help them modify it or learn to live with it. Every professional role has its limitations and a therapist cannot respond to all client needs at all times. A therapist who is truly committed to such clients would be of greater help by working for the establishment of necessary support services than by trying to offer such services him- or herself.

CONTACTING THE THERAPIST AFTER THERAPY HAS ENDED

Most clients often think of the therapist and would like to share information with him or her about certain events or accomplishments after therapy is terminated, but they hesitate to do so, fearing that the therapist is no longer interested and would consider it an intrusion. If your therapy was successful, you should be able to follow your impulses in this regard and do what you feel like doing. Although therapists rarely initiate follow-up contact with former clients, most will be very pleased to hear from you and appreciative of your wanting to keep them posted. Aside from the genuine interest that one person develops for another after such close contact, therapists are interested in what happens to you because they have a lot at stake in your continued progress. How you make out and what you do when you leave therapy reflects in part how effective the therapist has been. As it is less appropriate for the therapist to pry into your life after therapy is over, if any contact will be kept it will most likely be up to you to take the initiative. If the therapist does not care about you once you are no longer his or her client, that is a loss for both of you. However, unless your parting has been unpleasant, don't deprive both of you by acting on that assumption.

12 *Starting Again*

IF YOU have had a bad or nonproductive therapy experience you will be faced with a dilemma. You will probably be drawn back to therapy to work out the problems that remain unresolved. But having been burned, you will probably be hesitant about trying it again. This is not an uncommon situation. Because of the hazards of the field, many people have suffered disappointment in psychotherapy and had to go looking again. Fortunately, the second stab at psychotherapy usually works out better than the first. In fact, many therapy clients report that their most significant therapy experience was not with their first but their second (or third) therapist. The second time around you are more alert to shortcomings in the therapist and more focused on what you need in order to have successful therapy. In a sense, persisting until you find what you need is not really starting again, but continuing with an important task that you have committed yourself to undertaking.

People are drawn back to therapy not only after an unsuccessful try, but sometimes after a good therapy experience as well. Various circumstances can create a need for further therapy even when the first experience has been productive. Sometimes, if you leave therapy at the first signs of strength, you may not have had sufficient time to consolidate your gains. Sometimes it happens that after leaving therapy you find yourself coming up against new problems that you could not anticipate and that you feel you cannot handle on your own. It might happen that you find you cannot really progress as much as you would like or as much as you thought you would be able to, without help. Or you might feel a desire to work on more ambitious goals than you set the first time. Resuming therapy after good therapy can also be difficult.

Obstacles to Starting Again

When you are not able to get as much out of life as you want or find that problems are starting to bother you again, the thought naturally occurs to you to go back to therapy. If it helped you once, it should be able to help you again.

But this desire is often counterbalanced by a feeling that there is something wrong with you if you can't work things out on your own. Some people feel that once they have been in therapy they shouldn't need help anymore; admitting the need for help makes them feel like a failure. Sometimes one's friends and relatives may reinforce this feeling. They might mock the need for therapy as a sign of weakness or self-indulgence: "Oh, he can't live without a therapist"; "She needs somebody to make a fuss over her once a week"; "What's the matter with you—why don't you stop supporting a shrink and buy yourself a new suit?" To bolster the feeling that they are capable of managing on their own, these persons may not follow through with a desire to resume therapy.

It may also happen that as you feel a need for further therapy you start to feel angry at therapy. Why do you need more therapy? If it really works why are you still troubled? You start to feel that the original therapy has let you down, that it didn't do enough for you. This anger might disillusion you about your prospects and turn you against the idea of going back to therapy.

If you are doubtful about the merits of starting again, it is often helpful to review where you were when you terminated. The optimism you felt at that time about your newfound strengths probably encouraged you to stop therapy even though you knew you were not a finished person—and could never be. There is no final point at which you are complete, there is no way to be problem-free, and there is no way not to experience anxiety, unless you are dead. It is not necessarily a sign of your weakness or of the inadequacy of your previous therapy that you once again find yourself coming across new obstacles and new problems. If your life were static and not progressing, there would be no new challenges to throw you off. The new crises that you meet—should you take that new job, should you break off that relationship—indicate that you are open enough to expose yourself to new risks and broader possibilities.

Therapists, too, often find subsequent rounds of therapy helpful. Freud was the first to insist that therapists periodically undergo reanalysis. One can never know oneself perfectly at any given moment since one is always in the process of evolving. To be totally open to oneself means, therefore, to be always reexamining oneself. Reentering therapy, for client or therapist, is a testament to one's unending search for self-responsibility and autonomy.

THE SAME OR A DIFFERENT THERAPIST?

Whether you will do better with the same therapist you had before or with a new therapist will depend on your previous relationship and what you are going back for.

If you are returning for a short-term consultation about a particular problem, or for a "booster shot," it is probably best to see the same therapist again. Being familiar with you and your needs, that person will be better able to help you in a short series of concentrated sessions.

If you are returning for extended psychotherapy, the choice of the same or a different therapist hinges on a number of considerations. When people have had an exceptionally good therapy experience they not only are drawn back to the same therapist but, perhaps, afraid to try someone new. They might feel that no one else could possibly enable them to repeat the same kind of positive results. Such a feeling implies that the effectiveness of the therapy depends entirely on the therapist, and ignores that therapy can be productive only because of the combined efforts of you and the therapist. Given a competent therapist whom you like and respect, there is no reason why you cannot repeat your initial success. You might also feel drawn to the same therapist as before because you know his or her way of working and feel comfortable with a familiar situation, in which you know what to expect. It should be easier for you, however, to adapt to new ways of working and to new approaches once you already have been through therapy. You may be somewhat afraid of the unfamiliar, but it does afford the opportunity for new perspectives. If you have been with your previous therapist for a long time and want to develop new aspects of yourself, you are probably better off finding a new therapist. Each person, therapists included, has something different to offer and a slightly different way of looking at things, which help to enrich your experience.

In making a decision, it is helpful to ask yourself these questions:

- How well did you work with the previous therapist? Did you experience any barriers between you that you were not able to work through?
- Are your therapy needs now the same as before, or different?
- If they are the same, do you think that your therapist's approach still leaves room to shed new light on these problems? Do you think new perspectives or new techniques may make these old problems more accessible?
- If your needs now are different, why were these areas not explored before? Were they left for the future or never considered? Do you think your former therapist's approach is suitable for your new goals? If not, do you feel your former therapist can work with you in different ways? Did your former therapist work with you the way he or she did because that was the most suitable for you at the time or because that was the only way he or she knew or felt comfortable with?

Sometimes clients want to return to therapy not because of new problems to work out but because there are unresolved aspects of the old therapy relationship. Perhaps there are deep feelings of affection for the therapist: you miss him or her a great deal and returning to therapy is the only way that you can think of to reinstitute the relationship. If you harbor angry feelings toward a former therapist or feel that he or she never really appreciated you, you may want to go back to therapy to tell the therapist off or to show him or her how well you have done. In these instances you will be drawn not to therapy, but to the former therapist. Be clear on what you want to accomplish and if you do not want therapy perhaps you can bring your feelings to resolution in a more direct way. If such feelings cannot be resolved, they may be an issue for therapy, but in that case, it would probably be best to work them out with a new therapist.

WORKING WITH A NEW THERAPIST

If you decide on seeing a new therapist rather than the former one, the new therapist will, as a matter of course, want to talk to you about your former therapy experience. This is a responsible way to begin, providing a background and framework for the new work you will do together. You will want to talk about what brought you to therapy the first time, the goals you set for yourself, what you accomplished and were able to work out, what was most helpful to you in the therapy, how you felt about yourself when you left, and the reasons you want to come back to therapy. If the first therapy experience was unpleasant or unproductive there will probably be a lot of unresolved feelings remaining, which you will want to work through with the new therapist: how the experience affected you and how it made you feel about yourself and about therapy.

As a client resuming therapy you pose an extra challenge to the new therapist. There is a temptation for the new therapist in such a situation to want to do the job better than his or her colleague. Therapists, like other people, have their competitive instincts, but because they tend to work in isolation from their peers, they do not have much opportunity for playing these competitive needs out. Seeing somebody else's former client provides just such an opportunity. If you feel that the therapist is digging into the old relationship beyond what is useful, or that he or she is trying to show up your former therapist, this may be revealing a competitiveness and immaturity that does not bode well for the future of your new venture. Do not allow your new therapy experience to become the grounds for satisfying the unresolved needs of the therapist.

WHAT THERAPY IS LIKE THE SECOND TIME

Starting therapy again does not mean a boring repetition of the same old material. Just as in your previous therapy, you will find that some issues keep cropping up, but that as you review and rework them your perspective changes and the issues are experienced in a different way. Each time there may be something new to notice, some new configuration and repatterning that escaped you before. And, although there might be a lot of reworking to do, there will undoubtedly be a lot of new territory to cover as well. If you are in therapy with a new therapist then, of course, the different interaction between you two will also add spice to the proceedings. No matter whom you are with, therapy cannot be boring when you are growing and evolving.

Being in therapy a second time actually puts you at an advantage. Armed with your previous experience, you know how to use the therapy better and become a better client. You will find that you have more control of the therapy and will not have to rely so much on the therapist, but can use the therapist to help you focus more clearly on exactly what you want to do. As a more experienced client, you are more apt to avoid unproductive encounters and to get the best out of your therapist.

SUGGESTED READING

Social Issues and Psychotherapy

Clark, Ted, and Jaffe, Dennis T. *Toward a Radical Therapy.* New York: Gordon and Breach, 1973.

Halleck, Seymour L. *The Politics of Therapy.* New York: Science House, 1971.

Laing, R. D. *The Politics of Experience.* New York: Ballantine Books, 1967.

Szasz, Thomas S. *The Myth of Mental Illness.* New York: Harper & Row, 1961.

Psychotherapy Effectiveness

Smith, Mary Lee, Glass, Gene V., and Miller, T. I. *The Benefits of Psychotherapy.* Baltimore: Johns Hopkins University Press, 1980.

Williams, Janet B. W., and Spitzer, Robert L., eds. *Psychotherapy Research: Where Are We and Where Should We Go?* New York: Guilford Press, 1984.

The Major Approaches

FREUD AND PSYCHOANALYSIS

Freud, Sigmund. *New Introductory Lectures on Psychoanalysis.* New York: W. W. Norton, 1933.

———. *The Basic Writings of Sigmund Freud,* edited by A. A. Brill, New York: Modern Library, 1938.

———. *A General Introduction to Psychoanalysis.* Garden City, NY: Garden City Publishing Co., 1943.

EGO PSYCHOLOGY AND OBJECT RELATIONS THEORY

Blanck, Gertrude, and Blanck, Rubin. *Ego Psychology II.* New York: Columbia University Press, 1979.

Kernberg, Otto. *Object-Relations Theory and Clinical Psychoanalysis.* New York: Jason Aronson, 1976.

ADLER AND INDIVIDUAL PSYCHOLOGY

Adler, Alfred. *The Practice and Theory of Individual Psychology.* New York: Harcourt Brace, 1924.

JUNG AND ANALYTIC PSYCHOLOGY

Jung, Carl G. *Modern Man in Search of a Soul.* New York: Harcourt Brace, 1933.

———. *The Practice of Psychotherapy.* New York: Pantheon, 1954.

REICH AND VEGETOTHERAPY

Reich, Wilhelm. *The Function of the Orgasm.* New York: Orgone Institute, 1942.

———. *Character Analysis.* New York: Orgone Institute, 1949.

HORNEY AND THE CULTURAL APPROACH

Horney, Karen. *Our Inner Conflicts.* New York: W. W. Norton, 1945.

SULLIVAN AND INTERPERSONAL RELATIONS

Sullivan, Harry Stack. *The Interpersonal Theory of Psychiatry.* New York: W. W. Norton, 1953.

ROGERS AND CLIENT-CENTERED THERAPY

Rogers, Carl R. *Client-Centered Therapy.* Boston: Houghton Mifflin, 1951.

EXISTENTIAL THERAPY

Boss, Medard. *Psychoanalysis and Daseinsanalysis.* New York: Basic Books, 1963.

May, Rollo, Angel, Ernest, and Ellenberger, Henri F., eds. *Existence.* New York: Basic Books, 1958.

GESTALT THERAPY

Perls, Frederick, Hefferline, Ralph, and Goodman, Paul. *Gestalt Therapy.* New York: Julian Press, 1951.

Polster, Erving, and Polster, Miriam. *Gestalt Therapy In-*

tegrated: Contours of Theory and Practice. New York: Vintage Books, 1974.

LOWEN AND BIOENERGETICS
Lowen, Alexander. *Bioenergetics*. New York: Coward, McCann & Geoghegan, 1975.

JANOV AND PRIMAL THERAPY
Janov, Arthur. *The Primal Scream*. New York: G. P. Putnam's Sons, 1970.

TRANSACTIONAL ANALYSIS
Berne, Eric. *Games People Play*. New York: Grove Press, 1964.
Harris, Thomas A. *I'm OK—You're OK*. New York: Harper & Row, 1969.

ELLIS AND RATIONAL-EMOTIVE THERAPY
Ellis, Albert. *How to Live with a Neurotic*. New York: Crown, 1957.

BEHAVIOR MODIFICATION
Bandura, A. *Principles of Behavior Modification*. New York: Holt, Rinehart and Winston, 1969.
Wolpe, Joseph, and Lazarus, A. A. *Behavior Therapy Techniques*. New York: Pergamon, 1966.

SEX THERAPY
Kaplan, Helen Singer. *The New Sex Therapy*. New York: Brunner/Mazel, 1974.

NEURO LINGUISTIC PROGRAMING
Dilts, Robert B., Grinder, John, Bandler, Richard, DeLozier, Judith, and Cameron-Bandler, Leslie. *Neuro Linguistic Programming I*. Cupertino, CA: Meta Publications, 1979.

HYPNOTHERAPY
Wolberg, Lewis R. *Hypnosis: Is It For You?*, 2nd ed. New York: Dembner Books, 1982.

ECLECTIC PSYCHOTHERAPY
Goldfried, Marvin R., ed. *Converging Themes in Psychotherapy: Trends in Psychodynamic, Humanistic, and Behavioral Practice*. New York: Springer, 1982.

The Different Modalities

GROUP THERAPY

Jacobs, Alfred, and Spradlin, W. W., eds. *The Group As an Agent of Change.* New York: Behavioral Publications, 1974.

Yalom, I. W. *The Theory and Practice of Group Psychotherapy,* 2nd ed. New York: Basic Books, 1975.

FAMILY THERAPY

Minuchin, Salvador, and Fishman, H. Charles. *Family Therapy Techniques.* Cambridge, MA: Harvard University Press, 1981.

Weeks, Gerald R., and L'Abate, Luciano. *Paradoxical Psychotherapy.* New York: Brunner/Mazel, 1982.

COUPLES AND MARRIAGE THERAPY

Humphrey, Frederick G. *Marital Therapy.* Englewood Cliffs, NJ: Prentice-Hall, 1983.

Wile, Daniel B. *Couples Therapy: A Non-Traditional Approach.* New York: John Wiley & Sons, 1981.

CHILD THERAPY

Bush, Richard. *A Parent's Guide to Child Therapy.* New York: Delacorte Press, 1980.

Stein, Michael D., and Davis, J. Kent. *Therapies for Adolescents: Current Treatments for Behavior Problems.* San Francisco: Jossey-Bass, 1982.

Medical Treatment

DIAGNOSIS

American Psychiatric Association. *Diagnostic and Statistical Manual of Mental Disorders,* 3rd ed. Washington, D.C.: Author, 1980.

Reid, William H. *Treatment of the DSM-III Psychiatric Disorders.* New York: Brunner/Mazel, 1983.

PSYCHOACTIVE DRUGS

Donlon, Patrick T., Schaffer, Charles B., Erickson, Stephen E., Pepitone-Arreloa-Rockwell, Frances, and Schaffer, Linda A. *A Manual of Psychotropic Drugs: A Mental Health Resource.* Englewood Cliffs, NJ: M. D. Bowie-Robert J. Brady Co., Prentice-Hall, 1983.

Lickey, Marvin E., and Gordon, Barbara. *Drugs for Mental Illness: A Revolution in Psychiatry.* New York: W. H. Freeman, 1983.

Physician's Desk Reference. Oradell, NJ: Medical Economics, published and updated annually.

ELECTROCONVULSIVE THERAPY

Breggin, Peter Roger. *Electro-Shock: Its Brain-Disabling Effects.* New York: Springer Books, 1979.

Friedberg, John. *Shock Treatment Is Not Good for Your Brain.* San Francisco: Glide Publications, 1976.

PSYCHOSURGERY

Chavkin, Samuel. *The Mind Stealers: Psychosurgery and Mind Control.* Boston: Houghton Mifflin, 1978.

ORTHOMOLECULAR PSYCHIATRY

Feingold, Benjamin. *Why Your Child Is Hyperactive.* New York: Random House, 1975.

Hawkins, David, and Pauling, Linus, eds. *Orthomolecular Psychiatry.* San Francisco: Freeman, 1973.

Popular Electives

ENCOUNTER GROUPS

Lieberman, M. A., Yalom, I. D., and Miles, M. B. *Encounter Groups.* New York: Basic Books, 1973.

Schultz, William C. *Joy.* New York: Grove Press, 1967.

EST

Rhinehart, Luke. *The Book of est.* New York: Holt, Rinehart and Winston, 1976.

ARICA

Ichazo, Oscar. *Arica/Psychocalisthenics.* New York: Fireside Books, Simon and Schuster, 1976.

SILVA MIND CONTROL

Silva, José. *The Silva Mind Control Method for Business Managers.* Englewood Cliffs, NJ: Prentice-Hall, 1983.

TRANSCENDENTAL MEDITATION

Maharishi Mahesh Yogi. *Transcendental Meditation.* New York: Signet, 1968.

Naranjo, Claudio, and Ornstein, Robert E. *On the Psychology of Meditation.* New York: Viking Press, 1971.

Differences Among the Psychotherapy Professions

Burton, Arthur, and Associates. *Twelve Therapists.* San Francisco: Jossey-Bass, 1972.

Henry, William E., Sims, John H., and Spray, S. Lee. *Public and Private Lives of Psychotherapists.* San Francisco: Jossey-Bass, 1973.

———. *The Fifth Profession.* San Francisco: Jossey-Bass, 1971.

Rogow, Arnold A. *The Psychiatrists.* London: Allen and Unwin, 1971.

Psychotherapy and Ethnic Minorities

Dudley, G. Rita, and Rawlings, Maxines R., eds. "Psychotherapy with Ethnic Minorities." *Psychotherapy,* vol. 22, no. 2, Summer 1985.

Thomas, A., and Sillen, S. *Racism and Psychiatry.* New York: Brunner/Mazel, 1973.

Willie, C. V., Kramer, B. M., and Brown, B. S., eds. *Racism and Mental Health.* Pittsburgh: University of Pittsburgh Press, 1973.

Women and Feminist Therapy

Brodsky, Annette M., and Hare-mustin, Rachel, eds. *Women and Psychotherapy: An Assessment of Research and Practice.* New York: Guilford Press, 1980.

Robson, Elizabeth, and Edwards, Gwenyth. *Getting Help: A Woman's Guide to Therapy.* New York: E. P. Dutton, 1980.

Gay and Lesbian Therapy

Bell, A. P., and Weinberg, M. S. *Homosexualities: A Study of Diversity Among Men and Women.* New York: Simon and Schuster, 1978.

Gonsiorek, John C., ed. *A Guide to Psychotherapy with Gay and Lesbian Clients.* New York: Harrington Press, 1985.

Hodges, A., and Hutter, D. *With Downcast Gays: Aspects of Homosexual Self-Oppression.* Toronto: Pink Triangle Press, 1977.

Klaich, Dolores. *Woman Plus Woman: Attitudes Towards Lesbianism.* New York: Simon and Schuster, 1974.

Psychotherapy for Older People
> Brink, T. L. *Geriatric Psychotherapy*. New York: Human Sciences Press, 1979.
>
> Gottsegen, Gloria B., and Park, Paul D., eds. "Psychotherapy in Later Life." *Psychotherapy: Theory, Research and Practice*. vol. 19, no. 4, Winter 1982.

The Psychotherapy Contract
> Adams, Sallie, and Orgel, Michael, *Through the Mental Health Maze*. Washington, D.C.: Public Citizen's Health Research Group, 1975.

The Psychotherapy Process
> Singer, Erwin. *Key Concepts in Psychotherapy*. 2nd ed. New York: Basic Books, 1970.
>
> Weinberg, George. *The Heart of Psychotherapy*. New York: St. Martin's Press, 1984.

Index